MW01222198

WORD 6 FOR WINDOWS™

VISUAL PocketGuide

by: maranGraphics' Development Group

Canadian Trade Sales

Contact Prentice Hall Canada at (800) 567-3800 or Fax (416) 299-2529.

Corporate Sales

Contact maranGraphics at (800) 469-6616, ext. 206 or Fax (905) 890-9434.

Word 6 for Windows™ Visual PocketGuide

Published 1994
Canadian Cataloging in Publication Data
Maran, Ruth, 1970-
MaranGraphics Microsoft Word 6 for Windows : pocket guide

Includes index.
ISBN 0-9695666-6-2

1. Microsoft Word for Windows (Computer file).
2. Word processing - Computer programs. I. Title.
II. Title: Microsoft Word 6 for Windows.

Z52.5.M523M3 1994 652.5'5369 C94-932368-3

Printed in the United States of America

10 9 8 7 6 5 4 3 2

Trademark Acknowledgments

maranGraphics Inc. has attempted to include trademark information for products, services and companies referred to in this guide. Although maranGraphics Inc. has made reasonable efforts in gathering this information, it cannot guarantee its accuracy.

Microsoft, MS, MS-DOS and Microsoft Mouse are registered trademarks, and Windows is a trademark of Microsoft Corporation.

Credits

Author:
Ruth Maran

Consultant:
Wendi Blouin Ewbank

Layout Artist:
Carol Walthers

Designer:
David de Haas

Illustrator:
Dave Ross

Production Editor:
Kelleigh Wing

Editor:
Judy Maran

Post Production:
Robert Maran

Acknowledgments

Thanks to Hilaire Gagne and Matthew Price of Microsoft Canada Inc. for their support and consultation.

Special thanks to Wendi B. Ewbank for her patience, insight and humor throughout the project.

Thanks to José F. Pérez and Saverio C. Tropiano for their assistance and expert advice.

Thanks to the dedicated staff of maranGraphics including, Peters Ezers, David de Haas, David Hendricks, Jill Maran, Judy Maran, Maxine Maran, Robert Maran, Dave Ross, Christie Van Duin, Carol Walthers and Kelleigh Wing.

Finally, to Richard Maran who originated the easy-to-use graphic format of this guide. Thank you for your inspiration and guidance.

TABLE OF CONTENTS

Getting Started

Edit Your Documents

Smart Editing

Save and Open Your Documents

Using Multiple Documents

Print Your Documents

TABLE OF CONTENTS

Change Your Screen Display

Format Characters

Format Paragraphs

Format Pages

Working With Tables

INTRODUCTION

A typewriter makes editing your document a difficult task. If you want to make minor changes, you have to use correction fluid. For extensive changes, you may even have to retype your entire document.

Microsoft® Word 6.0 for Windows™ enables you to produce documents in less time and with greater accuracy. You can take advantage of the editing and formatting features provided to produce impressive-looking documents.

INTRODUCTION

This is what you can create with Word for Windows.

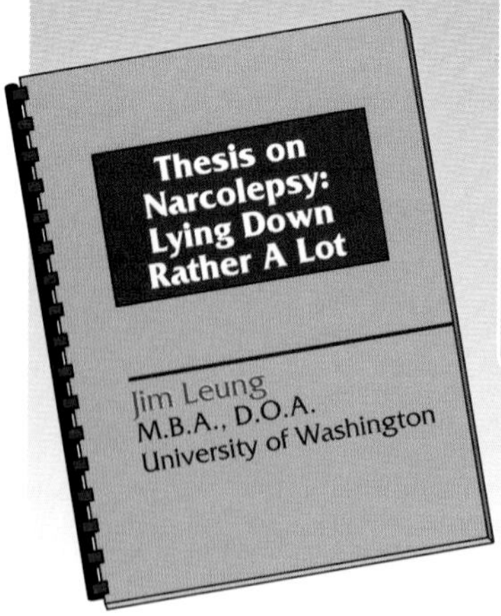
Thesis on Narcolepsy: Lying Down Rather A Lot
Jim Leung
M.B.A., D.O.A.
University of Washington

REPORTS AND MANUALS

Word for Windows provides editing and formatting features that make it ideal for producing longer documents such as reports and manuals.

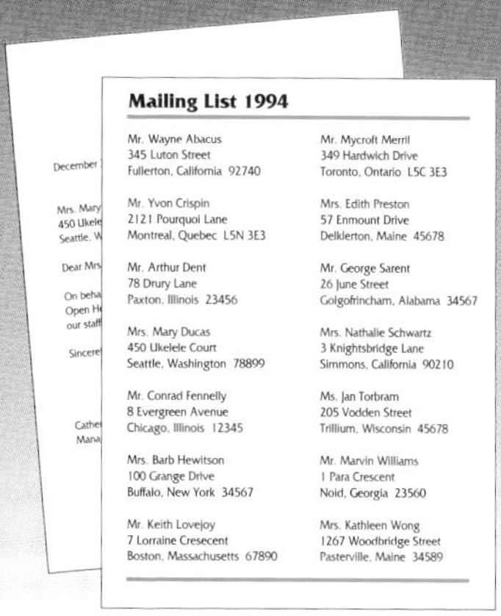
Mailing List 1994
Mr. Wayne Abacus
345 Luton Street
Fullerton, California 92740
Mr. Yvon Crispin
2121 Pourquoi Lane
Montreal, Quebec L5N 3E3
Mr. Arthur Dent
78 Drury Lane
Paxton, Illinois 23456
Mrs. Mary Ducas
450 Ukelele Court
Seattle, Washington 78899
Mr. Conrad Fennelly
8 Evergreen Avenue
Chicago, Illinois 12345
Mrs. Barb Hewitson
100 Grange Drive
Buffalo, New York 34567
Mr. Keith Lovejoy
7 Lorraine Cresecent
Boston, Massachusetts 67890
Mr. Mycroft Merril
349 Hardwich Drive
Toronto, Ontario L5C 3E3
Mrs. Edith Preston
57 Enmount Drive
Delklerton, Maine 45678
Mr. George Sarent
26 June Street
Golgofrincham, Alabama 34567
Mrs. Nathalie Schwartz
3 Knightsbridge Lane
Simmons, California 90210
Ms. Jan Torbram
205 Vodden Street
Trillium, Wisconsin 45678
Mr. Marvin Williams
1 Para Crescent
Noid, Georgia 23560
Mrs. Kathleen Wong
1267 Woodbridge Street
Pasterville, Maine 34589

MAILING LISTS

Word for Windows can merge documents with a list of names and addresses to produce personalized letters.

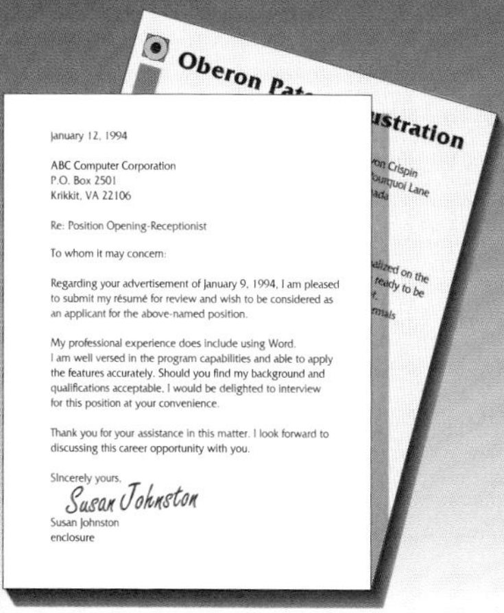
Oberon Pat
stration
January 12, 1994
ABC Computer Corporation
P.O. Box 2501
Krikkit, VA 22106
Re: Position Opening-Receptionist
To whom it may concern:
Regarding your advertisement of January 9, 1994, I am pleased to submit my résumé for review and wish to be considered as an applicant for the above-named position.
My professional experience does include using Word. I am well versed in the program capabilities and able to apply the features accurately. Should you find my background and qualifications acceptable, I would be delighted to interview for this position at your convenience.
Thank you for your assistance in this matter. I look forward to discussing this career opportunity with you.
Sincerely yours,
Susan Johnston
Susan Johnston
enclosure

PERSONAL AND BUSINESS LETTERS

Word for Windows helps you to produce letters quickly and accurately.

MOUSE BASICS

The mouse is a hand-held device that lets you quickly select commands and perform tasks.

USING THE MOUSE

Hold the mouse as shown in the diagram. Use your thumb and two rightmost fingers to guide the mouse while your two remaining fingers press the mouse buttons.

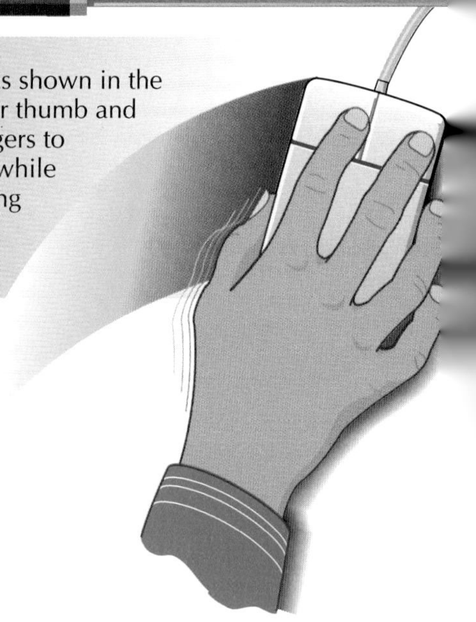

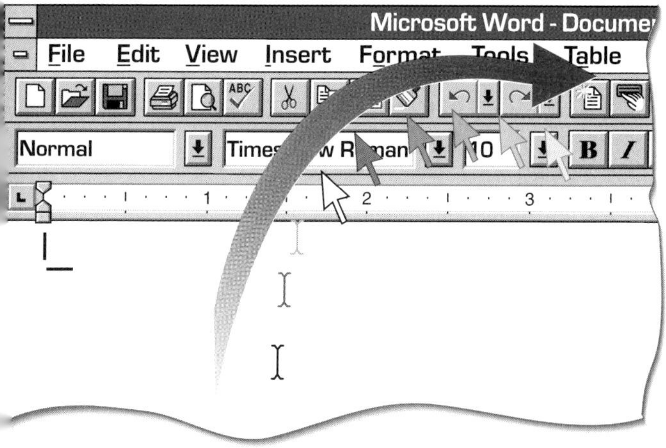

When you move the mouse on your
esk, the mouse pointer (or) on your
creen also moves. The mouse pointer
hanges shape depending on its location
n your screen.

PARTS OF THE MOUSE

The mouse has a left and right button. You can use these buttons to:

- open menus
- select commands
- choose options

Note: You will use the left button most of the time.

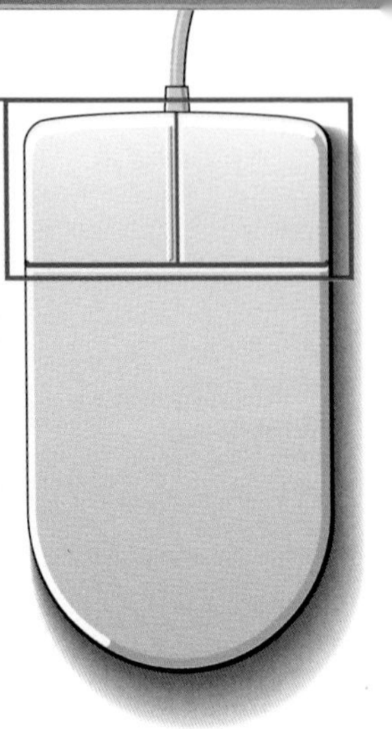

MOUSE TERMS

CLICK

Quickly press and release the left mouse button once.

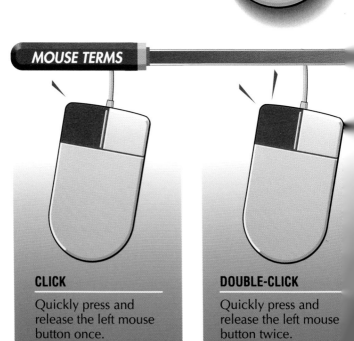

DOUBLE-CLICK

Quickly press and release the left mouse button twice.

◆ Under the mouse is a ball that senses movement. To ensure smooth motion of the mouse, you should occasionally remove and clean this ball.

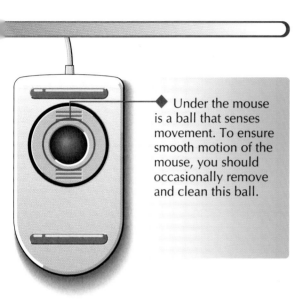

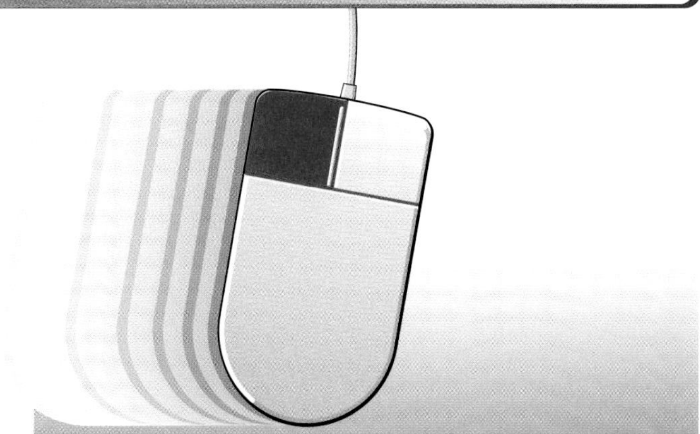

DRAG

When the mouse pointer (↖ or I) is over an object on your screen, press and hold down the left mouse button and then move the mouse.

START WORD

When you start Word for Windows, a blank document appears.
Page 1 Sec 1 1/1 At 1" Ln 1 Col 1

START WORD FOR WINDOWS

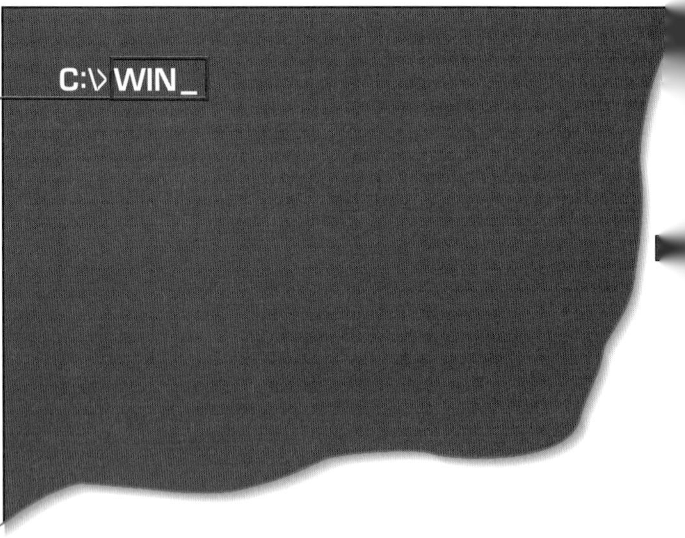
C:\> WIN_

1 To start Word for Windows from MS-DOS, type **WIN** and then press **Enter** .

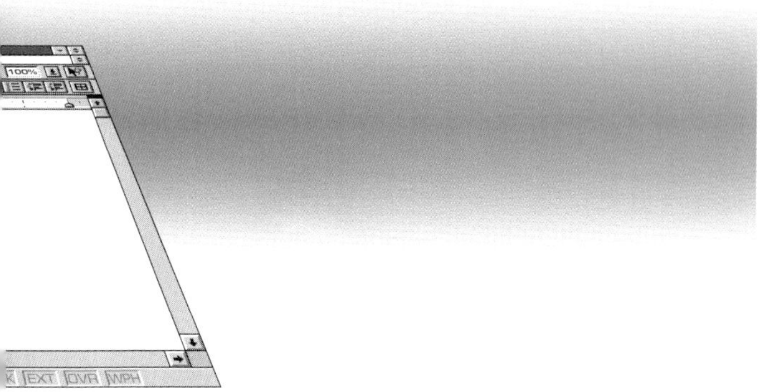

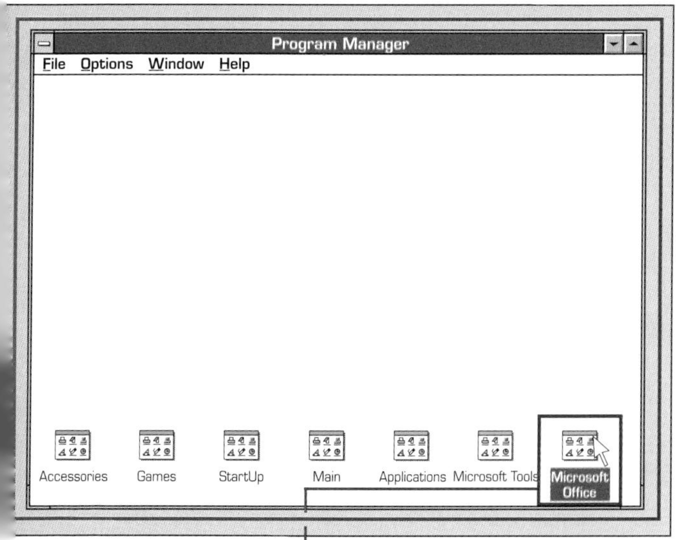

The **Program Manager** window appears.

2 To open the group window that contains Word, move the mouse over the icon (example: **Microsoft Office**) and then quickly press the left button twice.

Note: To continue, refer to the next page.

START WORD

You can type text into the document displayed on your screen.

START WORD (Continued)

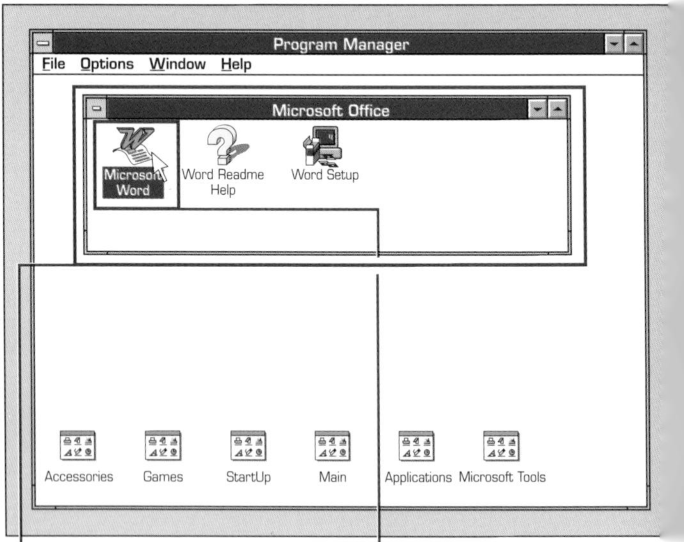

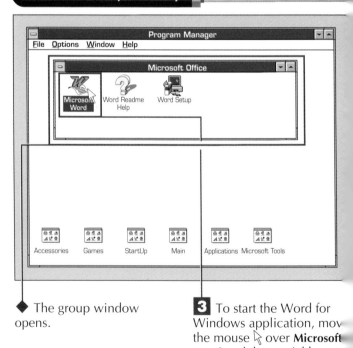

◆ The group window opens.

3 To start the Word for Windows application, mov the mouse over **Microsoft Word** and then quickly pre the left button twice.

TIP

The flashing line on your screen indicates where the text you type will appear. It is called the ***insertion point****.*

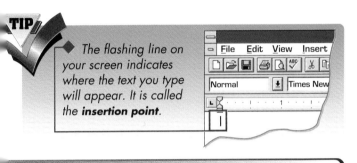

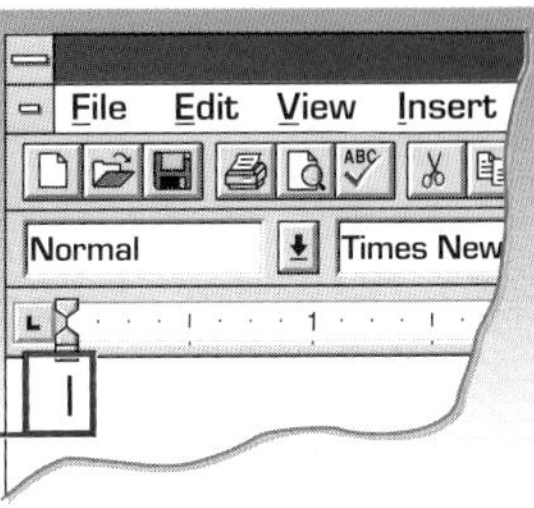

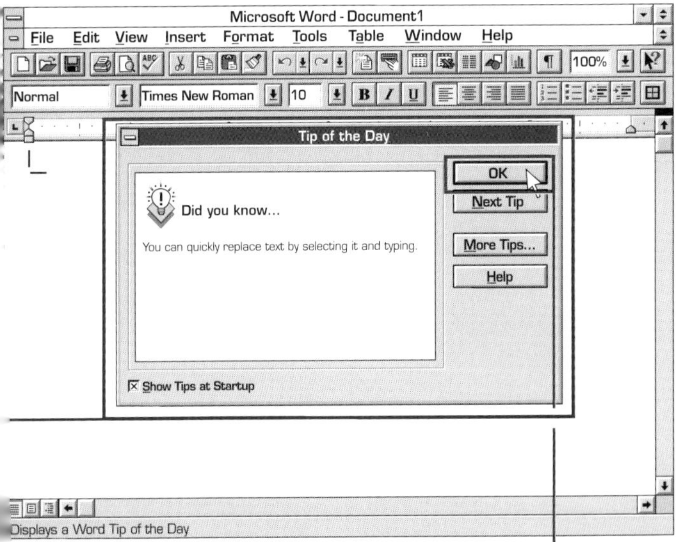

- The **Microsoft Word** vindow appears, displaying blank document.
- Each time you start Vord, a tip about using the rogram appears.

4 To close the **Tip of the Day** dialog box, move the mouse over **OK** and then press the left button.

ENTER TEXT

When typing text
in your document yo
do not need to pres
Enter at the end of
line. Word automatic
moves the text to th
next line. This is
called word
wrapping.

ENTER TEXT

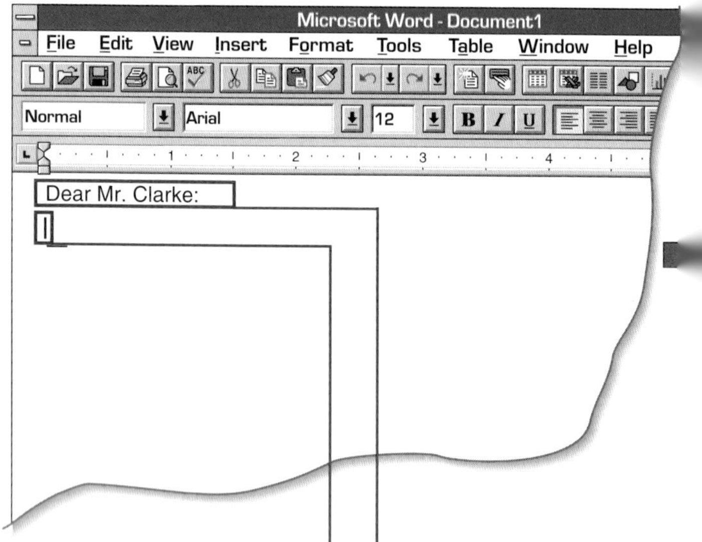
Microsoft Word - Document1
File Edit View Insert Format Tools Table Window Help
Normal
Arial
12
Dear Mr. Clarke:

◆ The flashing line (|) on your screen indicates where the text you type will appear. It is called the **insertion point**.

1 Type the first line of text

2 To start a new line, pres Enter .

3 To start a new paragrap press Enter again.

Important!

◆ In this book, the design and size of text were changed to make the document easier to read.

Note: To change the design and size of text, refer to page 164.

Initial or default font	►	New font
Times New Roman 10 point		Arial 12 point

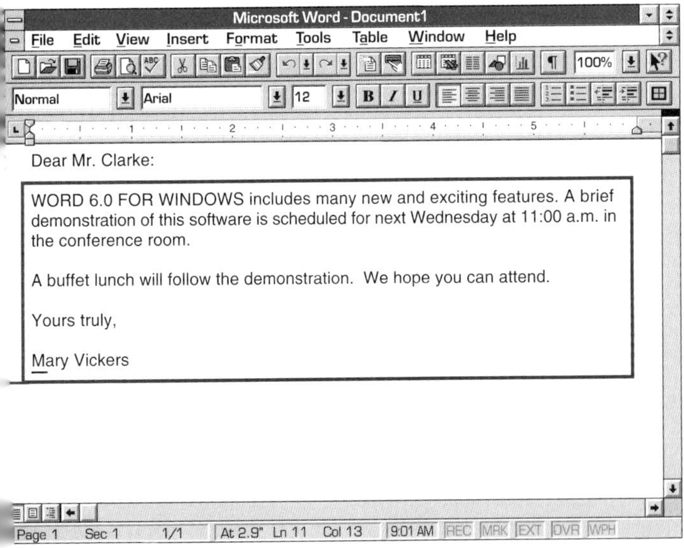
Microsoft Word - Document1
File Edit View Insert Format Tools Table Window Help
100%
Normal
Arial
12
Dear Mr. Clarke:
WORD 6.0 FOR WINDOWS includes many new and exciting features. A brief demonstration of this software is scheduled for next Wednesday at 11:00 a.m. in the conference room.
A buffet lunch will follow the demonstration. We hope you can attend.
Yours truly,
Mary Vickers
Page 1 Sec 1 1/1 At 2.9" Ln 11 Col 13 9:01 AM REC MRK EXT OVR WPH

4 Type the remaining text.

◆ Press **Enter** only when you want to start a new line or paragraph.

THE STATUS BAR

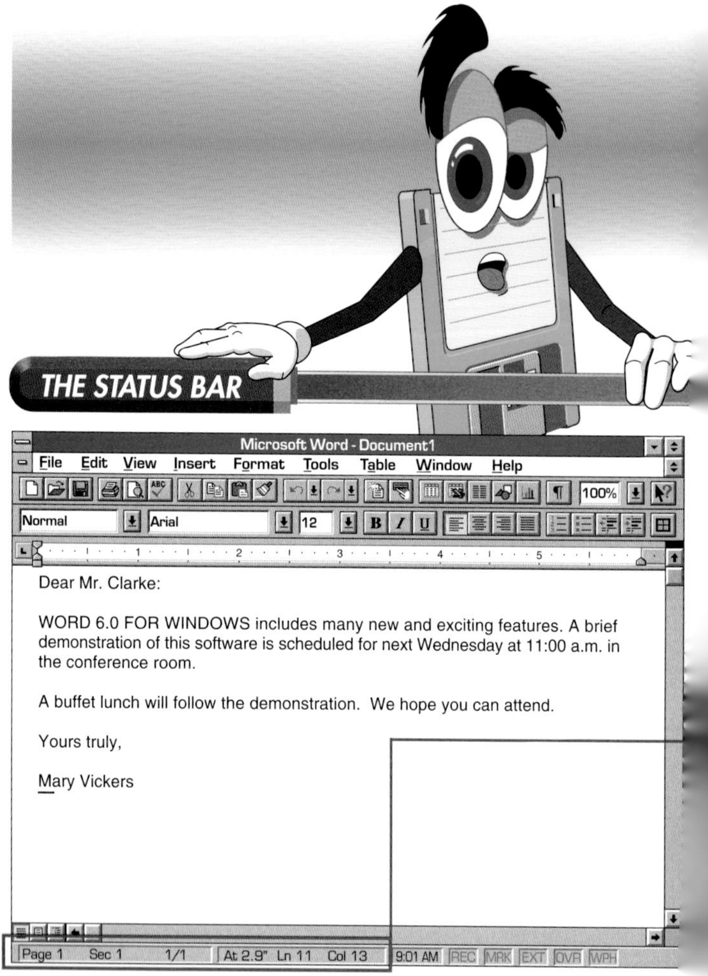
THE STATUS BAR
Microsoft Word - Document1
File Edit View Insert Format Tools Table Window Help
100%
Normal
Arial
12
Dear Mr. Clarke:
WORD 6.0 FOR WINDOWS includes many new and exciting features. A brief demonstration of this software is scheduled for next Wednesday at 11:00 a.m. in the conference room.
A buffet lunch will follow the demonstration. We hope you can attend.
Yours truly,
Mary Vickers
Page 1 Sec 1 1/1 At 2.9" Ln 11 Col 13
9:01 AM REC MRK EXT OVR WPH

The Status bar provides information about the position of the insertion point and the text displayed on your screen.

◆ **Page 1**
The page displayed on your screen.

◆ **Sec 1**
The section of the document displayed on your screen.

◆ **1/1**
The page displayed on your screen/The total number of pages in your document.

◆ **At 2.9''**
The distance (in inches) from the top of the page to the insertion point.

◆ **Ln 11**
The number of lines from the top of the page to the insertion point.

◆ **Col 13**
The number of characters from the left margin to the insertion point, including spaces.

SELECT COMMANDS

USING THE MOUSE

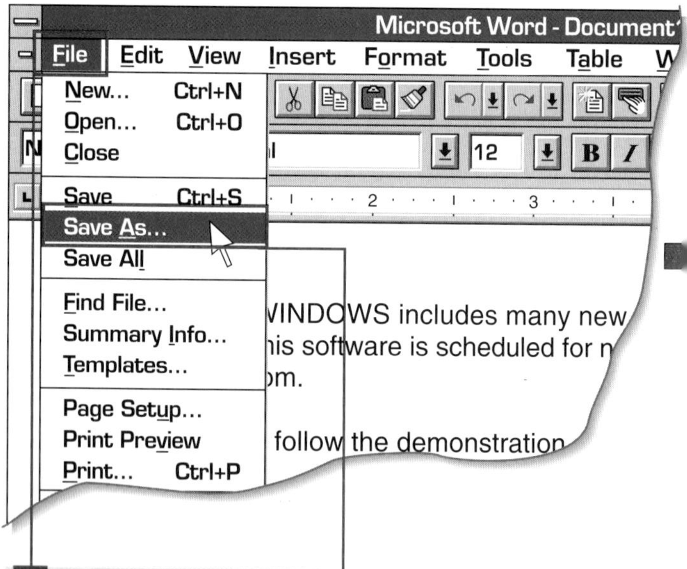

1 To open a menu, move the mouse over the menu name (example: **File**) and then press the left button.

◆ A menu appears displaying a list of related commands.

Note: To close a menu, move the mouse anywhere over your document and then press the left button.

2 To select a command, move the mouse over the command name (example: **Save As**) and then press the left button.

You can open a menu to display a list of related commands. You can then select the command you want to use.

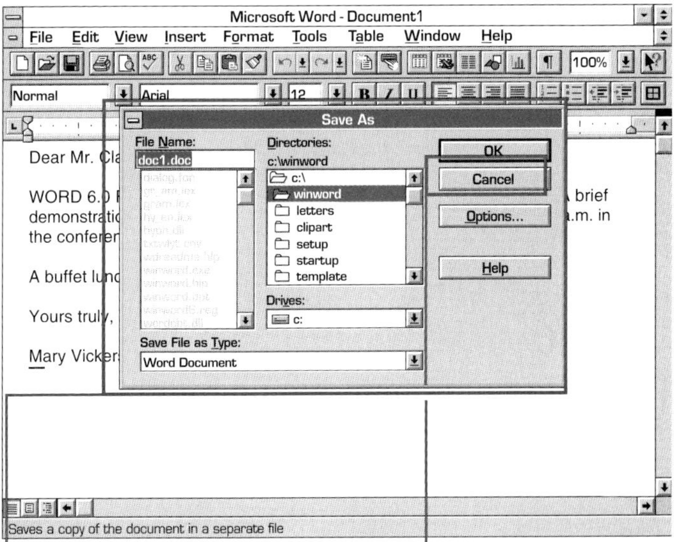

◆ A dialog box appears if Word requires more information to carry out the command.

3 To close a dialog box, move the mouse over **Cancel** and then press the left button.

SELECT COMMANDS

USING THE KEYBOARD

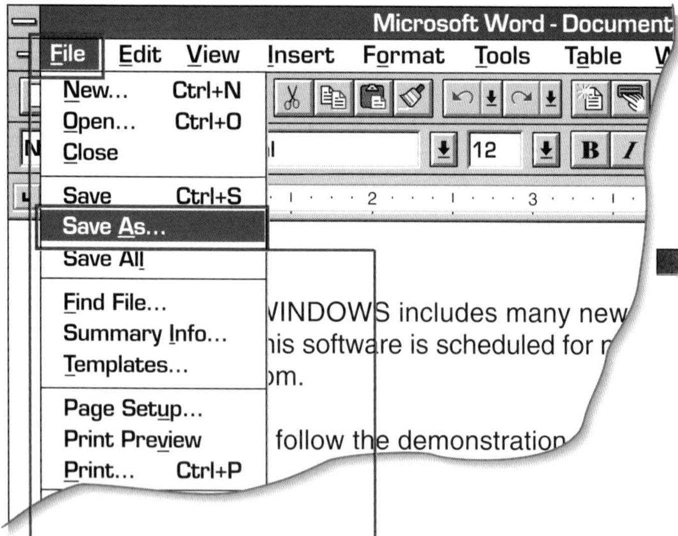

1 To open a menu, press Alt followed by the underlined letter in the menu name (example: F for **File**).

Note: To close a menu, press Alt.

2 To select a command, press the underlined letter in the command name (example: A for **Save As**).

TIP

◆ *Some commands display a keyboard shortcut. For example, you can press* Ctrl + N *to select the* ***New*** *command.*

◆ *If key names are separated by a plus sign (+), press and hold down the first key before pressing the second key (example:* Ctrl + N *).*

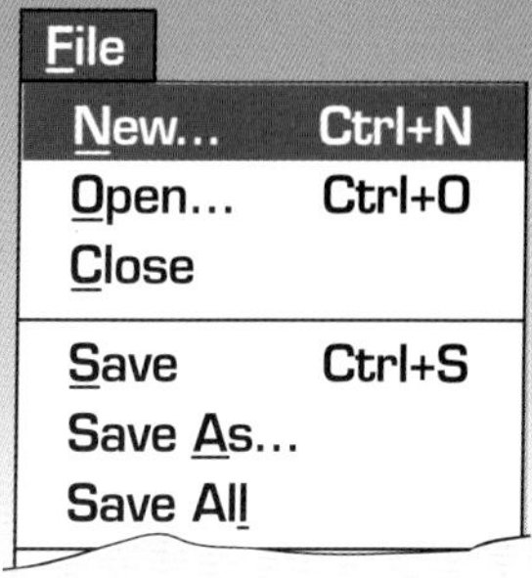

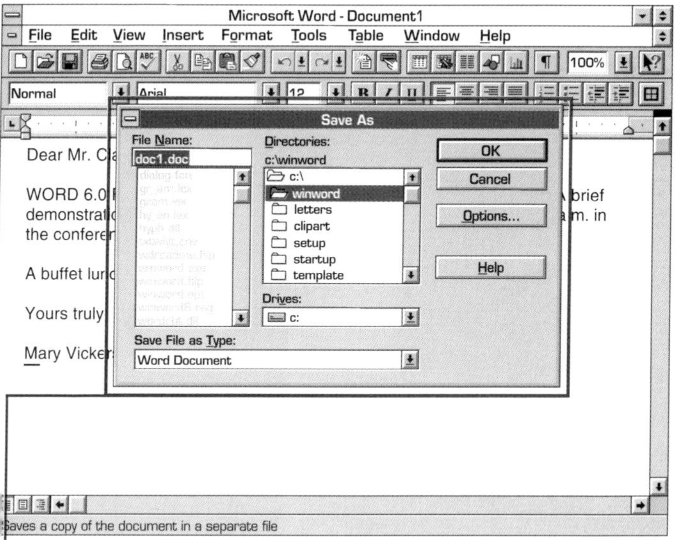

◆ A dialog box appears
Word requires more
nformation to carry out
ne command.

3 To close a dialog box, press Esc .

SELECT COMMANDS

You can use the Word buttons to quickly select the most commonly used commands.

THE WORD BUTTONS

Each button displayed on your screen provides a fast method of selecting a menu command.

For example, you can use to quickly select the **Save** command.

File	
<u>N</u>ew...	Ctrl+N
<u>O</u>pen...	Ctrl+O
<u>C</u>lose	
<u>S</u>ave	Ctrl+S
Save <u>A</u>s...	
Save Al<u>l</u>	

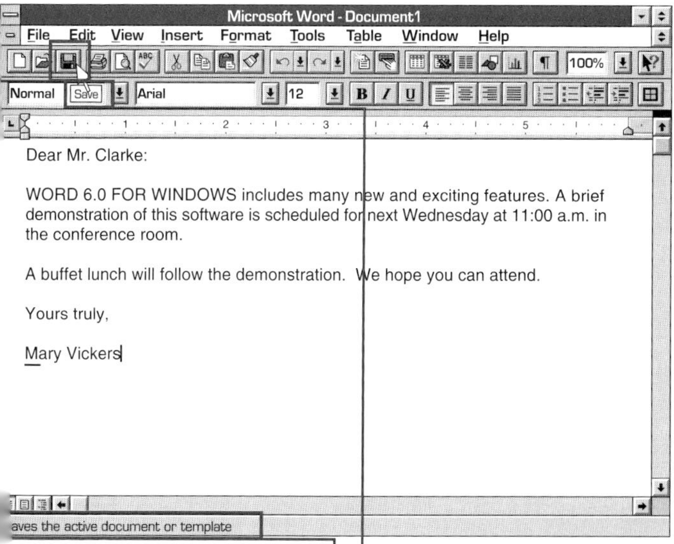
Microsoft Word - Document1
File Edit View Insert Format Tools Table Window Help
Normal
Save
Arial
12
100%
Dear Mr. Clarke:
WORD 6.0 FOR WINDOWS includes many new and exciting features. A brief demonstration of this software is scheduled for next Wednesday at 11:00 a.m. in the conference room.
A buffet lunch will follow the demonstration. We hope you can attend.
Yours truly,
Mary Vickers
aves the active document or template

1 To display a escription of a button n your screen, move the ıouse over the button of ıterest (example:).

◆ After a few seconds, the name of the button appears (example: **Save**).

◆ A short description of the button also appears at the bottom of your screen.

MOVE THROUGH A DOCUMENT

Important!

You cannot move the insertion point past the horizontal line (▁) displayed on your screen. To move this line, position the insertion point after the last character in your document and then press **Enter**.

If you create a long document, your computer screen cannot display all the text at the same time. You must scroll up or down to view other parts of your document.

MOVE TO ANY POSITION ON YOUR SCREEN

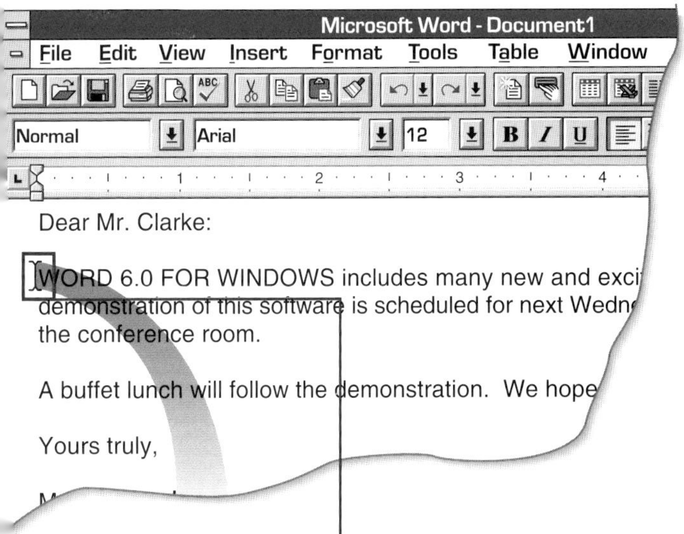
Microsoft Word - Document1
File Edit View Insert Format Tools Table Window
Normal
Arial
12
Dear Mr. Clarke:
WORD 6.0 FOR WINDOWS includes many new and exci
demonstration of this software is scheduled for next Wedn
the conference room.
A buffet lunch will follow the demonstration. We hope
Yours truly,

he insertion point indicates 'here the text you type will ppear in your document.

1 To position the insertion point at another location on your screen, move the mouse I over the new location and then press the left button.

MOVE THROUGH A DOCUMENT

SCROLL UP OR DOWN

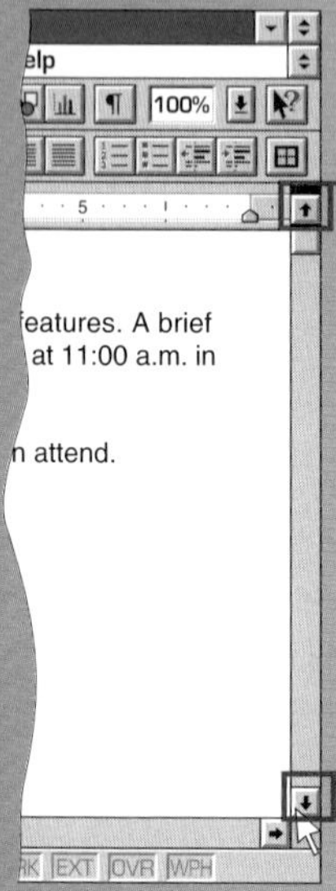

◆ To scroll up one line, move the mouse over and then press the left button.

◆ To scroll down one line, move the mouse over and then press the left button.

KEYBOARD SHORTCUTS

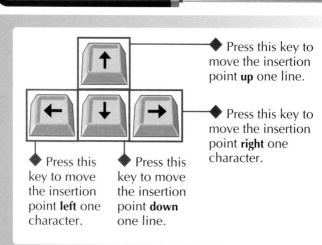

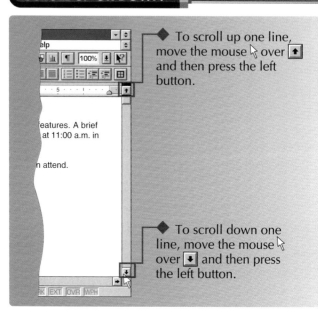

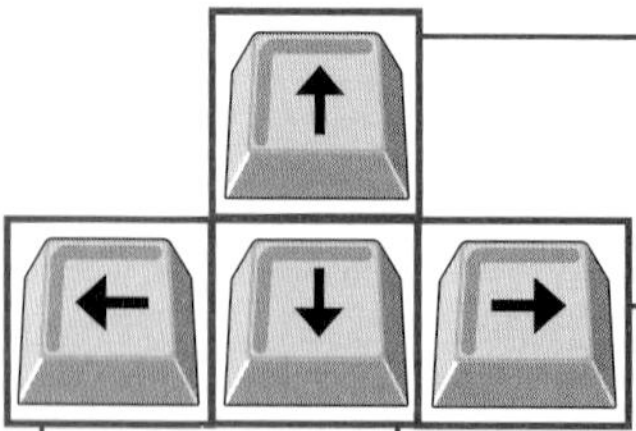

◆ Press this key to move the insertion point **up** one line.

◆ Press this key to move the insertion point **right** one character.

◆ Press this key to move the insertion point **left** one character.

◆ Press this key to move the insertion point **down** one line.

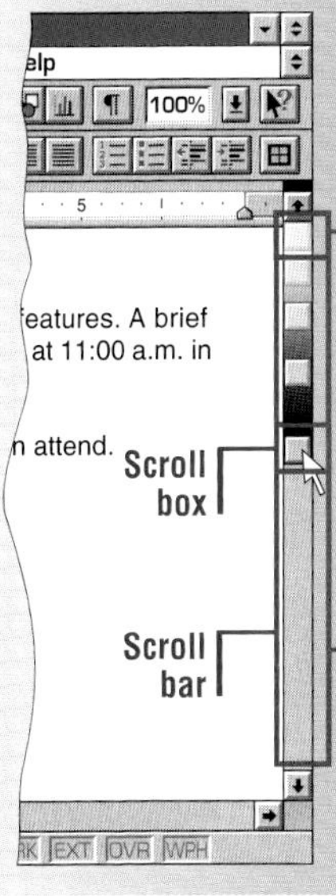

The location of the scroll box on the scroll bar indicates which part of your document is displayed on the screen.

For example, when the scroll box is in the middle of the scroll bar, you are viewing the middle part of your document.

1 To move the scroll box, position the mouse over the box and then press and hold down the left button.

2 Still holding down the button, drag the scroll box down the scroll bar. Then release the button.

Press this key to move **up** one screen.

Press this key to move **down** one screen.

Press these keys to move to the **beginning** of your document.

Press these keys to move to the **end** of your document.

SELECT TEXT

SELECT A SENTENCE

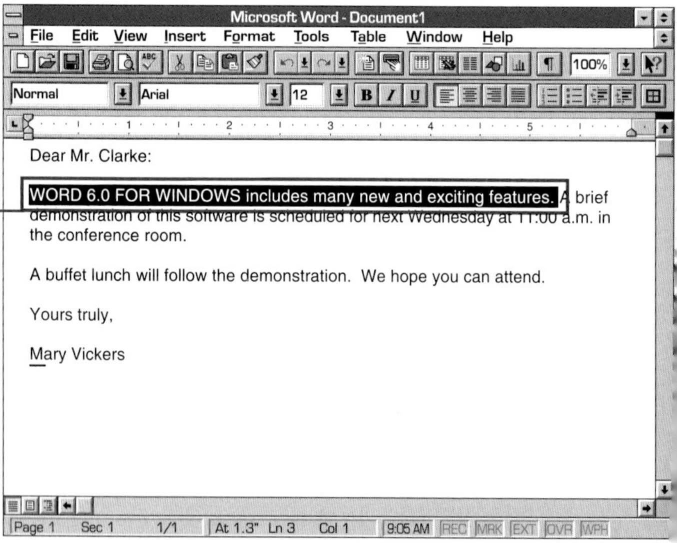
Microsoft Word - Document1
File Edit View Insert Format Tools Table Window Help
100%
Normal
Arial
12
Dear Mr. Clarke:
WORD 6.0 FOR WINDOWS includes many new and exciting features. A brief demonstration of this software is scheduled for next Wednesday at 11:00 a.m. in the conference room.
A buffet lunch will follow the demonstration. We hope you can attend.
Yours truly,
Mary Vickers
Page 1 Sec 1 1/1 At 1.3" Ln 3 Col 1 9:05 AM REC MRK EXT OVR WPH

1 Press and hold down **Ctrl**.

2 Still holding down **Ctrl**, move the mouse I anywhere over the sentence you want to select and then press the left button. Release **Ctrl**.

TO CANCEL A TEXT SELECTION

Move the mouse I outside the selected area and then press the left button.

Before you can use many Word features, you must first select the text you want to change.

SELECT A PARAGRAPH

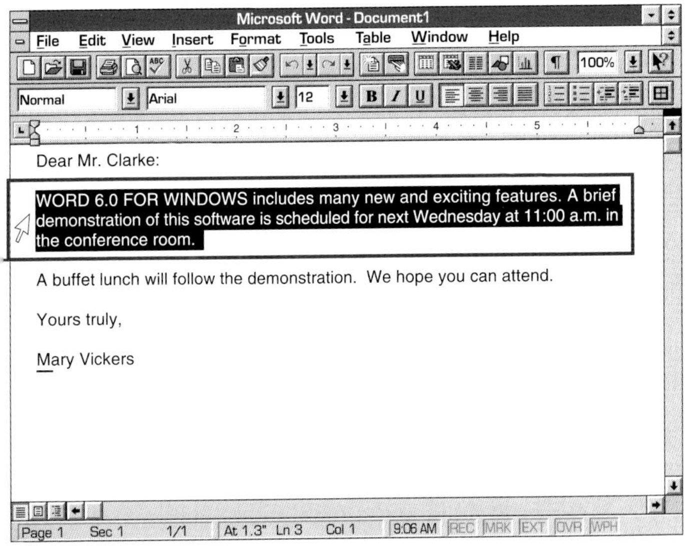
Microsoft Word - Document1
File Edit View Insert Format Tools Table Window Help
100%
Normal
Arial
12
Dear Mr. Clarke:
WORD 6.0 FOR WINDOWS includes many new and exciting features. A brief demonstration of this software is scheduled for next Wednesday at 11:00 a.m. in the conference room.
A buffet lunch will follow the demonstration. We hope you can attend.
Yours truly,
Mary Vickers
Page 1 Sec 1 1/1 At 1.3" Ln 3 Col 1 9:06 AM REC MRK EXT OVR WPH

1 Move the mouse I to the left of the paragraph you want to select (I changes to ↖) and then quickly press the left button twice.

SELECT TEXT

Selected text appears highlighted on your screen.

SELECT YOUR ENTIRE DOCUMENT

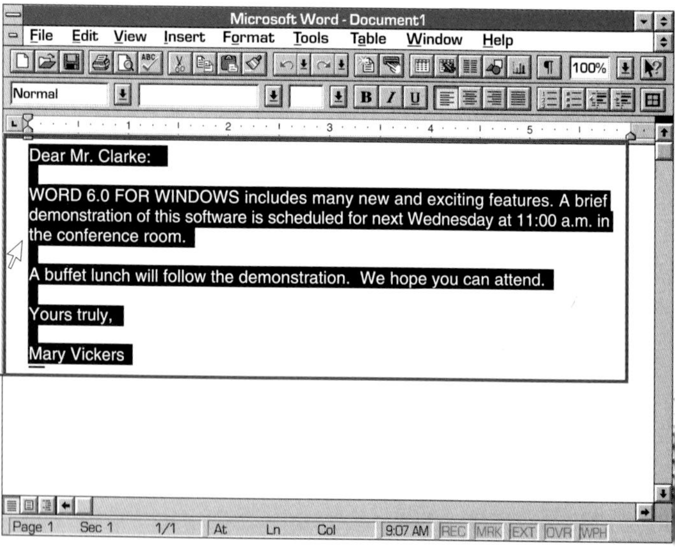
Microsoft Word - Document1
File Edit View Insert Format Tools Table Window Help
100%
Normal
Dear Mr. Clarke:
WORD 6.0 FOR WINDOWS includes many new and exciting features. A brief demonstration of this software is scheduled for next Wednesday at 11:00 a.m. in the conference room.
A buffet lunch will follow the demonstration. We hope you can attend.
Yours truly,
Mary Vickers
Page 1 Sec 1 1/1 At Ln Col 9:07 AM REC MRK EXT OVR WPH

1 Move the mouse I anywhere to the left of the text in your document (I changes to ↗) and then quickly press the left button three times.

TO CANCEL A TEXT SELECTION

Move the mouse I outside the selected area and then press the left button.

SELECT A WORD

Dear Mr. Clarke:

WORD 6.0 FOR WINDOWS in
demonstration of this software
the conference room.

A buffet lunch will follow

1 Move the mouse I anywhere over the word you want to select and then quickly press the left button twice.

SELECT ANY AMOUNT OF TEXT

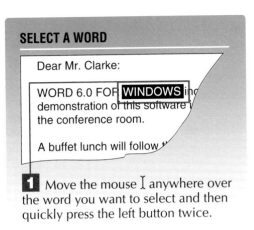

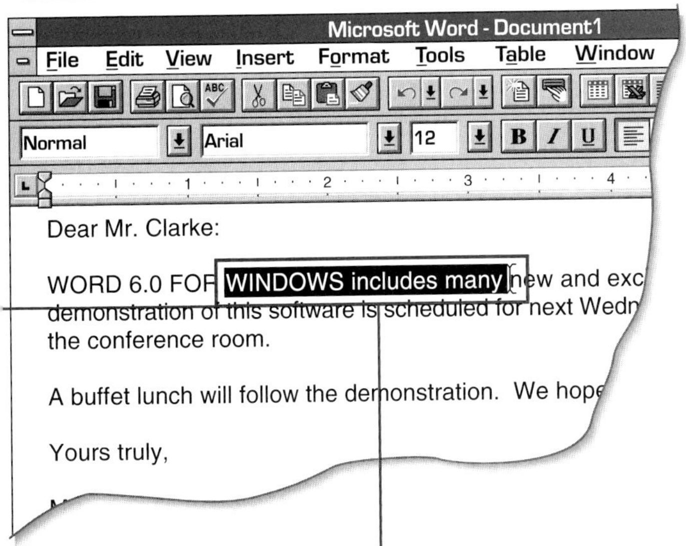

1 Move the mouse I to the left of the first character you want to select.

2 Press and hold down the left button as you drag the mouse I over the text. Then release the button.

HELP

HELP

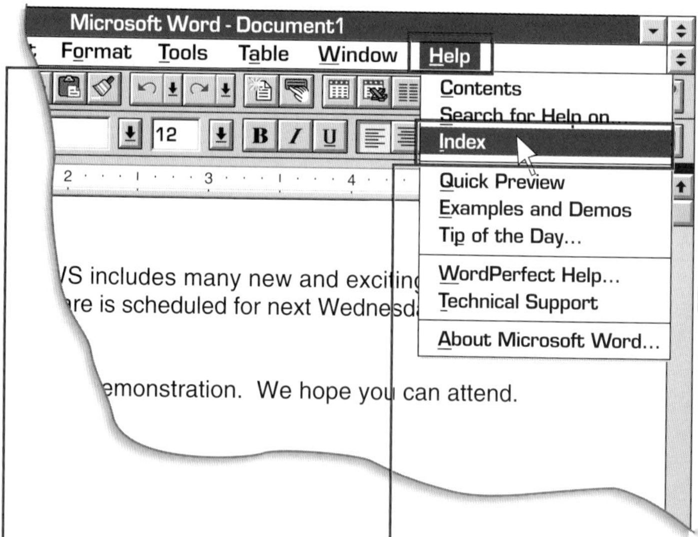

1 To display the Word Help Index, move the mouse over **Help** and then press the left button.

2 Move the mouse over **Index** and then press the left button.

If you forget how to perform a task, you can use the Word Help feature to obtain information.

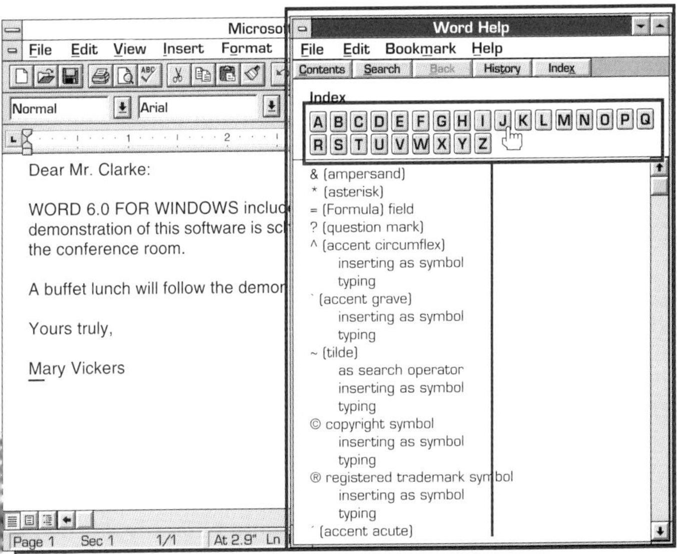

◆ The **Word Help** window appears.

3 Move the mouse over the first letter of the topic you want information on (example: J for **Justification**) and then press the left button.

Note: To continue, refer to the next page.

HELP (Continued)

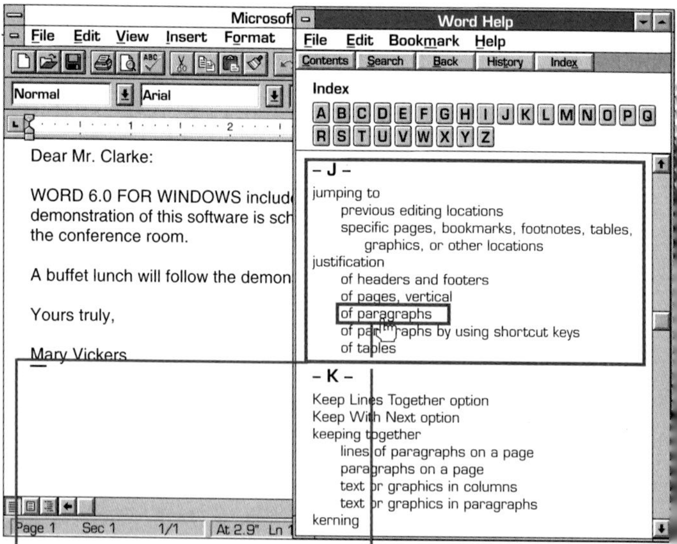

◆ Topics beginning with the letter you selected appear.

◆ To view more topics beginning with that letter, press PageDown on your keyboard.

4 Move the mouse over the topic of interest (example: **justification of paragraphs**) and then press the left button.

TIP

To print the help topic displayed on your screen:

◆ *Move the mouse over* Print *in the* ***How To*** *window and then press the left button.*

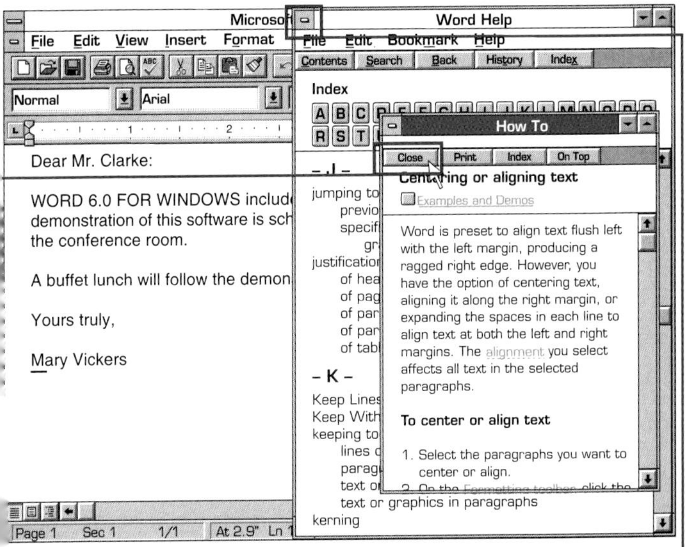

Microsoft
File Edit View Insert Format
Normal
Arial
Dear Mr. Clarke:
WORD 6.0 FOR WINDOWS includ
demonstration of this software is sch
the conference room.
A buffet lunch will follow the demon
Yours truly,
Mary Vickers
Page 1 Sec 1 1/1 At 2.9" Ln 1
Word Help
File Edit Bookmark Help
Contents Search Back History Index
Index
– J –
jumping to
justification
– K –
Keep Lines
Keep With
keeping to
text or graphics in paragraphs
kerning
How To
Close Print Index On Top
Centering or aligning text
Examples and Demos
Word is preset to align text flush left with the left margin, producing a ragged right edge. However, you have the option of centering text, aligning it along the right margin, or expanding the spaces in each line to align text at both the left and right margins. The alignment you select affects all text in the selected paragraphs.
To center or align text
1. Select the paragraphs you want to center or align.

◆ Information on the topic you selected appears.

5 To close the **How To** window, move the mouse over **Close** and then press the left button.

6 To close the **Word Help** window, move the mouse over its **Control-menu** box and then quickly press the left button twice.

INSERT A BLANK LINE

INSERT A BLANK LINE

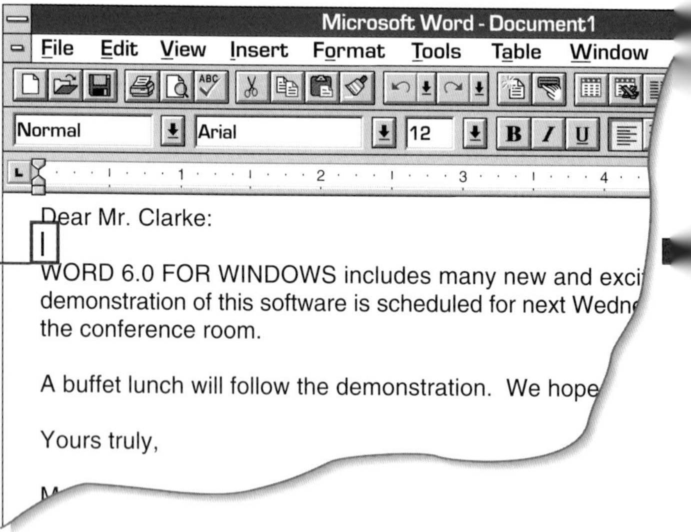
Microsoft Word - Document1
File Edit View Insert Format Tools Table Window
Normal
Arial
12
Dear Mr. Clarke:
WORD 6.0 FOR WINDOWS includes many new and exci
demonstration of this software is scheduled for next Wedn
the conference room.
A buffet lunch will follow the demonstration. We hope
Yours truly,

1 Position the insertion point where you want to insert a blank line.

Word makes it easy to edit your document. To make changes, you no longer have to use correction fluid or retype a page.

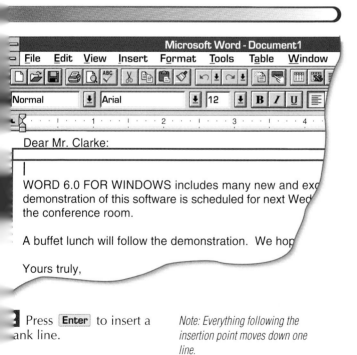

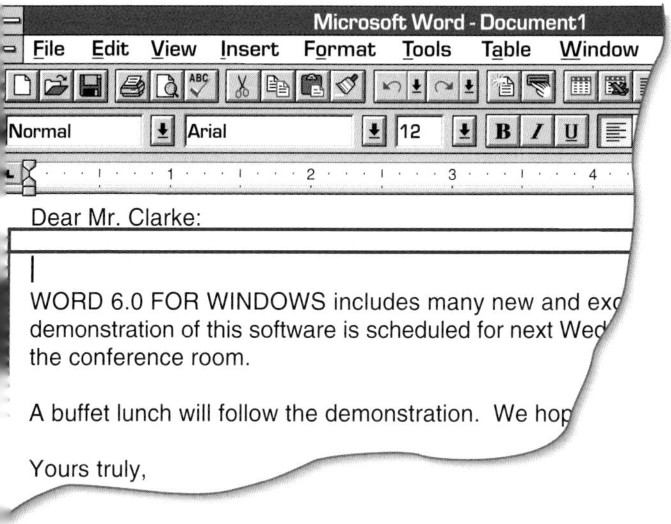
Microsoft Word - Document1
File Edit View Insert Format Tools Table Window
Normal
Arial
12
Dear Mr. Clarke:
WORD 6.0 FOR WINDOWS includes many new and exc
demonstration of this software is scheduled for next Wed
the conference room.
A buffet lunch will follow the demonstration. We hop
Yours truly,

Press **Enter** to insert a
ank line.

Note: Everything following the insertion point moves down one line.

SPLIT AND JOIN PARAGRAPHS

You can easily split or join paragraphs in your document.

SPLIT AND JOIN PARAGRAPHS

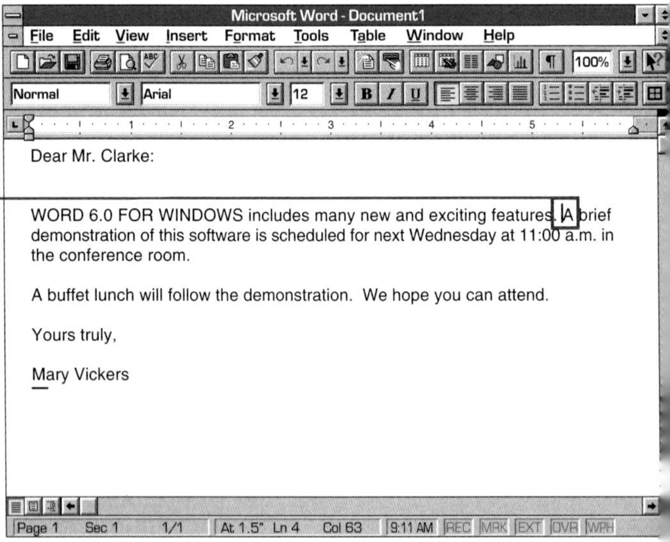

Split a Paragraph

1 Position the insertion point where you want to split a paragraph in two.

Important!

Make sure you save your document to store it for future use. If you do not save your document, it will disappear when you turn off your computer.

Note: To save a document, refer to page 96.

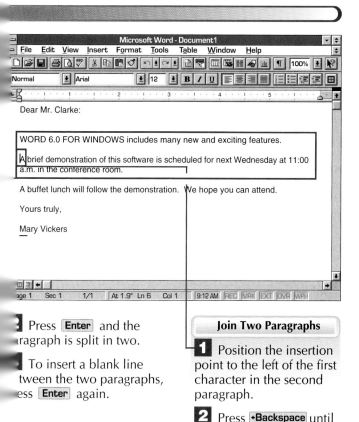

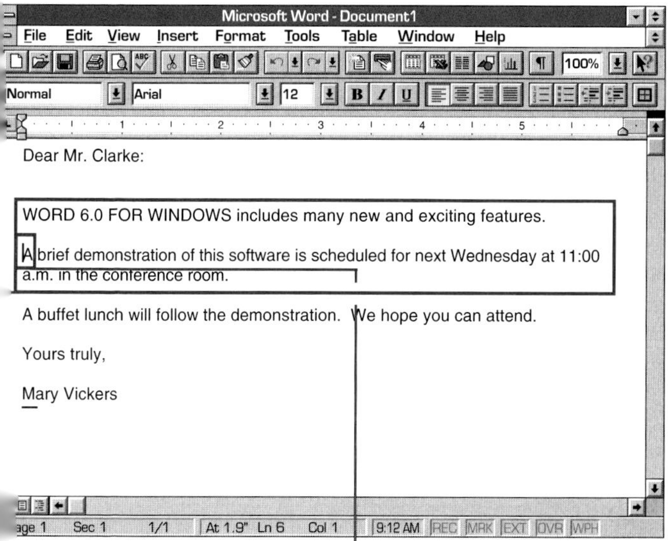
Microsoft Word - Document1
File Edit View Insert Format Tools Table Window Help
Normal
Arial
12
100%
Dear Mr. Clarke:
WORD 6.0 FOR WINDOWS includes many new and exciting features.
A brief demonstration of this software is scheduled for next Wednesday at 11:00 a.m. in the conference room.
A buffet lunch will follow the demonstration. We hope you can attend.
Yours truly,
Mary Vickers
age 1 Sec 1 1/1 At 1.9" Ln 6 Col 1 9:12 AM REC MRK EXT OVR WPH

Press **Enter** and the ıragraph is split in two.

To insert a blank line tween the two paragraphs, ess **Enter** again.

Join Two Paragraphs

1 Position the insertion point to the left of the first character in the second paragraph.

2 Press **←Backspace** until the paragraphs are joined.

INSERT TEXT

In the Insert mode, the text you type appears at the current insertion point location. Any existing text moves forward to make room for the new text.

INSERT TEXT

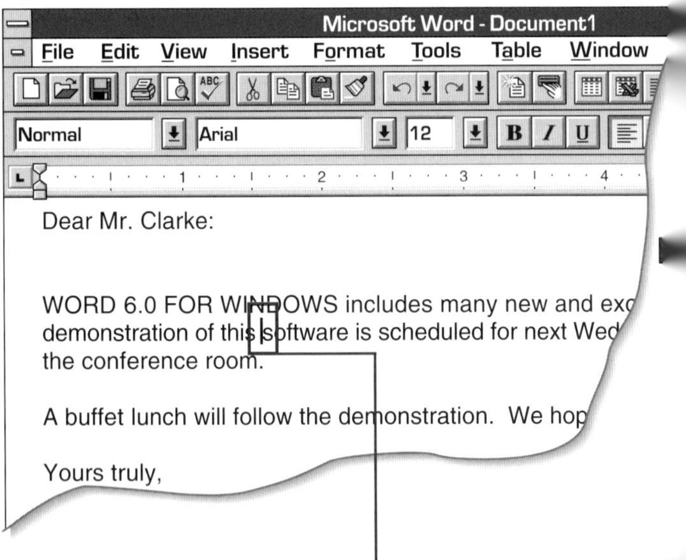

Microsoft Word - Document1
File Edit View Insert Format Tools Table Window
Normal
Arial
12
Dear Mr. Clarke:
WORD 6.0 FOR WINDOWS includes many new and exc
demonstration of this software is scheduled for next Wed
the conference room.
A buffet lunch will follow the demonstration. We hop
Yours truly,

When you start Word, the program is in the Insert mode.

1 Position the insertion point where you want to insert the new text.

*Note: If the letters **OVR** appear in bla(OVR) at the bottom of your screen, press Insert on your keyboard to switch to the **Insert** mode.*

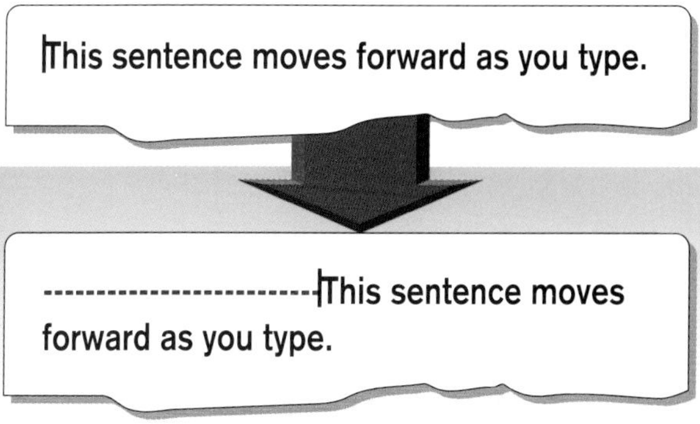
This sentence moves forward as you type.
------------------------This sentence moves
forward as you type.

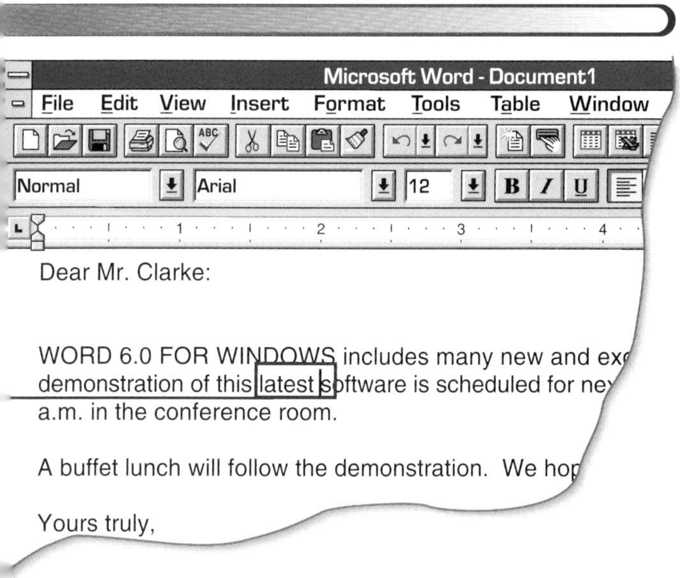
Microsoft Word - Document1
File Edit View Insert Format Tools Table Window
Normal
Arial
12
Dear Mr. Clarke:
WORD 6.0 FOR WINDOWS includes many new and ex
demonstration of this latest software is scheduled for ne
a.m. in the conference room.
A buffet lunch will follow the demonstration. We hop
Yours truly,

2 Type the text you want
insert (example: **latest**).

3 To insert a blank space,
ess the **Spacebar**.

Note: The words to the right of the inserted text are pushed forward.

OVERTYPE TEXT

In the Overtype mode, the text you type appears at the current insertion point location. The new text replaces (types over) any existing text.

OVERTYPE TEXT

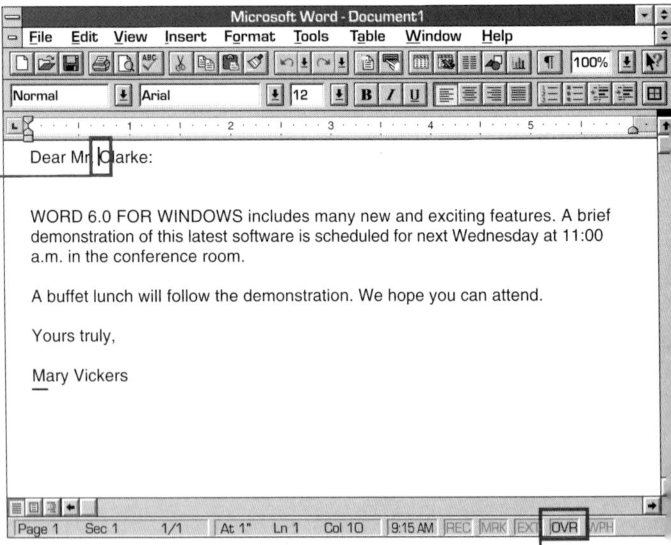

1 Position the insertion point to the left of the first character you want to replace.

2 To turn on the **Overtype** mode, move the mouse over OVR and then quickly press the left button twice (OVR changes to OVR).

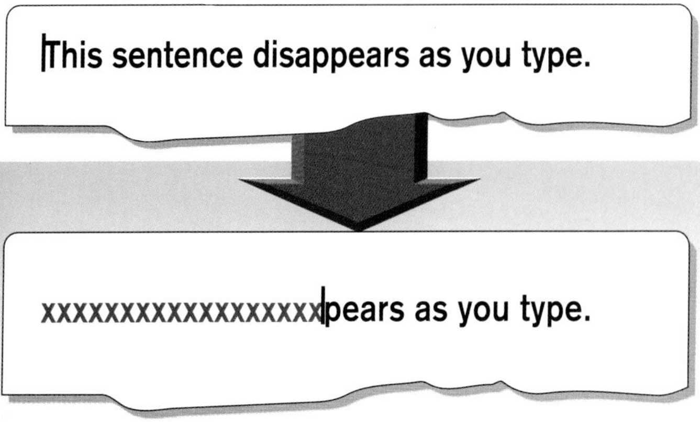
This sentence disappears as you type.
xxxxxxxxxxxxxxxxxxpears as you type.

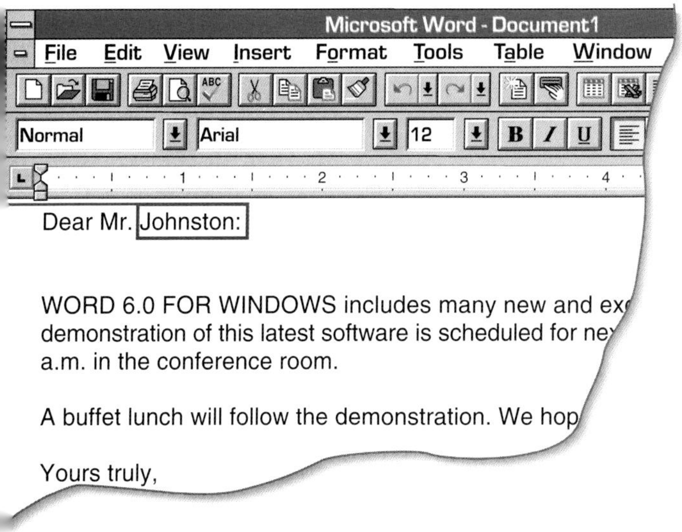
Microsoft Word - Document1
File Edit View Insert Format Tools Table Window
Normal
Arial
12
Dear Mr. Johnston:
WORD 6.0 FOR WINDOWS includes many new and ex
demonstration of this latest software is scheduled for ne
a.m. in the conference room.
A buffet lunch will follow the demonstration. We hop
Yours truly,

3 Type the text you want) replace the existing text ʼith (example: **Johnston:**).

ɔte: The new text types over the ɨisting text.

4 To turn off the **Overtype** mode, repeat step **2** (OVR changes to OVR).

Note: You can also press Insert *on your keyboard to turn on or off the* ***Overtype*** *mode.*

DELETE A BLANK LINE

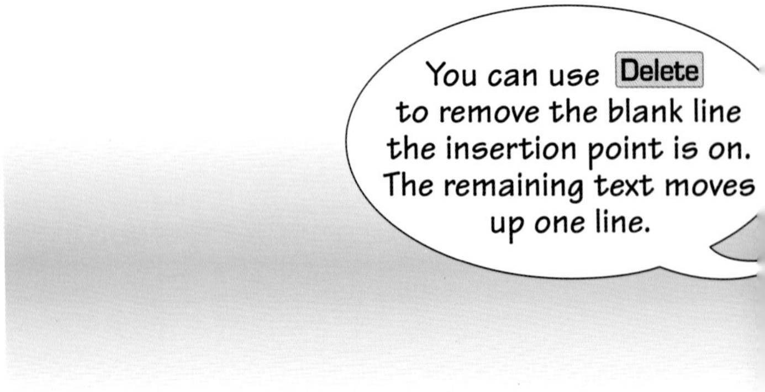

You can use Delete to remove the blank line the insertion point is on. The remaining text moves up one line.

Delete DELETE A BLANK LINE

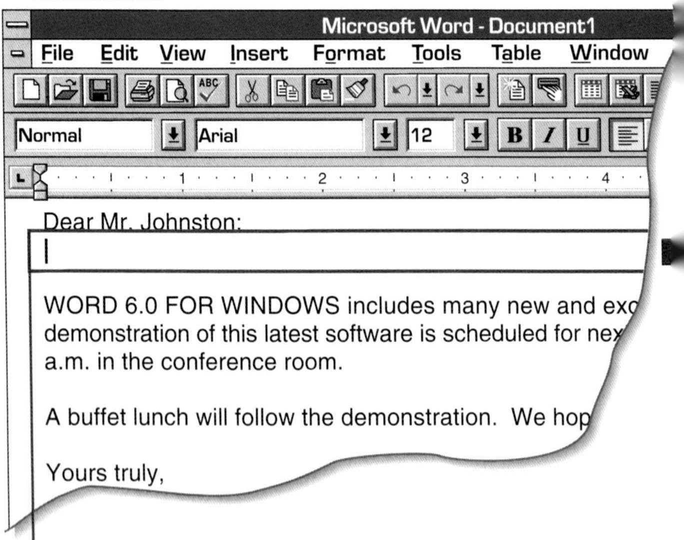

Microsoft Word - Document1
File Edit View Insert Format Tools Table Window
Normal
Arial
12
Dear Mr. Johnston:
WORD 6.0 FOR WINDOWS includes many new and exc
demonstration of this latest software is scheduled for nex
a.m. in the conference room.
A buffet lunch will follow the demonstration. We hop
Yours truly,

1 Position the insertion point at the beginning of the blank line you want to delete.

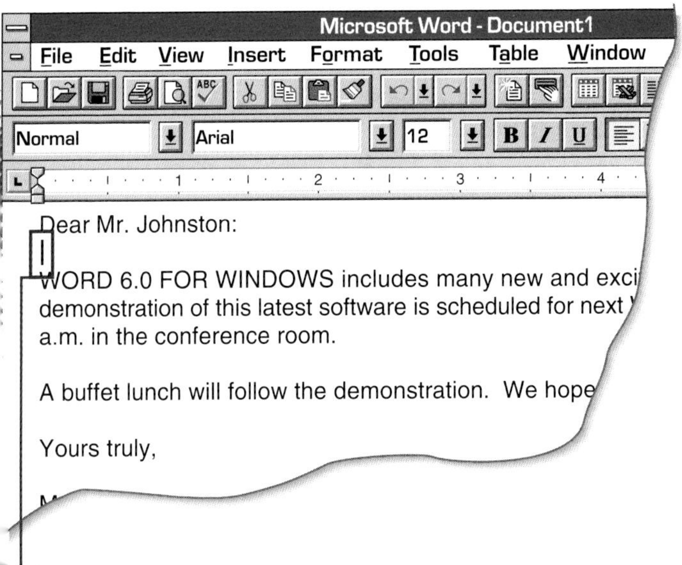
Microsoft Word - Document1
File Edit View Insert Format Tools Table Window
Normal
Arial
12
Dear Mr. Johnston:
WORD 6.0 FOR WINDOWS includes many new and exci
demonstration of this latest software is scheduled for next
a.m. in the conference room.
A buffet lunch will follow the demonstration. We hope
Yours truly,

2 Press **Delete** to remove the blank line.

Note: The remaining text moves up one line.

DELETE A CHARACTER

You can use Delete to remove the character to the right of the insertion point. The remaining text moves to the left.

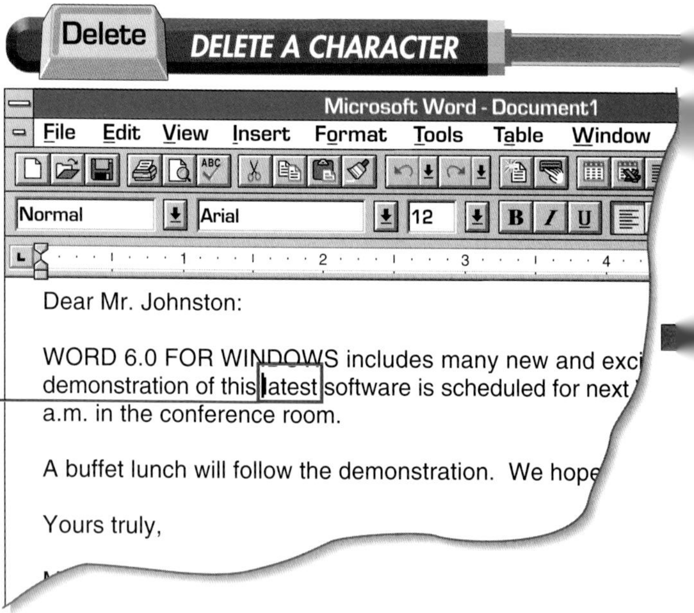
Delete
DELETE A CHARACTER
Microsoft Word - Document1
File Edit View Insert Format Tools Table Window
Normal
Arial
12
Dear Mr. Johnston:
WORD 6.0 FOR WINDOWS includes many new and exc
demonstration of this latest software is scheduled for next
a.m. in the conference room.
A buffet lunch will follow the demonstration. We hope
Yours truly,

1 Position the insertion point to the left of the character you want to delete (example: **l** in **l**atest).

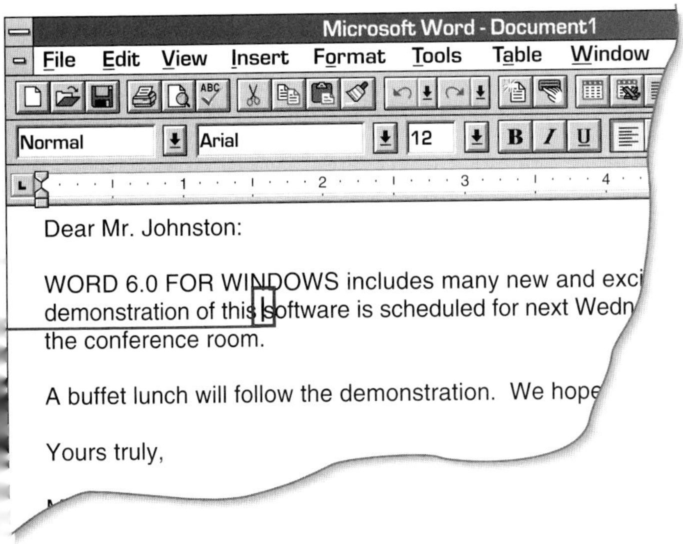
Microsoft Word - Document1
File Edit View Insert Format Tools Table Window
Normal
Arial
12
Dear Mr. Johnston:
WORD 6.0 FOR WINDOWS includes many new and exci
demonstration of this software is scheduled for next Wedn
the conference room.
A buffet lunch will follow the demonstration. We hope
Yours truly,

2 Press Delete once for each character you want to delete (example: press Delete seven times).

You can also use this key to delete characters. Position the insertion point to the right of the character(s) you want to delete and then press ←Backspace.

←Backspace

DELETE SELECTED TEXT

Delete   DELETE SELECTED TEXT

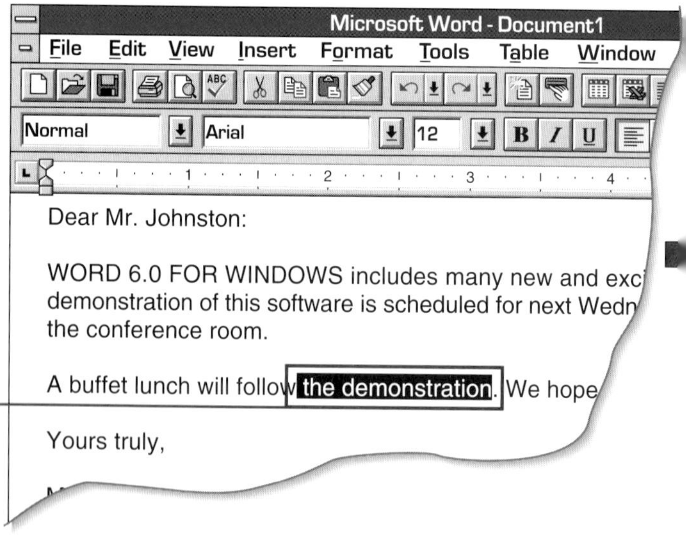

1 Select the text you want to delete.

Note: To select text, refer to pages 28 to 31.

You can use Delete to remove text you have selected. The remaining text moves up or to the left.

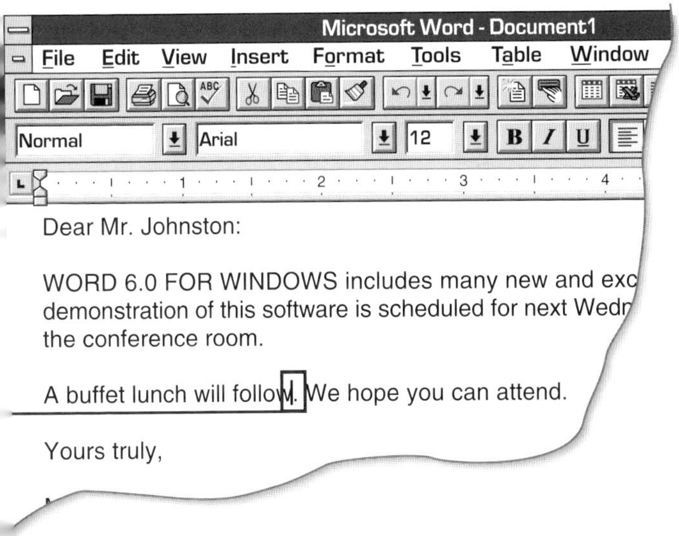
Microsoft Word - Document1
File Edit View Insert Format Tools Table Window
Normal
Arial
12
Dear Mr. Johnston:
WORD 6.0 FOR WINDOWS includes many new and exc
demonstration of this software is scheduled for next Wedn
the conference room.
A buffet lunch will follow. We hope you can attend.
Yours truly,

2 Press Delete to remove he text.

UNDO CHANGES

Word remembers the last 100 changes you made to your document. If you regret these changes, you can cancel them by using the Undo feature.

UNDO CHANGES

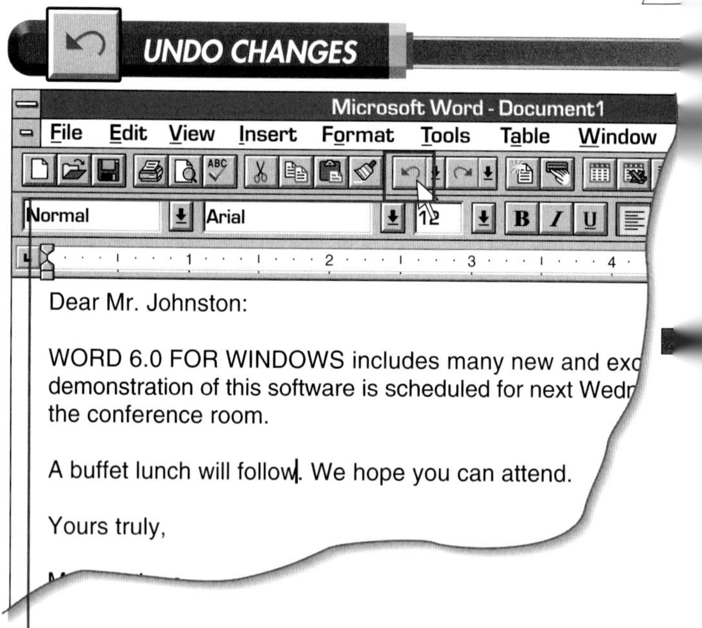

Microsoft Word - Document1
File Edit View Insert Format Tools Table Window
Normal
Arial
12
Dear Mr. Johnston:
WORD 6.0 FOR WINDOWS includes many new and exc
demonstration of this software is scheduled for next Wedn
the conference room.
A buffet lunch will follow. We hope you can attend.
Yours truly,

1 To cancel the last change you made to your document, move the mouse over the Undo button and then press the left button.

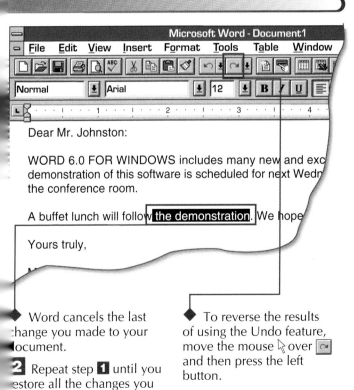

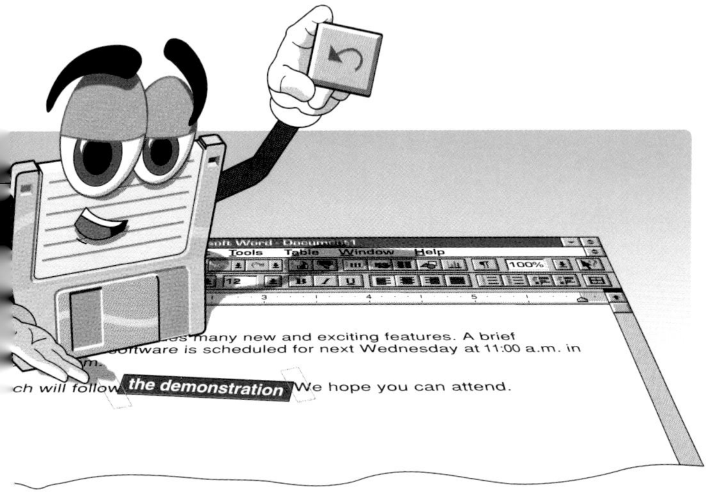
Tools Table Window Help
100%
12
many new and exciting features. A brief
oftware is scheduled for next Wednesday at 11:00 a.m. in
ch will follow the demonstration. We hope you can attend.

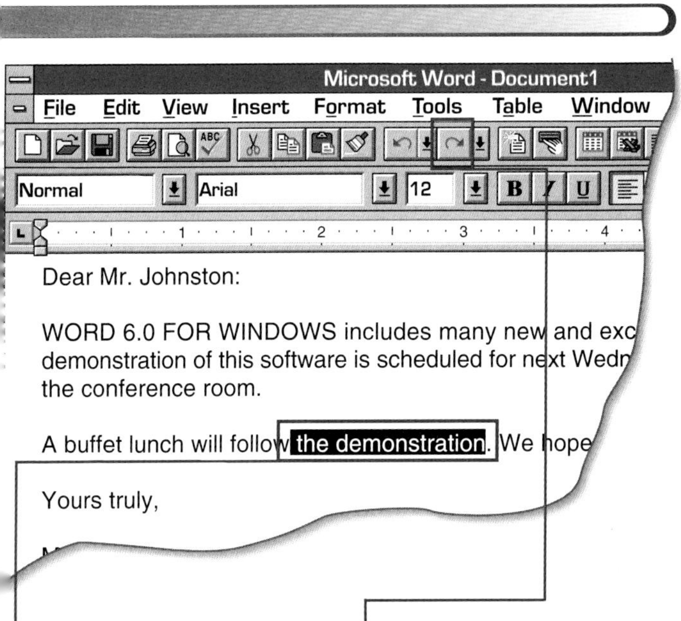
Microsoft Word - Document1
File Edit View Insert Format Tools Table Window
Normal
Arial
12
Dear Mr. Johnston:
WORD 6.0 FOR WINDOWS includes many new and exc
demonstration of this software is scheduled for next Wedn
the conference room.
A buffet lunch will follow the demonstration. We hope
Yours truly,

◆ Word cancels the last change you made to your document.

2 Repeat step **1** until you restore all the changes you regret.

◆ To reverse the results of using the Undo feature, move the mouse over and then press the left button.

MOVE TEXT

DRAG AND DROP TEXT

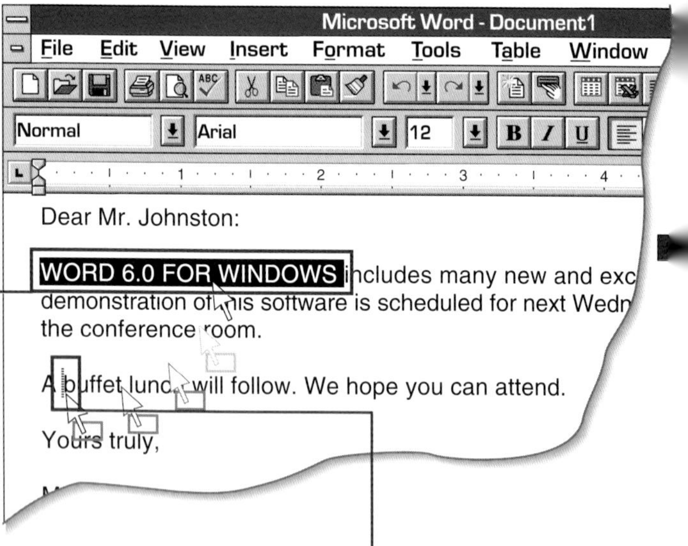

Microsoft Word - Document1
File Edit View Insert Format Tools Table Window
Normal
Arial
12
Dear Mr. Johnston:
WORD 6.0 FOR WINDOWS includes many new and exc
demonstration of this software is scheduled for next Wedn
the conference room.
A buffet lunch will follow. We hope you can attend.
Yours truly,

1 Select the text you want to move.

2 Move the mouse I anywhere over the selected text (I becomes ↖).

3 Press and hold down the left button (↖ becomes ↖).

4 Still holding down the left button, move the mouse ↖ where you want to place the text.

Note: The text will appear where you position the dotted insertion point on your screen.

You can use the Drag and Drop feature to move text from one location in your document to another. The original text disappears.

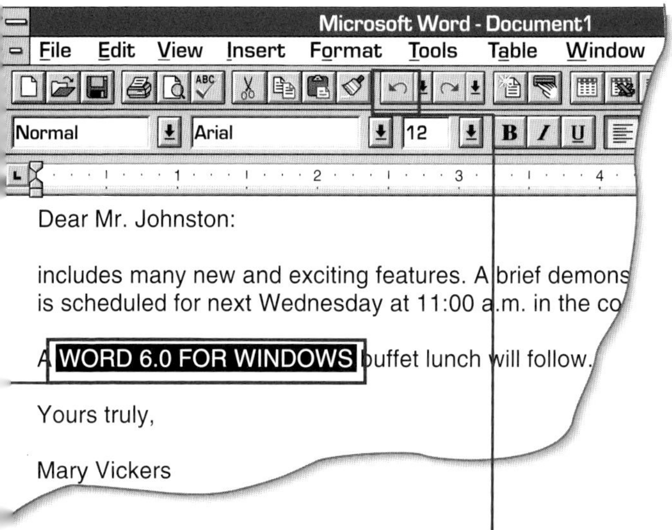
Microsoft Word - Document1
File Edit View Insert Format Tools Table Window
Normal
Arial
12
Dear Mr. Johnston:
includes many new and exciting features. A brief demons
is scheduled for next Wednesday at 11:00 a.m. in the co
A WORD 6.0 FOR WINDOWS buffet lunch will follow.
Yours truly,
Mary Vickers

Release the button
nd the text moves to
e new location.

CANCEL THE MOVE

◆ To immediately cancel the move, position the mouse over [undo button] and then press the left button.

MOVE TEXT

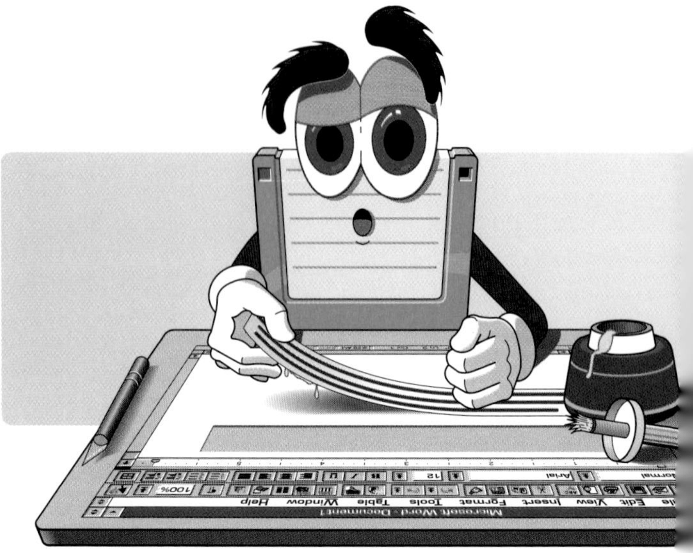

CUT AND PASTE TEXT

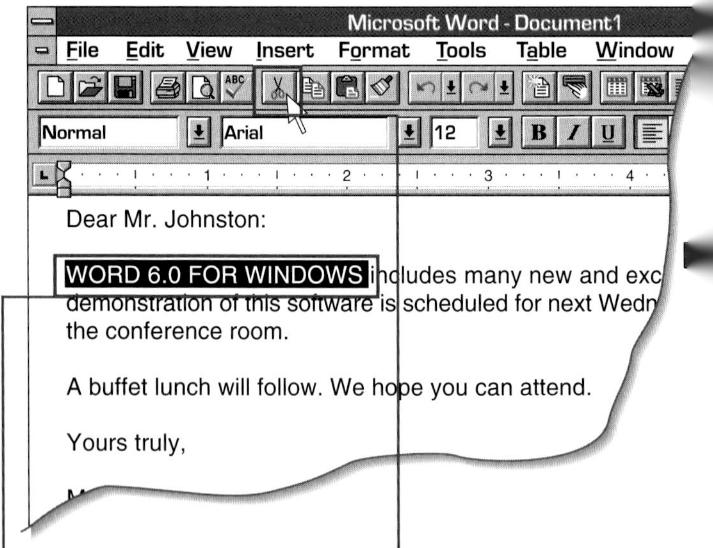
Microsoft Word - Document1
File Edit View Insert Format Tools Table Window
Normal
Arial
12
Dear Mr. Johnston:
WORD 6.0 FOR WINDOWS includes many new and exc
demonstration of this software is scheduled for next Wedn
the conference room.
A buffet lunch will follow. We hope you can attend.
Yours truly,

1 Select the text you want to move.

2 Move the mouse over and then press the left button. The text you selected disappears from your screen.

The Cut and Paste features let you move text from one location in your document to another. The original text disappears.

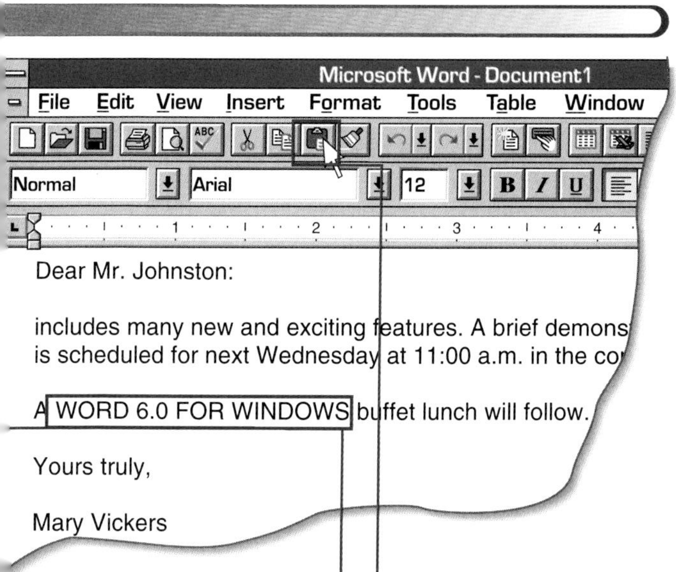
Microsoft Word - Document1
File Edit View Insert Format Tools Table Window
Normal
Arial
12
B I U
Dear Mr. Johnston:
includes many new and exciting features. A brief demons
is scheduled for next Wednesday at 11:00 a.m. in the co
A WORD 6.0 FOR WINDOWS buffet lunch will follow.
Yours truly,
Mary Vickers

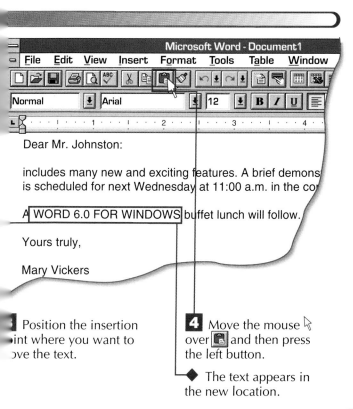

Position the insertion int where you want to ve the text.

4 Move the mouse over and then press the left button.

◆ The text appears in the new location.

COPY TEXT

You can use the Drag and Drop feature to copy text from one location in your documen to another. The origina text remains in its place.

DRAG AND DROP TEXT

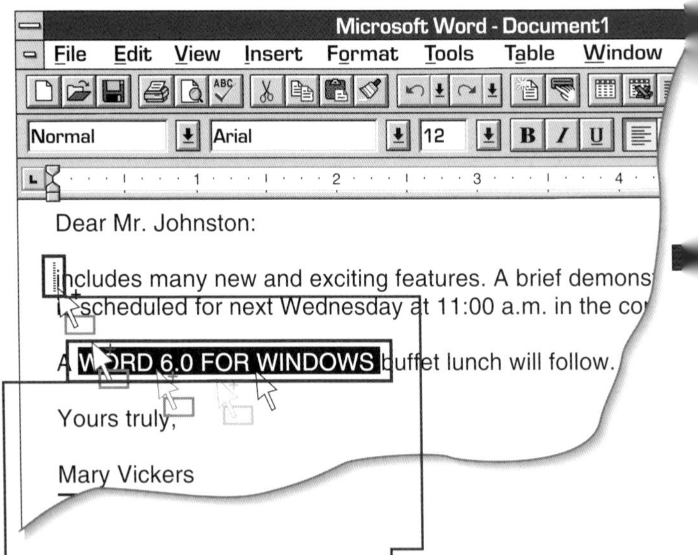

Microsoft Word - Document1
File Edit View Insert Format Tools Table Window
Normal
Arial
12
Dear Mr. Johnston:
includes many new and exciting features. A brief demons
scheduled for next Wednesday at 11:00 a.m. in the co
A WORD 6.0 FOR WINDOWS buffet lunch will follow.
Yours truly,
Mary Vickers

1 Select the text you want to copy.

2 Move the mouse anywhere over the selected text (becomes).

3 Press and hold down Ctrl and press and hold down the left button (becomes).

4 Still holding down Ctrl and the left button, drag the mouse where you want to place the copy.

Note: The text will appear where you position the dotted insertion point on your screen.

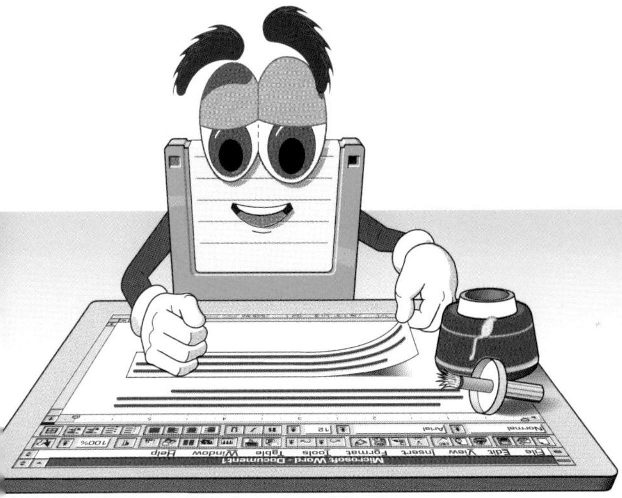

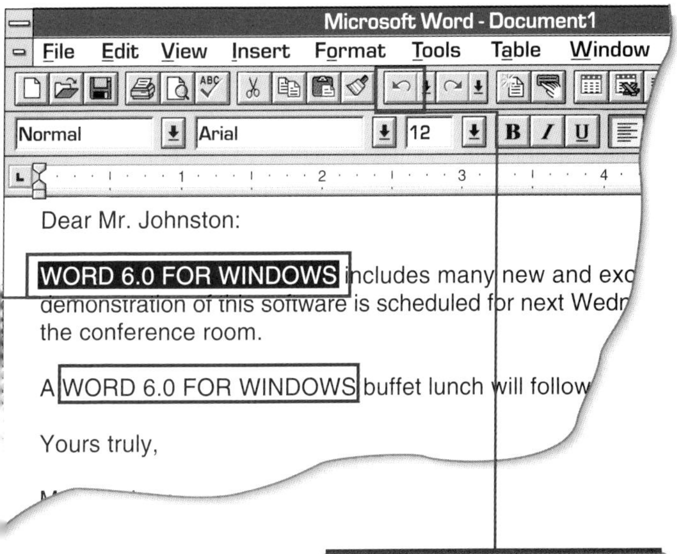
Microsoft Word - Document1
File Edit View Insert Format Tools Table Window
Normal
Arial
12
Dear Mr. Johnston:
WORD 6.0 FOR WINDOWS includes many new and exc
demonstration of this software is scheduled for next Wedn
the conference room.
A WORD 6.0 FOR WINDOWS buffet lunch will follow
Yours truly,

5 Release the button nd then Ctrl.

◆ A copy of the text ppears in the new ocation.

CANCEL THE COPY

◆ To immediately cancel the copy, position the mouse over the undo button and then press the left button.

COPY TEXT

The Copy and Paste features let you copy text from one location in your document to another. The original text remains in its place.

COPY AND PASTE TEXT

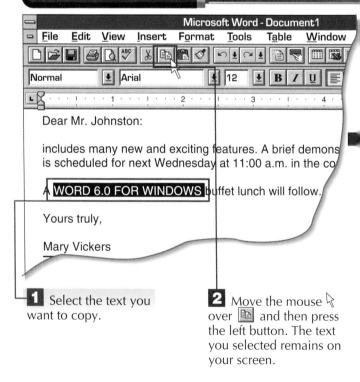

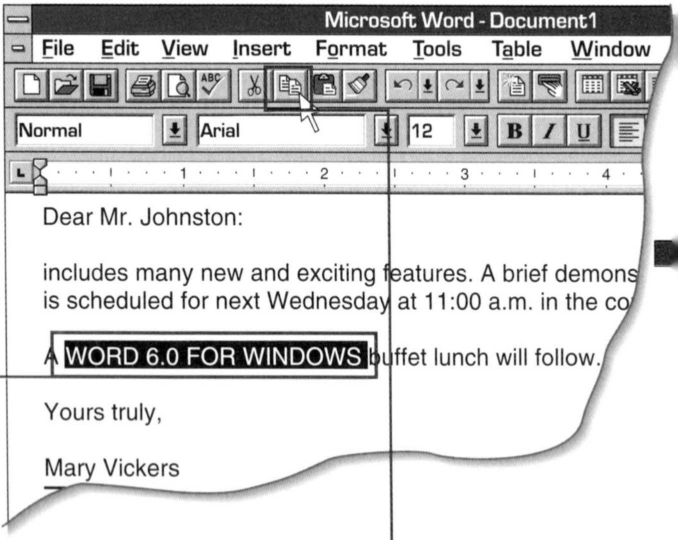

Microsoft Word - Document1
File Edit View Insert Format Tools Table Window
Normal
Arial
12
Dear Mr. Johnston:
includes many new and exciting features. A brief demons
is scheduled for next Wednesday at 11:00 a.m. in the co
A WORD 6.0 FOR WINDOWS buffet lunch will follow.
Yours truly,
Mary Vickers

1 Select the text you want to copy.

2 Move the mouse over the copy button and then press the left button. The text you selected remains on your screen.

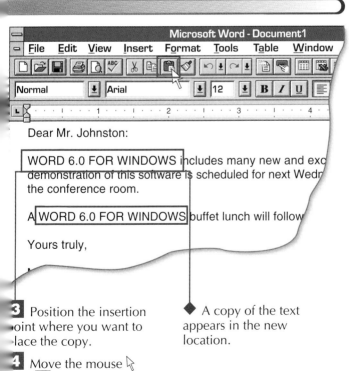

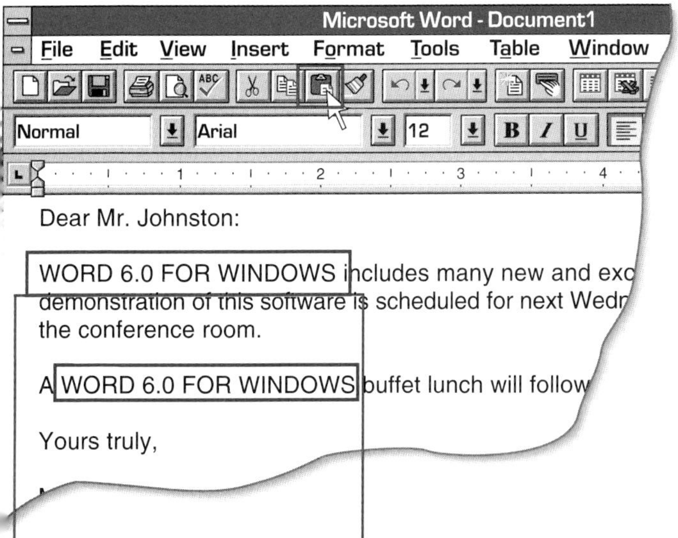
Microsoft Word - Document1
File Edit View Insert Format Tools Table Window
Normal
Arial
12
Dear Mr. Johnston:
WORD 6.0 FOR WINDOWS includes many new and exc
demonstration of this software is scheduled for next Wedn
the conference room.
A WORD 6.0 FOR WINDOWS buffet lunch will follow
Yours truly,

3 Position the insertion oint where you want to lace the copy.

4 Move the mouse ver and then press e left button.

◆ A copy of the text appears in the new location.

CHANGE THE CASE OF TEXT

Change Case
Sentence case.
lowercase
UPPERCASE
Title Case
tOGGLE cASE
OK
Cancel
Help
Dear Mr. Johnston:
A buffet lunch will follow.
Yours truly,
Mary Vickers

CHANGE THE CASE OF TEXT

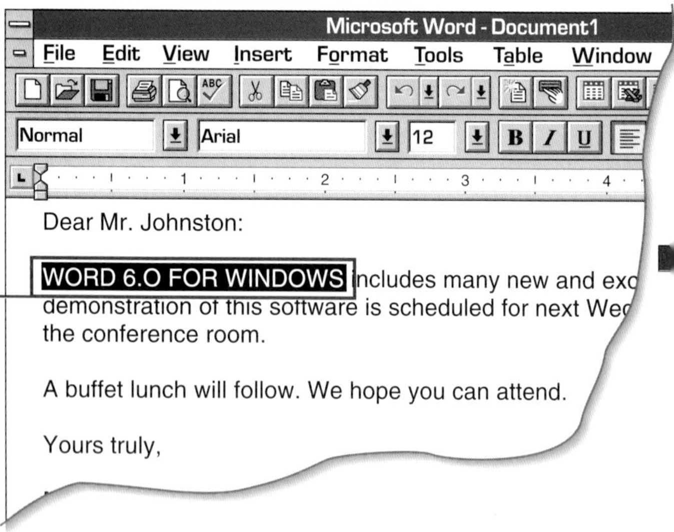

Microsoft Word - Document1
File Edit View Insert Format Tools Table Window
Normal
Arial
12
Dear Mr. Johnston:
WORD 6.O FOR WINDOWS includes many new and exc
demonstration of this software is scheduled for next We
the conference room.
A buffet lunch will follow. We hope you can attend.
Yours truly,

1 To change the case of text in your document, select the text you want to change.

Note: To select text, refer to pages 28 to 31.

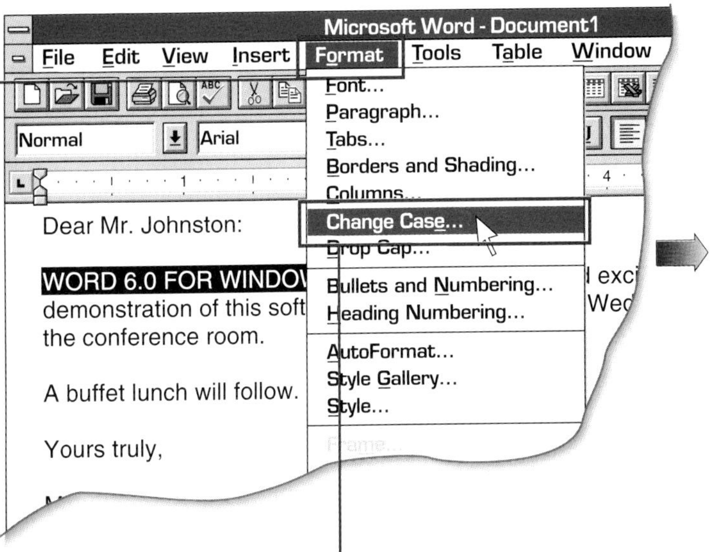

2 Move the mouse over **Format** and then press the left button.

3 Move the mouse over **Change Case** and then press the left button.

Note: To continue, refer to the next page.

CHANGE THE CASE OF TEXT

CHANGE THE CASE OF TEXT (Continued)

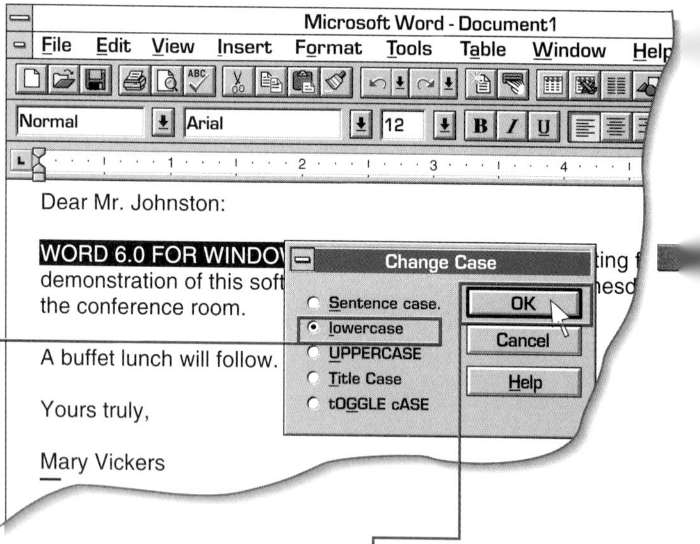

◆ The **Change Case** dialog box appears.

4 Move the mouse over the case you want to use (example: **lowercase**) and then press the left button (○ changes to ◉).

5 Move the mouse over **OK** and then press the left button.

Word offers
five case
options.

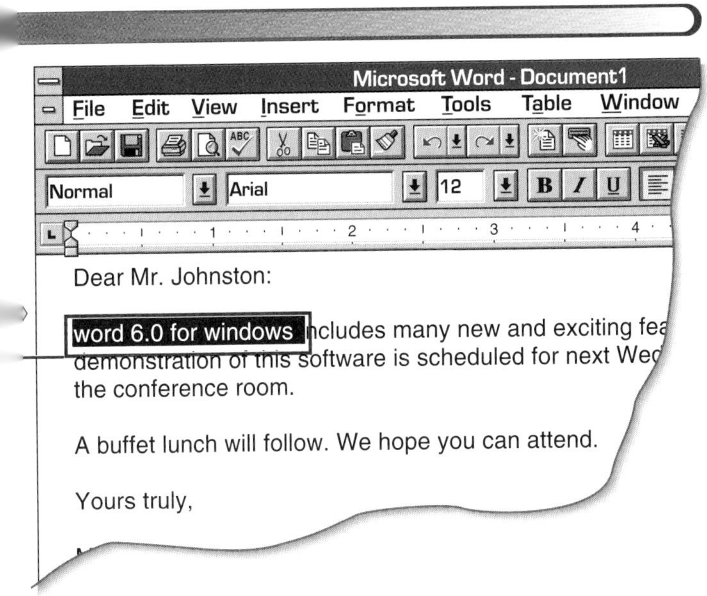
Microsoft Word - Document1
File
Edit
View
Insert
Format
Tools
Table
Window
Normal
Arial
12
Dear Mr. Johnston:
word 6.0 for windows includes many new and exciting fea
demonstration of this software is scheduled for next We
the conference room.
A buffet lunch will follow. We hope you can attend.
Yours truly,

◆ The text you selected changes to the new case.

FIND TEXT

FIND TEXT

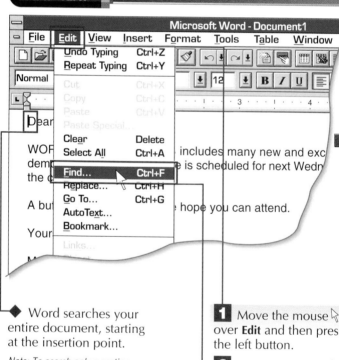

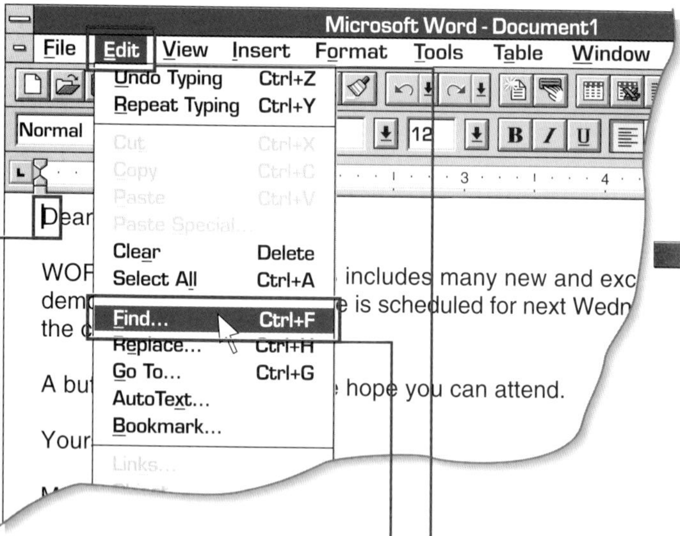

◆ Word searches your entire document, starting at the insertion point.

*Note: To search only a section of your document, select the text before performing step **1**. To select text, refer to pages 28 to 31.*

1 Move the mouse over **Edit** and then press the left button.

2 Move the mouse over **Find** and then press the left button.

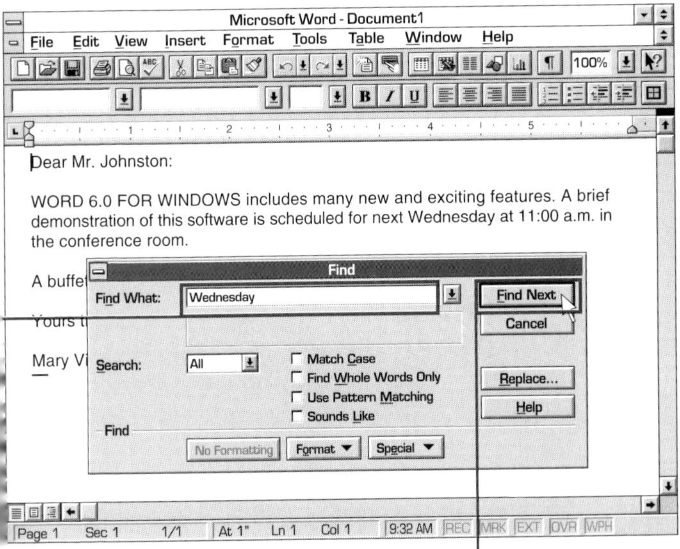

◆ The **Find** dialog box appears.

3 Type the text you want to find (example: **Wednesday**).

4 To find the next matching word in your document, move the mouse over **Find Next** and then press the left button.

Note: To continue, refer to the next page.

FIND TEXT

FIND TEXT (Continued)

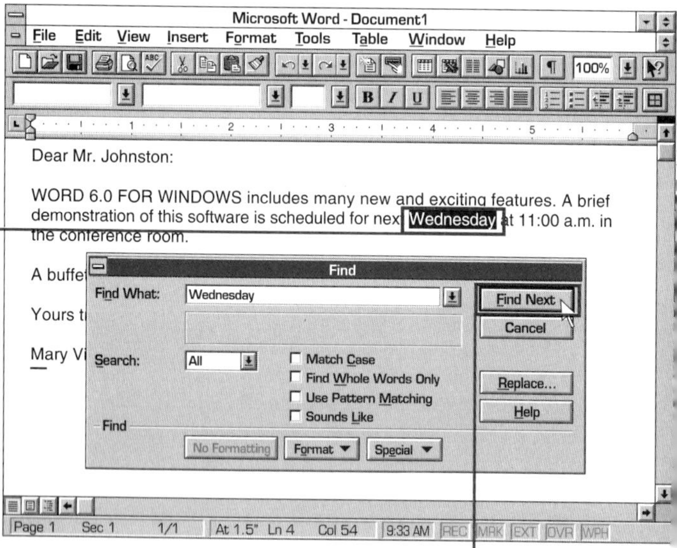

◆ Word highlights the first matching word it finds.

5 To find the next matching word, move the mouse ⇖ over **Find Next** and then press the left button.

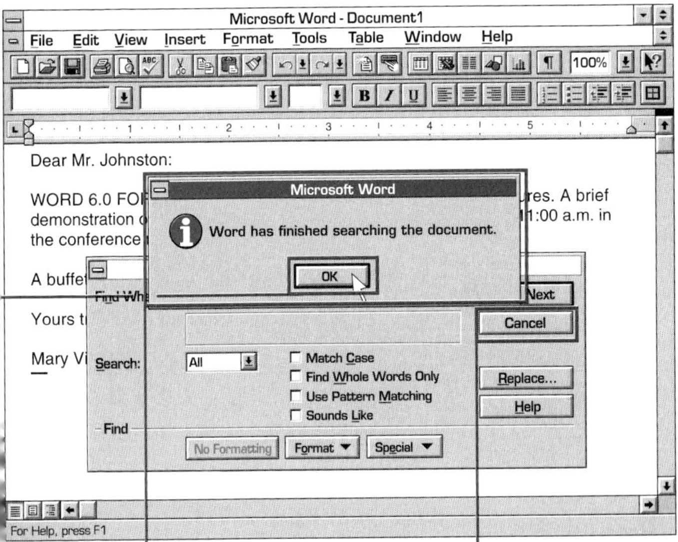

◆ This dialog box appears when there are no more matching words in your document.

6 To close the dialog box, move the mouse over **OK** and then press the left button.

7 To close the **Find** dialog box, move the mouse over **Cancel** and then press the left button.

REPLACE TEXT

Well Andrew, I was as surprised that you didn't win the Nobel prize thingy for chem... I mean honestly, who could possibly be doing anything more important in chemistry than you, and your subzero activated bug spray.

Obviously these Nobel types don't have any major bug problems. I refuse to believe that Europeans don't want a better bug spray, especially the more northern countries. And where do these Nobel prizes come from anyway - Switzerland! They probably have lots of uses for a subzero repellent in the Alps, but they're probably so busy swatting blackflies, they can't make a rational choice.

Send them a free sample, and you'll get the Noble prize next year...

REPLACE TEXT

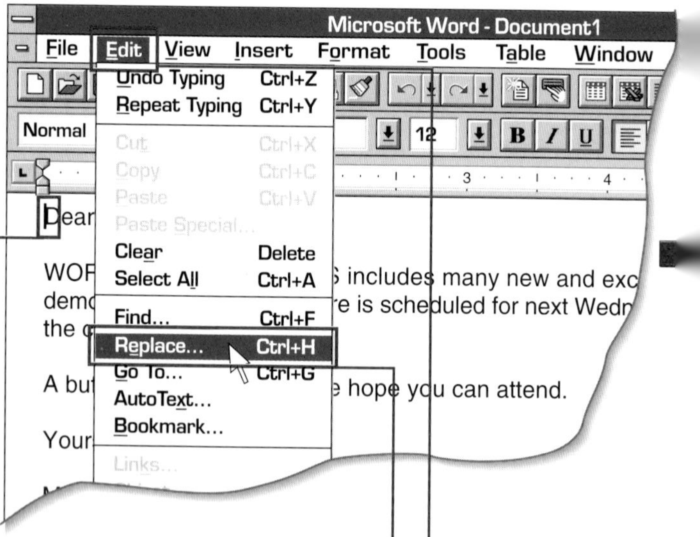

◆ Word searches your entire document, starting at the insertion point.

Note: To search only a section of your document, select the text before performing step **1**. *To select text, refer to pages 28 to 31.*

1 Move the mouse ⌖ over **Edit** and then press the left button.

2 Move the mouse ⌖ over **Replace** and then press the left button.

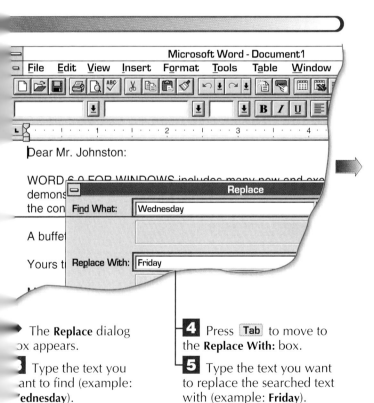

You can use
the Replace feature
to locate and replace
every occurrence of a word
or phrase in your
document.

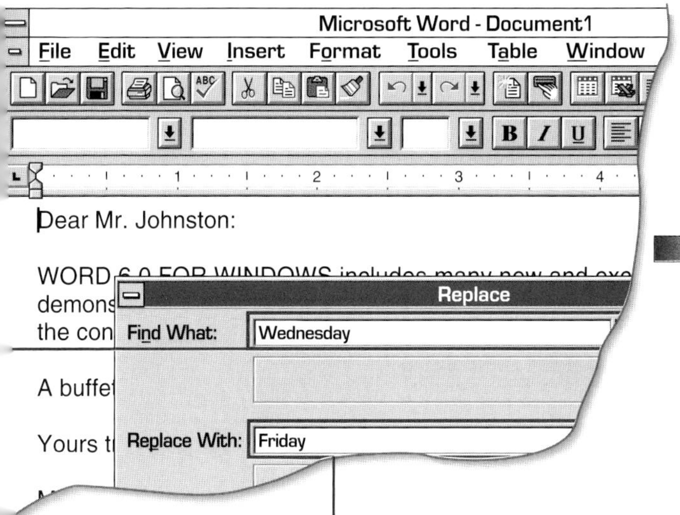
Microsoft Word - Document1
File Edit View Insert Format Tools Table Window
Dear Mr. Johnston:
Replace
Find What: Wedneday
Replace With: Friday

- The **Replace** dialog box appears.

3 Type the text you want to find (example: **Wednesday**).

4 Press Tab to move to the **Replace With:** box.

5 Type the text you want to replace the searched text with (example: **Friday**).

Note: To continue, refer to the next page.

REPLACE TEXT

The Replace feature is useful when you have to make the same change several times in a document.

...ndrew, I w... ...urprised that you didn't win the Nobel ...hingy for chem... ...I mean honestly, who could possibly be ...g anything more ...portant in chemistry than you, and your ...ubzero activated bu... spray.

Obviously these Nobel ...ypes don't have any major bug problems. I refuse to believe that Europeans don't want a better bug spray, especially the more northern countries. And where do the Nobel prizes come from anyway - Switzerland! They probably have lots of uses for a subzero repellent in the Alps, but they're probably so busy swatting blackflies, they can't make a rational choice.

Send them a free sample, and you'll get the Noble prize next year...

REPLACE TEXT (Continued)

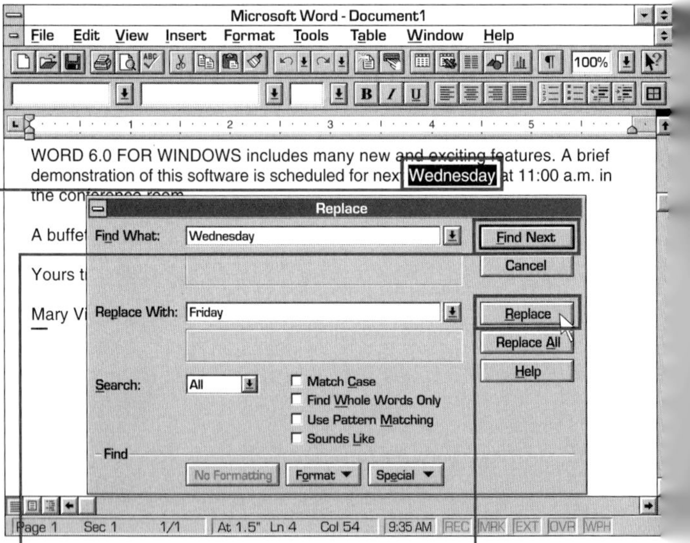

6 To start the search, move the mouse ⌖ over **Find Next** and then press the left button.

◆ Word highlights the first matching word it finds.

7 To replace the word, move the mouse ⌖ over **Replace** and then press the left button.

Note: If you do not want to replace the word, repeat step 6 to find the next matching word in your document.

TIP

You can replace all matching words or phrases in your document at the same time.

Replace steps **6** *to* **8** *below with the following:*

Replace All

◆ *Move the mouse over* ***Replace All*** *and then press the left button.*

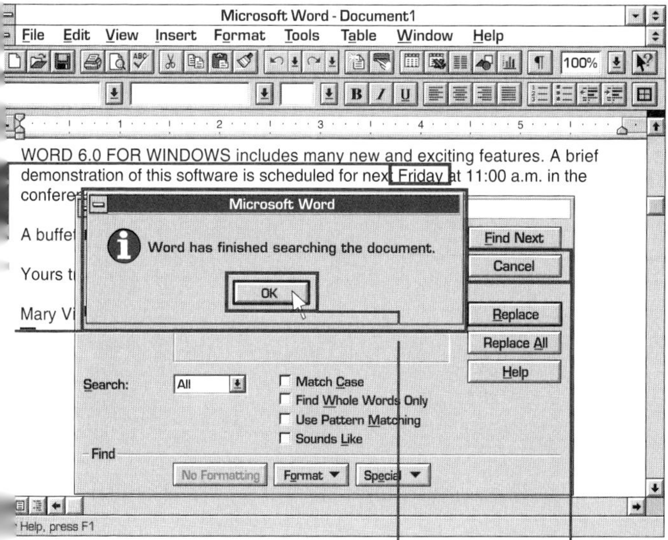

· Word replaces the word
d searches for the next
atching word.

Repeat step **7** for each
ord you want to replace.

This dialog box appears
en there are no more
atching words in your
cument.

9 To close this dialog box, move the mouse over **OK** and then press the left button.

10 To close the **Replace** dialog box, move the mouse over **Cancel** or **Close** and then press the left button.

CHECK SPELLING

You can use the Spelling feature to find and correct spelling errors in your document.
Word Dictionary

CHECK SPELLING

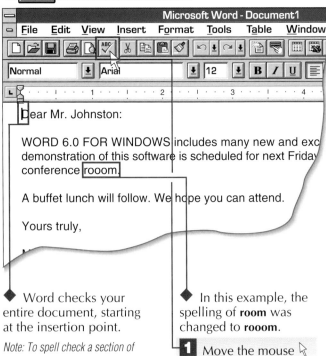

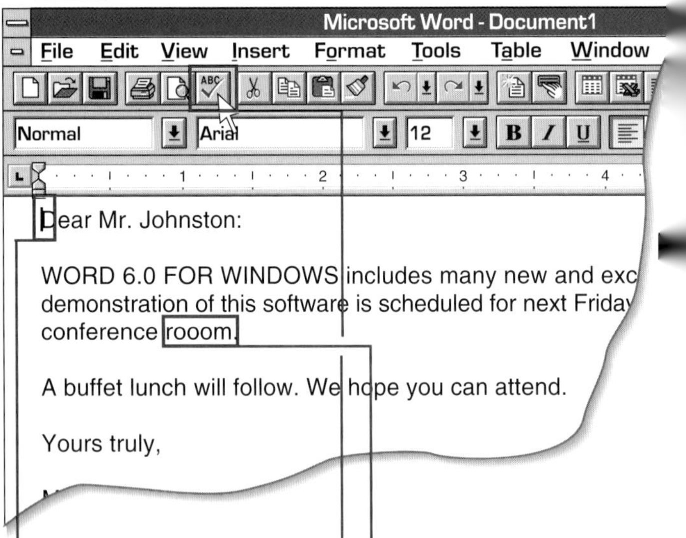
Microsoft Word - Document1
File Edit View Insert Format Tools Table Window
Normal
Arial
12
Dear Mr. Johnston:
WORD 6.0 FOR WINDOWS includes many new and exc
demonstration of this software is scheduled for next Friday
conference rooom.
A buffet lunch will follow. We hope you can attend.
Yours truly,

◆ Word checks your entire document, starting at the insertion point.

Note: To spell check a section of your document, select the text before performing step **1**. *To select text, refer to pages 28 to 31.*

◆ In this example, the spelling of **room** was changed to **rooom**.

1 Move the mouse over the Spelling button and then press the left button.

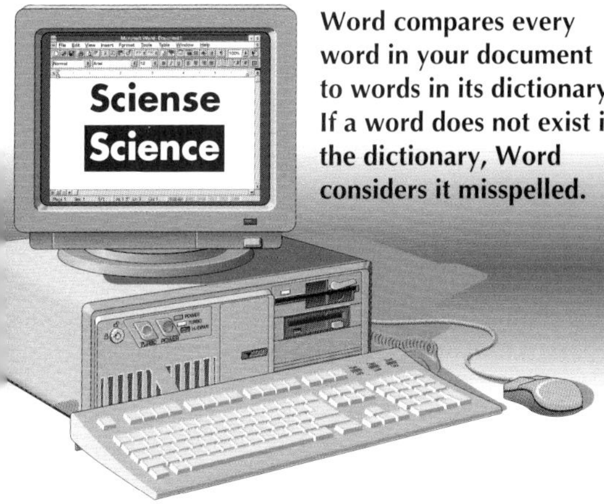

Word compares every word in your document to words in its dictionary. If a word does not exist in the dictionary, Word considers it misspelled.

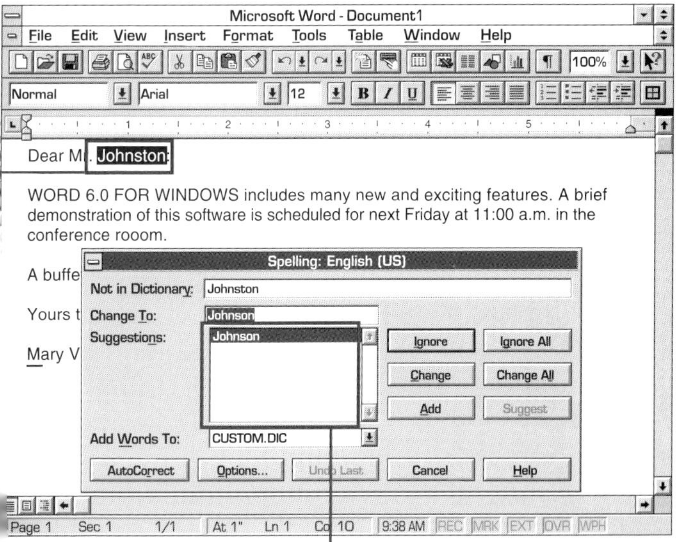

◆ The **Spelling** dialog box ppears.

◆ Word highlights the first vord it does not recognize xample: **Johnston**).

◆ The **Suggestions:** box displays alternative spellings.

Note: To continue, refer to the next page.

CHECK SPELLING

The Spell check will find many types of errors in your document.

CHECK SPELLING (Continued)

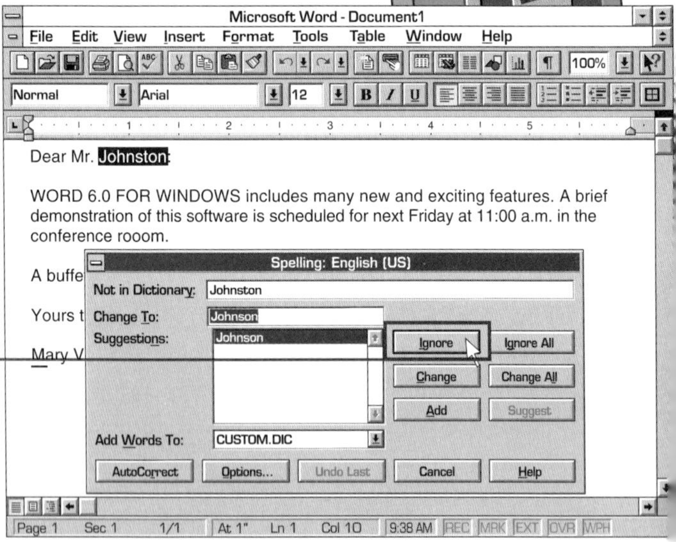
Microsoft Word - Document1
File Edit View Insert Format Tools Table Window Help
Normal
Arial
12
100%
Dear Mr. Johnston:
WORD 6.0 FOR WINDOWS includes many new and exciting features. A brief demonstration of this software is scheduled for next Friday at 11:00 a.m. in the conference rooom.
A buffe
Yours t
Mary V
Spelling: English (US)
Not in Dictionary: Johnston
Change To: Johnson
Suggestions: Johnson
Ignore
Ignore All
Change
Change All
Add
Suggest
Add Words To: CUSTOM.DIC
AutoCorrect
Options...
Undo Last
Cancel
Help
Page 1 Sec 1 1/1 At 1" Ln 1 Col 10 9:38 AM REC MRK EXT OVR WPH

Ignore misspelled word

2 If you do not want to change the spelling of the highlighted word, move the mouse over **Ignore** and then press the left button.

Note: To change the spelling of a word and continue the spell check, refer to the next page.

The spell check will find:	Example:
Misspelled words	The girl is six **yeers** old.
Duplicate words	The girl is **six six** years old.

The spell check will not find:	Example:
A correctly spelled word used in the wrong context	The girl is **sit** years old.

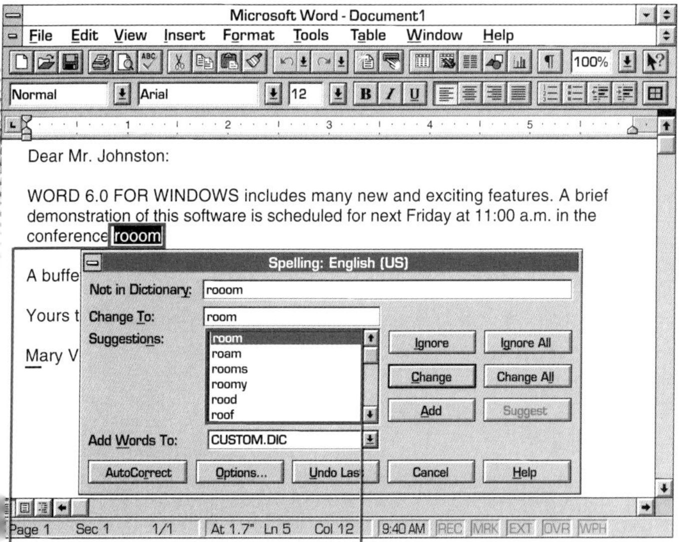

◆ Word highlights the next vord it does not recognize xample: **rooom**).

◆ The **Suggestions:** box displays alternative spellings.

Note: To continue, refer to the next page.

CHECK SPELLING

CHECK SPELLING (Continued)

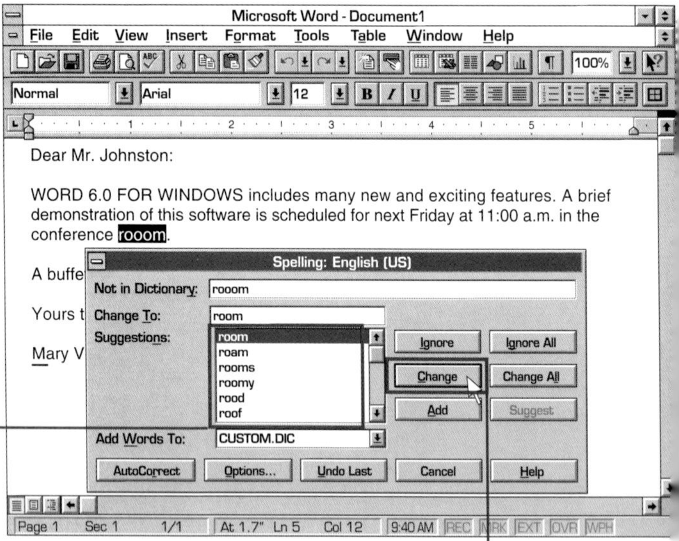

Correct misspelled word

3 To select the correct spelling, move the mouse over the word you want to use (example: **room**) and then press the left button.

4 To replace the misspelle word in your document with the correct spelling, move th mouse over **Change** and then press the left button.

To cancel the spell check at any time, move the mouse over **Close** or **Cancel** and then press the left button.

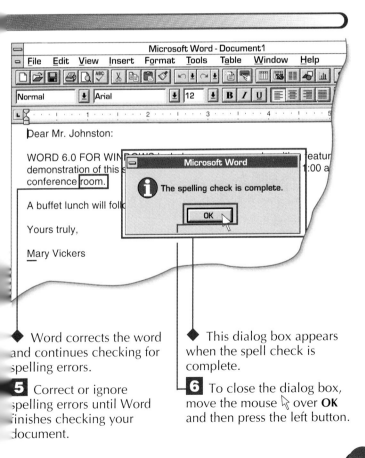

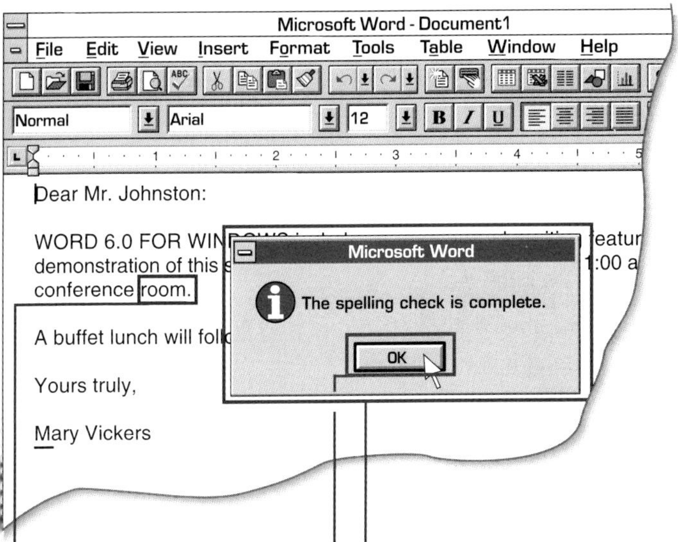

◆ Word corrects the word and continues checking for spelling errors.

5 Correct or ignore spelling errors until Word finishes checking your document.

◆ This dialog box appears when the spell check is complete.

6 To close the dialog box, move the mouse over **OK** and then press the left button.

USING AUTOCORRECT

ADD TEXT TO AUTOCORRECT

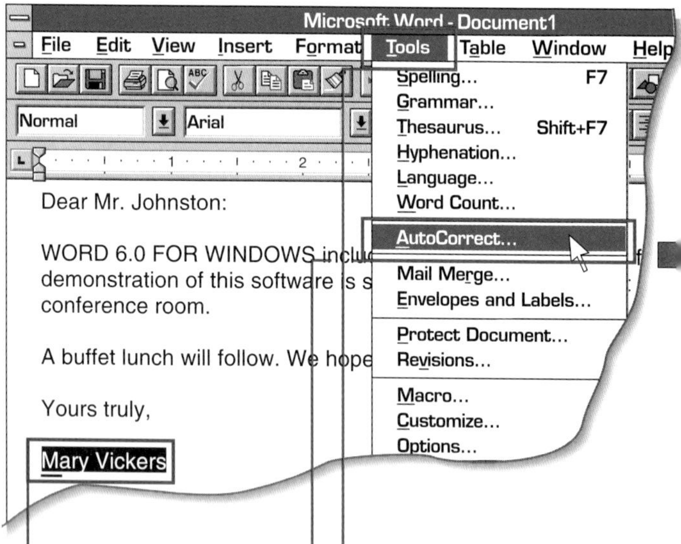
Microsoft Word - Document1
File
Edit
View
Insert
Format
Tools
Table
Window
Help
Normal
Arial
Spelling... F7
Grammar...
Thesaurus... Shift+F7
Hyphenation...
Language...
Word Count...
AutoCorrect...
Mail Merge...
Envelopes and Labels...
Protect Document...
Revisions...
Macro...
Customize...
Options...
Dear Mr. Johnston:
WORD 6.0 FOR WINDOWS inclu
demonstration of this software is s
conference room.
A buffet lunch will follow. We hope
Yours truly,
Mary Vickers

1 Select the text you want Word to automatically place in your documents.

Note: To select text, refer to pages 28 to 31.

2 Move the mouse ⇖ over **Tools** and then press the left button.

3 Move the mouse ⇖ over **AutoCorrect** and then press the left button.

Word automatically corrects common spelling errors as you type. You can customize the AutoCorrect list to include words you often misspell or words you frequently use.

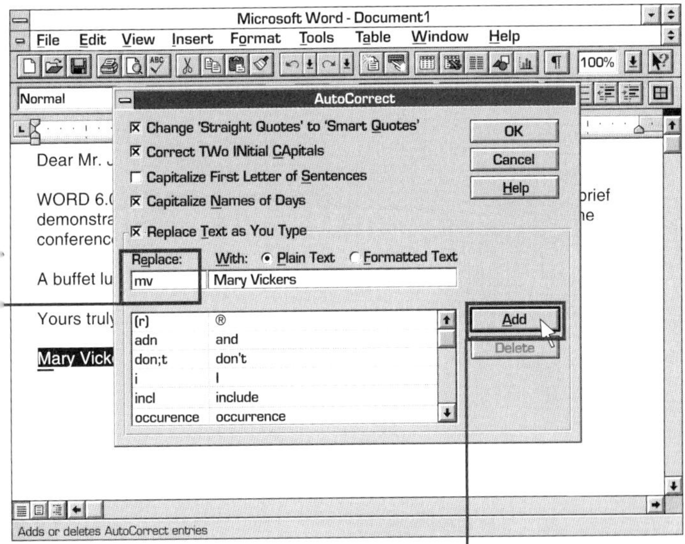

◆ The **AutoCorrect** dialog box appears.

4 Type the text you want Word to automatically replace every time you type it in a document (example: **mv**).

Note: This text cannot contain any spaces. Also, do not use a real word.

5 Move the mouse over **Add** and then press the left button.

Note: To continue, refer to the next page.

If you type one of the following words and then press the Spacebar, Word will automatically change the word for you.

ADD TEXT TO AUTOCORRECT (Continued)

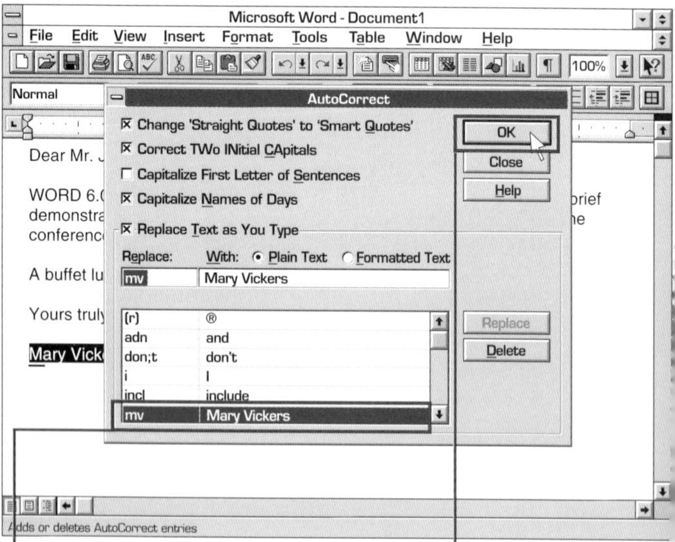

◆ The entry appears in the AutoCorrect list.

6 To close the **AutoCorrect** dialog box and return to your document, move the mouse over **OK** and then press the left button.

Text You Type	Replace With
(r)	®
adn	and
don;t	don't
i	I
incl	include
occurence	occurrence
recieve	receive
seperate	separate
teh	the

USING AUTOCORRECT

After you add text to the AutoCorrect list, Word will automatically change the text each time you type it in your document.

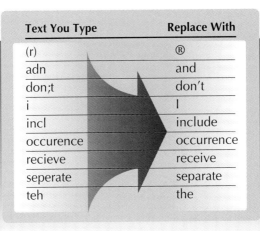

1 Position the insertion point where you want the text to appear.

2 Type the text (example: **mv**).

3 Press the **Spacebar** and the AutoCorrect text replaces the text you typed.

Note: The text will not change until you press the ***Spacebar****.*

USING AUTOTEXT

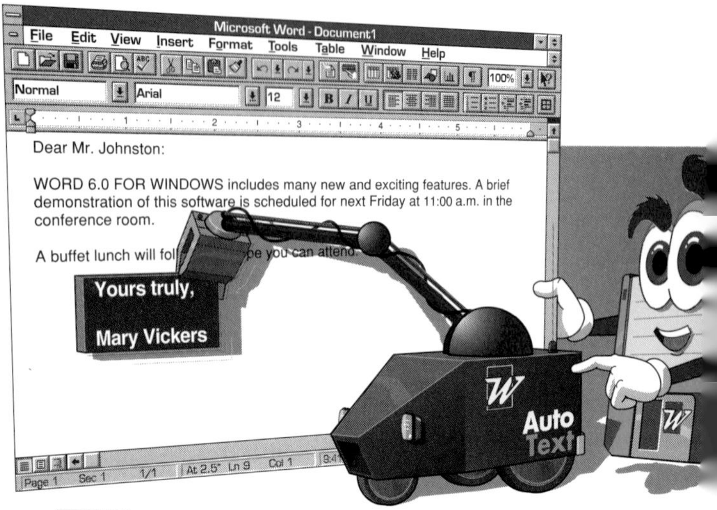
Microsoft Word - Document1
File Edit View Insert Format Tools Table Window Help
Dear Mr. Johnston:
WORD 6.0 FOR WINDOWS includes many new and exciting features. A brief demonstration of this software is scheduled for next Friday at 11:00 a.m. in the conference room.
Yours truly,
Mary Vickers
Auto Text

ADD TEXT TO AUTOTEXT

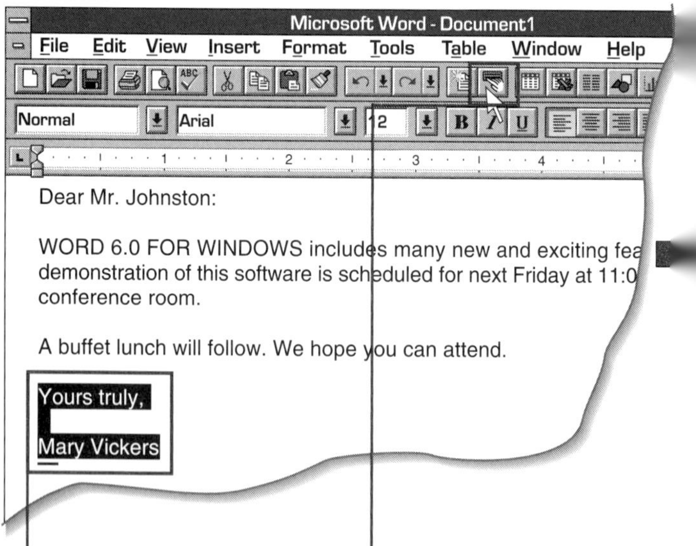
Microsoft Word - Document1
File Edit View Insert Format Tools Table Window Help
Normal
Arial
Dear Mr. Johnston:
A buffet lunch will follow. We hope you can attend.
Yours truly,
Mary Vickers

1 Select the text you want to appear in your document each time you type its abbreviated name.

Note: To select text, refer to pages 28 to 31.

2 Move the mouse over the AutoText button and then press the left button.

The AutoText feature lets you store frequently used words, phrases and sentences. You can then insert them into your document by typing an abbreviated version of the text.

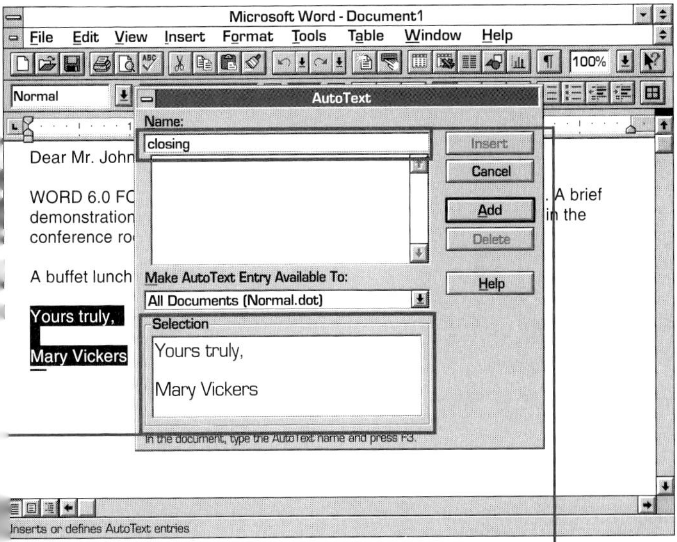

◆ The **AutoText** dialog ɔox appears.

◆ The text you selected n your document appears n the **Selection** box.

3 Type an abbreviated name for the text (example: **closing**).

Note: To continue, refer to the next page.

ADD TEXT TO AUTOTEXT (Continued)

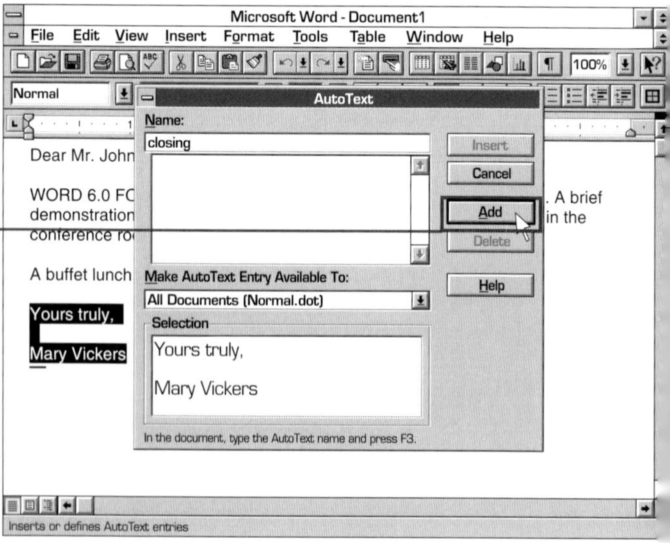

4 Move the mouse over **Add** and then press the left button.

The AutoText and AutoCorrect features both insert text into your document. However, there are two distinct differences:

AUTOTEXT

◆ Use AutoText to insert groups of text or to insert text you use occasionally.

◆ Word inserts the text only when you instruct it to do so.

AUTOCORRECT

◆ Use AutoCorrect to correct your most common spelling errors or to insert text you use frequently (i.e., every day).

◆ Word automatically inserts the text as you type.

USING AUTOTEXT

After you add text to the AutoText list, you can insert the text into your document.

1 Position the insertion point where you want the text to appear.

2 Type the name of the AutoText entry (example: **closing**).

3 Move the mouse over the AutoText button and then press the left button.

◆ The AutoText entry replaces the text you typed in your document.

USING THE THESAURUS

The Thesaurus lets you replace a word in your document with one that is more suitable.
Word Thesaurus

USING THE THESAURUS

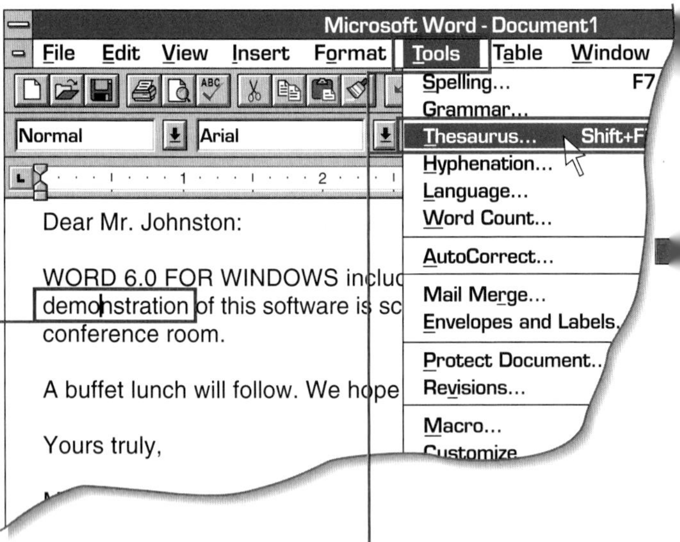

1 Move the mouse I anywhere over the word you want to look up (example: **demonstration**) and then press the left button.

2 Move the mouse over **Tools** and then press the left button.

3 Move the mouse over **Thesaurus** and then press the left button.

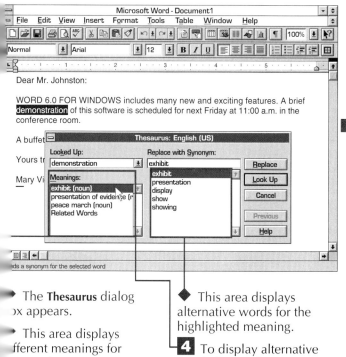

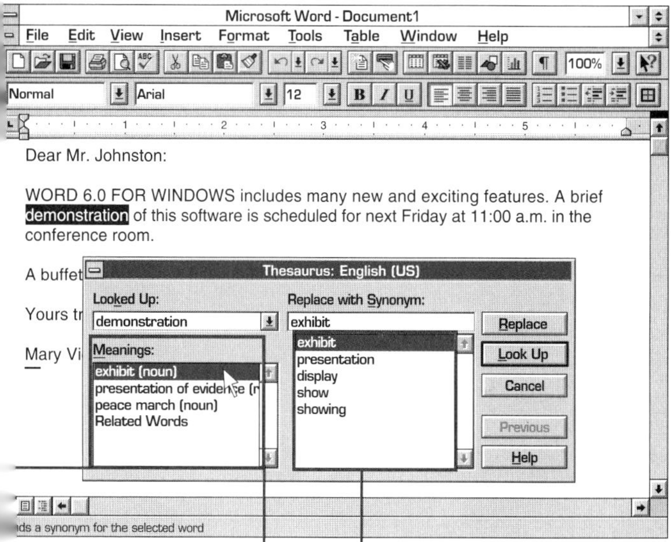

◆ The **Thesaurus** dialog ›x appears.

◆ This area displays fferent meanings for e word.

◆ This area displays alternative words for the highlighted meaning.

4 To display alternative words for another meaning, move the mouse ⇖ over the meaning and then press the left button.

Note: To continue, refer to the next page.

USING THE THESAURUS

You can use the Thesaurus to add variety to your writing.
Word Thesaur

USING THE THESAURUS (Continued)

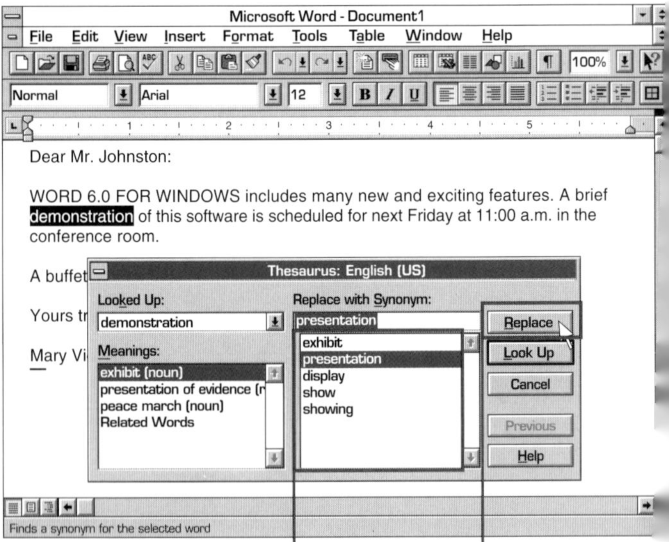
Microsoft Word - Document1
File Edit View Insert Format Tools Table Window Help
100%
Normal
Arial
12
Dear Mr. Johnston:
WORD 6.0 FOR WINDOWS includes many new and exciting features. A brief demonstration of this software is scheduled for next Friday at 11:00 a.m. in the conference room.
A buffet
Yours tr
Mary Vi
Thesaurus: English (US)
Looked Up:
demonstration
Meanings:
exhibit (noun)
presentation of evidence (r
peace march (noun)
Related Words
Replace with Synonym:
presentation
exhibit
presentation
display
show
showing
Replace
Look Up
Cancel
Previous
Help
Finds a synonym for the selected word

5 To select the word you want to use, move the mouse over the word (example: **presentation**) and then press the left button.

6 Move the mouse over **Replace** and then press the left button.

Make
-create
-produce

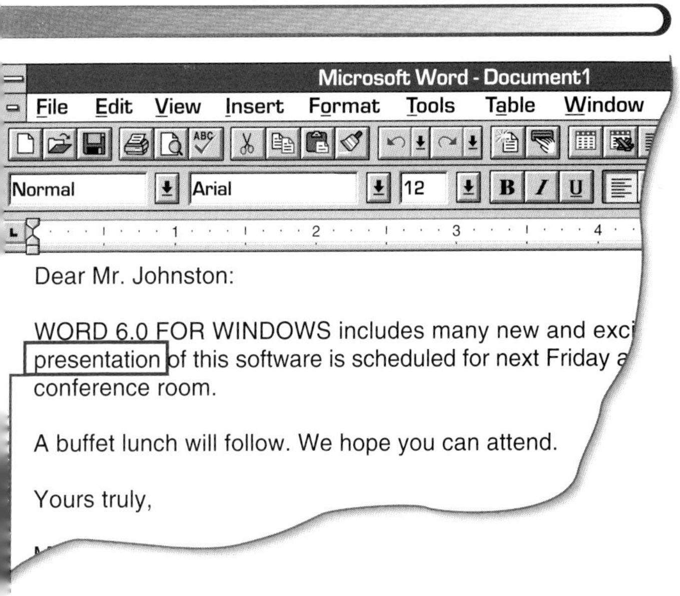
Microsoft Word - Document1
File Edit View Insert Format Tools Table Window
Normal
Arial
12
Dear Mr. Johnston:
WORD 6.0 FOR WINDOWS includes many new and exci
presentation of this software is scheduled for next Friday a
conference room.
A buffet lunch will follow. We hope you can attend.
Yours truly,

The word from the
hesaurus replaces the
ord in your document.

DRIVES

Your computer stores programs and data in devices called "drives." Like a filing cabinet, a drive stores information in an organized way.

Drives

Most computers have one hard drive and one or two floppy drives to store information.

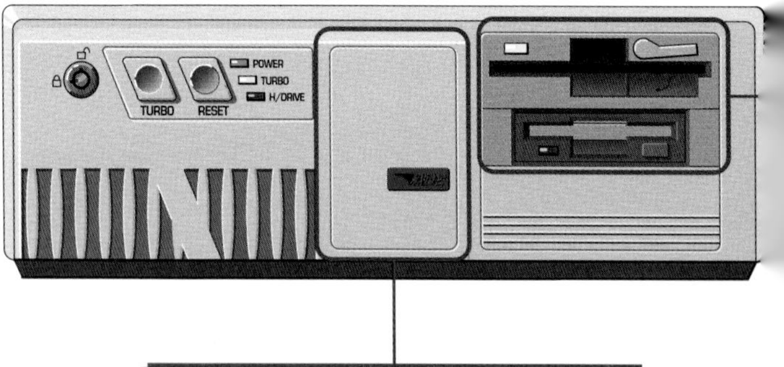

Hard drive (C:)

◆ A hard drive permanently stores programs and data. Most computers have at least one hard drive, called drive **C**.

Note: Your computer may be set up to have additional hard drives (example: ***drive D****).*

DRIVE NAME

A: A drive name consists of two parts: the letter and a colon (:). The colon represents the word "drive." For example, **A:** refers to the **A drive**.

Floppy drives (A: and B:)

A floppy drive stores programs and data on removable diskettes (or floppy disks). A diskette operates slower and stores less data than a hard drive.

Diskettes are used to:

- Load new programs.
- Store backup copies of data.
- Transfer data to other computers.

If your computer has only one floppy drive, it is called drive **A**.

If your computer has two floppy drives, the second drive is called drive **B**.

DIRECTORIES

Directories are like the drawers and folders in a filing cabinet. They help you organize the information stored in the drives.
C:
notice.doc
winword

◆ Hard drive (C:)

A hard drive stores programs and data. It contains many directories to help organize your information.

◆ Files

When you save a document, Word stores it as a file.

◆ Directories

A directory usually contains related information. For example, the **winword** directory contains the Microsoft Word files.

NAME A DOCUMENT

When you save a document for the first time, you must give it a name.

A file name consists of two parts: a name and an extension. You must separate these parts with a period.

notice . doc

Name

The name should describe the contents of a file. It can have up to eight characters.

Period

A period must separate the name and the extension.

Extension

The extension describes the type of information a file contains. It can have up to three characters.

*Note: **doc** stands for **document**.*

You should give your document a descriptive name to remind you of the information it contains.

A file name *can* contain the following characters:

◆ The letters A to Z, upper or lower case

◆ The numbers 0 to 9

◆ The symbols
_ ^ $ ~ ! # % & { } @ ( )

A file name *cannot* contain the following characters:

◆ A comma (,)

◆ A blank space

◆ The symbols
* ? ; [ ] + = \ / : < >

Each file in a directory must have a unique name.

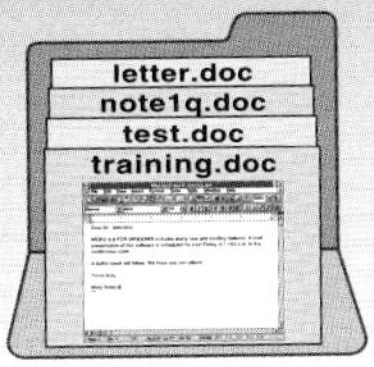

SAVE A NEW DOCUMENT

SAVE A NEW DOCUMENT

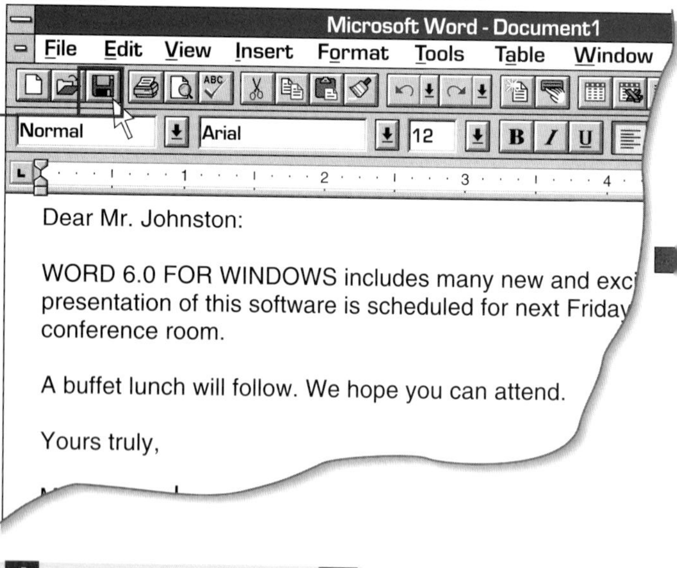
Microsoft Word - Document1
File Edit View Insert Format Tools Table Window
Normal
Arial
12
Dear Mr. Johnston:
WORD 6.0 FOR WINDOWS includes many new and exc
presentation of this software is scheduled for next Friday
conference room.
A buffet lunch will follow. We hope you can attend.
Yours truly,

1 Move the mouse over and then press the left button.

*Note: If you previously saved your document, the **Save As** dialog box will **not** appear since you have already named the file.*

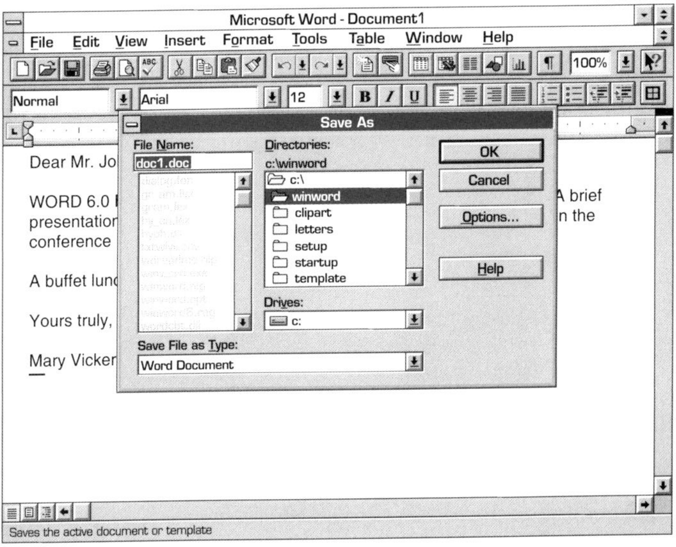

◆ The **Save As** dialog box appears.

Note: To continue, refer to the next page.

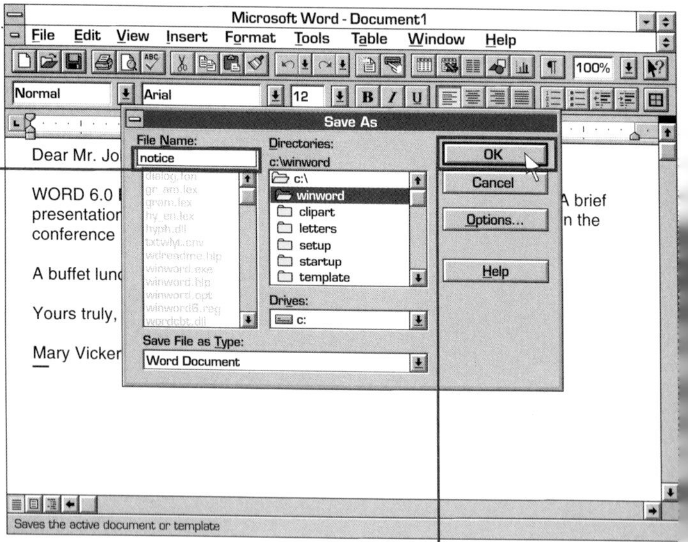

2 Type a name for your document (example: **notice**).

*Note: To make it easier to find your document later on, do not type an extension. Word will then automatically add the **doc** extension to the file name.*

3 Move the mouse over **OK** and then press the left button.

Saving a document enables you to later retrieve the document for reviewing or editing purposes.

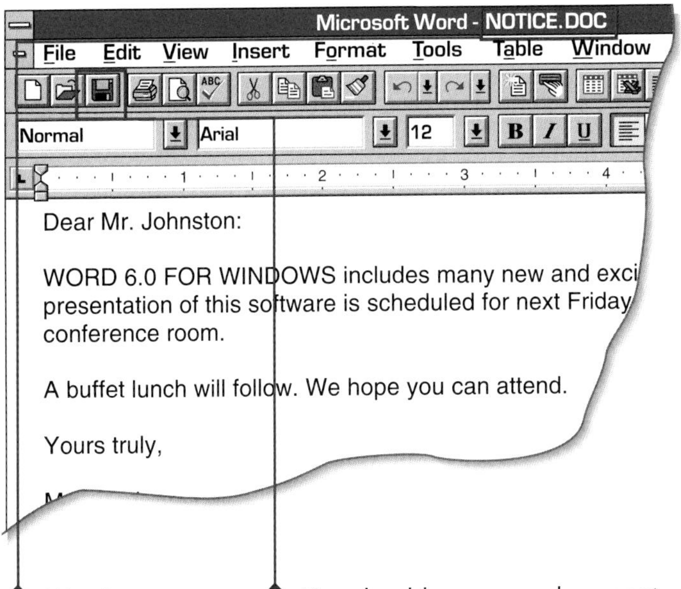
Microsoft Word - NOTICE.DOC
File Edit View Insert Format Tools Table Window
Normal
Arial
12
Dear Mr. Johnston:
WORD 6.0 FOR WINDOWS includes many new and exci
presentation of this software is scheduled for next Friday
conference room.
A buffet lunch will follow. We hope you can attend.
Yours truly,

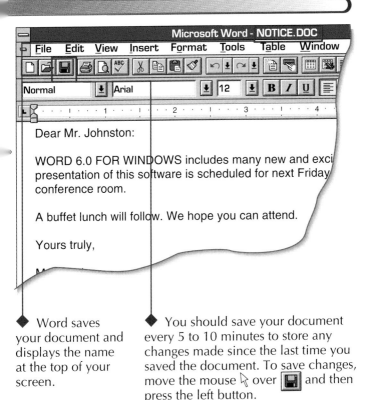

◆ Word saves your document and displays the name at the top of your screen.

◆ You should save your document every 5 to 10 minutes to store any changes made since the last time you saved the document. To save changes, move the mouse over the save button and then press the left button.

SAVE A DOCUMENT TO A DISKETTE

SAVE A DOCUMENT TO A DISKETTE

1 Insert a diskette into a floppy drive (example: **drive a**).

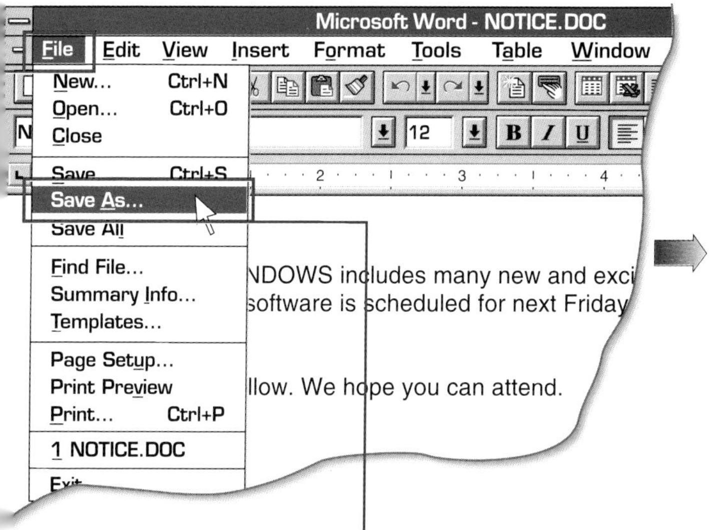

2 Move the mouse ⇖ ver **File** and then press e left button.

3 Move the mouse ⇖ over **Save As** and then press the left button.

Note: To continue, refer to the next page.

SAVE A DOCUMENT TO A DISKETTE

SAVE A DOCUMENT TO A DISKETTE (Continued)

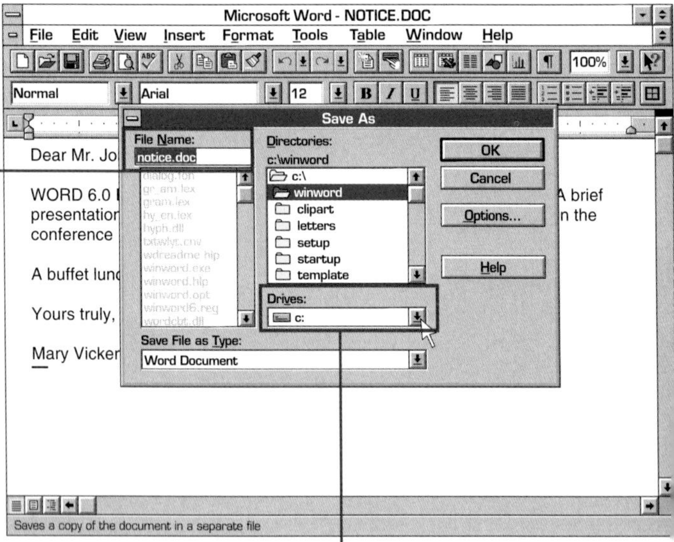

◆ The **Save As** dialog box appears.

◆ The **File Name:** box displays the current file name (example: **notice.doc**).

Note: To save your document with a different name, type a new name.

◆ The **Drives:** box displays the current drive (example: **c:**).

4 To save the file to a different drive, move the mouse ⇖ over ⬇ in the **Drives:** box and then press the left button.

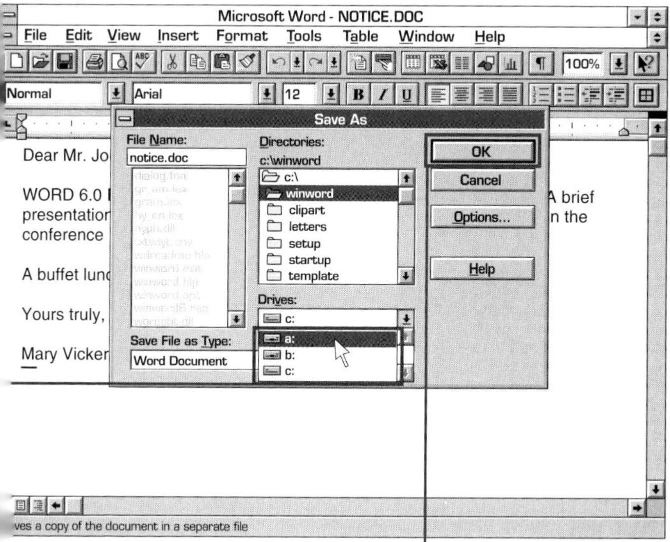

• A list of the available
ives for your computer
pears.

Move the mouse
er the drive you want to
e (example: **a:**) and then
ess the left button.

6 To save your document to the diskette, move the mouse over **OK** and then press the left button.

EXIT WORD

EXIT WORD

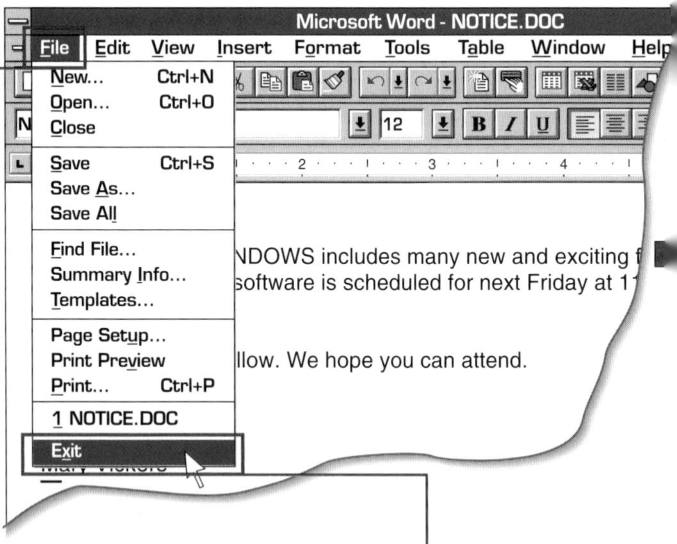

1 To exit Word, move the mouse over **File** and then press the left button.

2 Move the mouse over **Exit** and then press the left button.

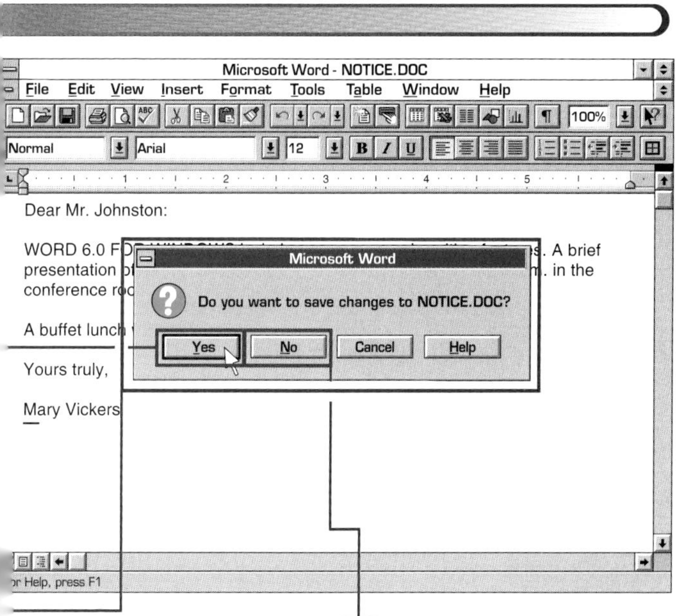

This dialog box appears if
ɔu have not saved changes
ade to your document.

To save changes, move
e mouse over **Yes** and
en press the left button.

te: For more information on saving
ocument, refer to page 96.

3 To close the document without saving the changes, move the mouse over **No** and then press the left button.

OPEN A DOCUMENT

OPEN A DOCUMENT

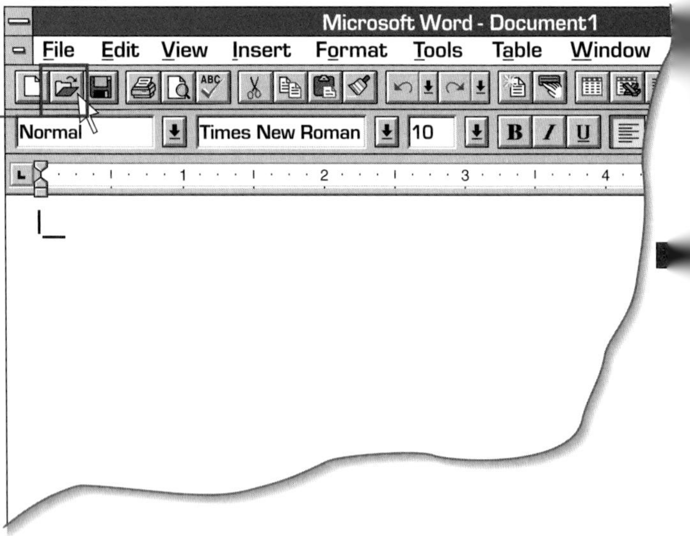

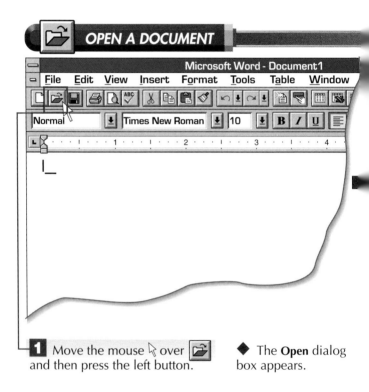

1 Move the mouse over and then press the left button.

◆ The **Open** dialog box appears.

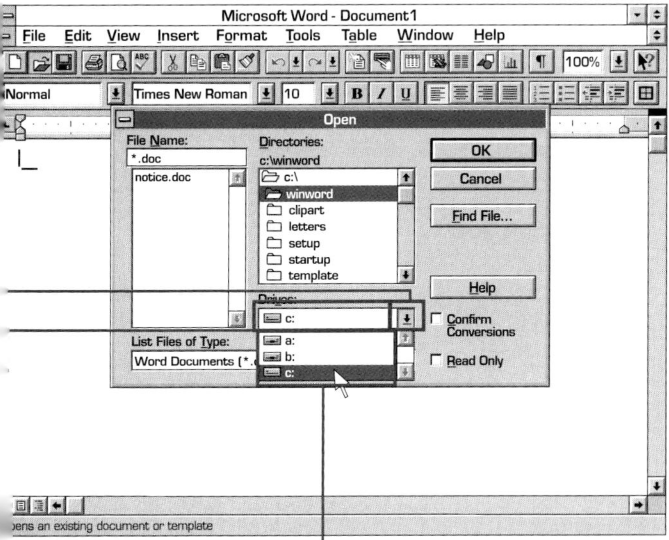

◆ The **Drives:** box
splays the current drive
xample: **c:**).

3 To open a file on
nother drive, move the
ouse ⇖ over ⬇ in the
ives: box and then press
e left button.

◆ A list of the available drives for your computer appears.

3 Move the mouse ⇖ over the drive containing the file you want to open and then press the left button.

Note: To continue, refer to the next page.

OPEN A DOCUMENT

After you open a document, you can review and edit your work.

OPEN A DOCUMENT (Continued)

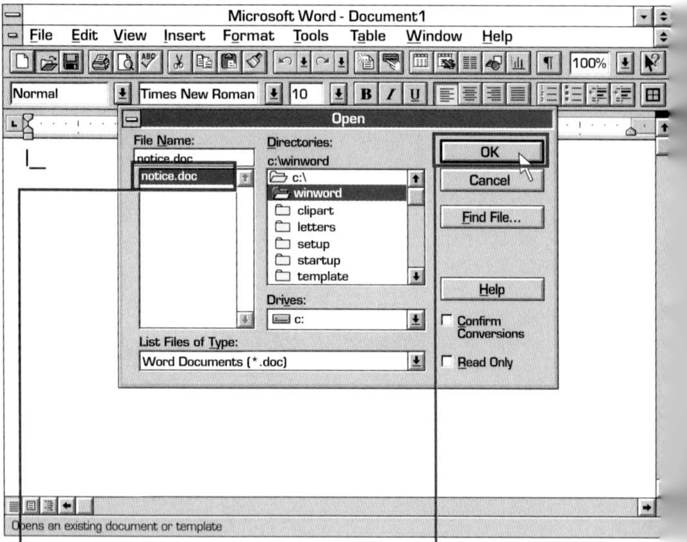

4 Move the mouse over the name of the file you want to open (example: **notice.doc**) and then press the left button.

Note: If you cannot remember the name or location of the file you want to open, refer to page 110 to find the file.

5 Move the mouse over **OK** and then pres the left button.

notice.doc

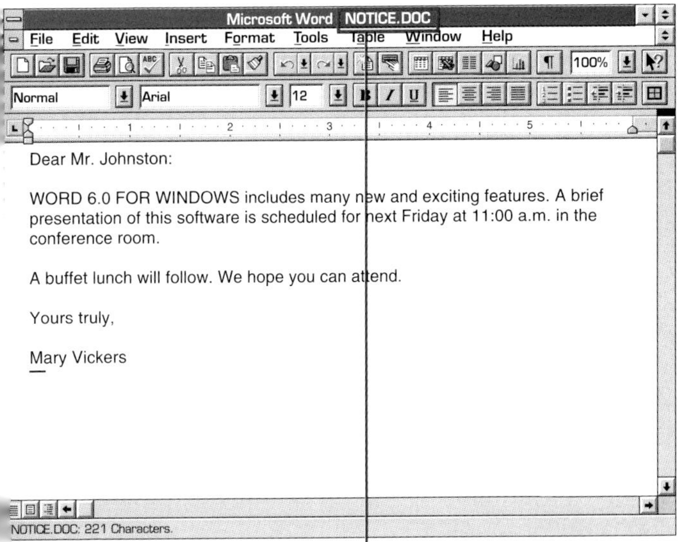
Microsoft Word NOTICE.DOC
File Edit View Insert Format Tools Table Window Help
Normal
Arial
12
100%
Dear Mr. Johnston:
WORD 6.0 FOR WINDOWS includes many new and exciting features. A brief presentation of this software is scheduled for next Friday at 11:00 a.m. in the conference room.
A buffet lunch will follow. We hope you can attend.
Yours truly,
Mary Vickers
NOTICE.DOC: 221 Characters.

- Word opens the ocument and displays it n your screen. You can ow make changes to the ocument.

- The name of the document appears at the top of your screen.

FIND A DOCUMENT

FIND A DOCUMENT

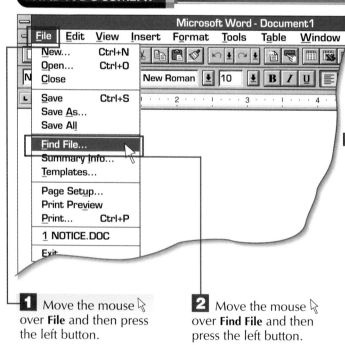

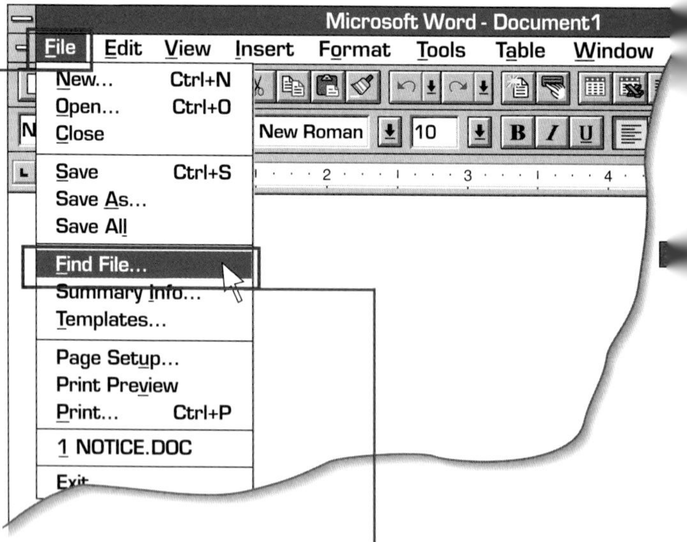

1 Move the mouse over **File** and then press the left button.

2 Move the mouse over **Find File** and then press the left button.

If you cannot remember the location of the document you want to open, you can use the Find File feature to search for the document.

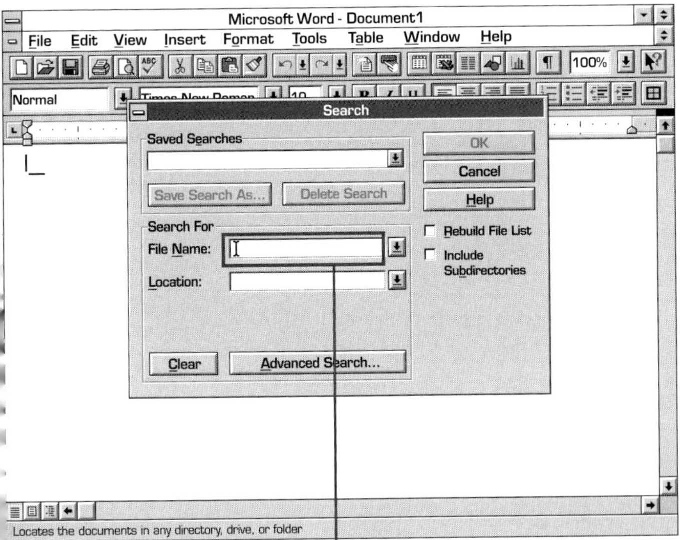

◆ The **Search** dialog box appears.

*Note: If the **Find File** dialog box appears, see IMPORTANT at the top of page 113.*

3 Move the mouse I over the box beside **File Name:** and then press the left button.

Note: To continue, refer to the next page.

FIND A DOCUMENT

FIND A DOCUMENT (Continued)

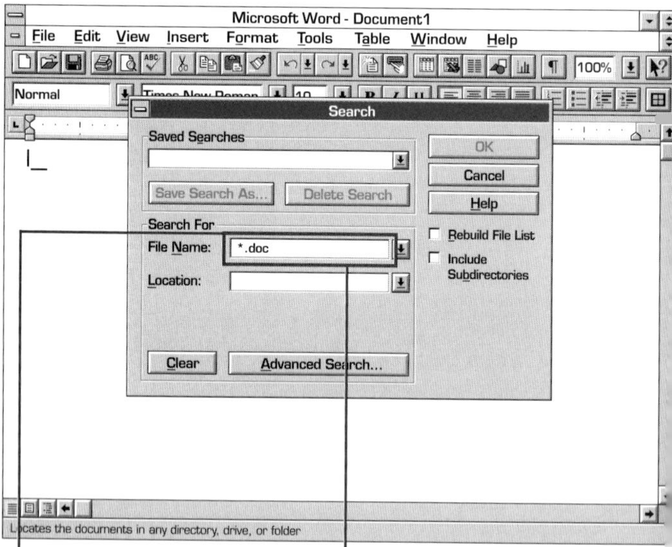

4 To search for a file with a particular extension, type ***.** followed by the extension. For example, type ***.doc** to find all files with the **doc** extension.

◆ To search for a file that begins with a particular sequence of letters, type the letters followed by the ***.*** characters. For example, type **n*.*** to find all files starting with **n**.

Important!

The Find File dialog box appears if you have previously used the Find File command. To display the Search dialog box and start a new search:

1 Move the mouse over **Search** and then press the left button. The **Search** dialog box appears.

2 To clear all the options you set for your last search, move the mouse over **Clear** and then press the left button.

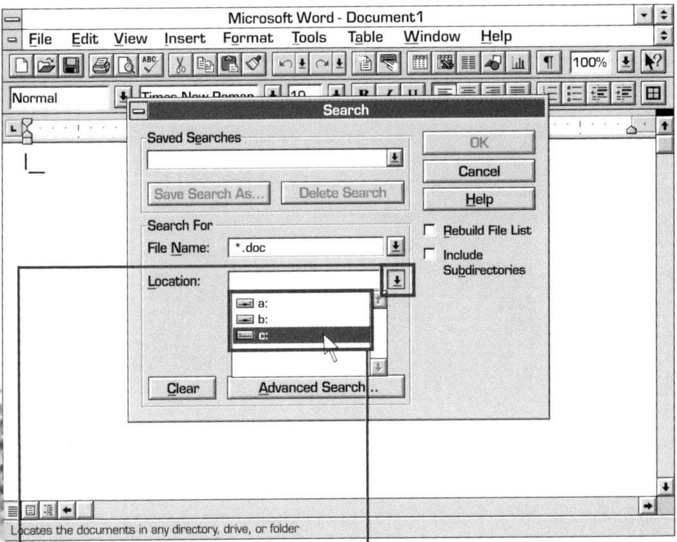

5 To select the drive you want to search, move the mouse over beside the **Location:** box and then press the left button.

6 Move the mouse over the drive (example: **c:**) and then press the left button.

Note: To continue, refer to the next page.

FIND A DOCUMENT

When Word finishes the search, a list of matching files appears on your screen. You can open any of these files.

FIND A DOCUMENT (Continued)

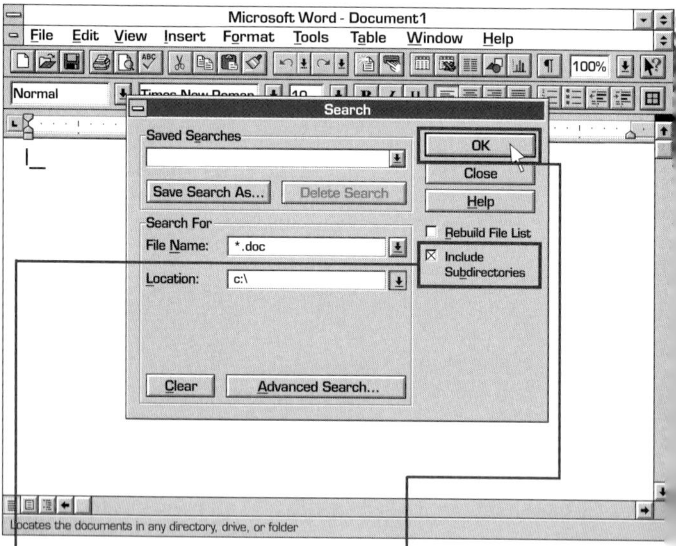

7 To search all subdirectories of the drive you selected, move the mouse ⇖ over **Include Subdirectories** and then press the left button (☐ changes to ☒).

8 To start the search, move the mouse ⇖ over **OK** and then press the left button.

TIP

To open a file displayed in the Find File dialog box:

1 *Move the mouse over the file name and then quickly press the left button twice.*

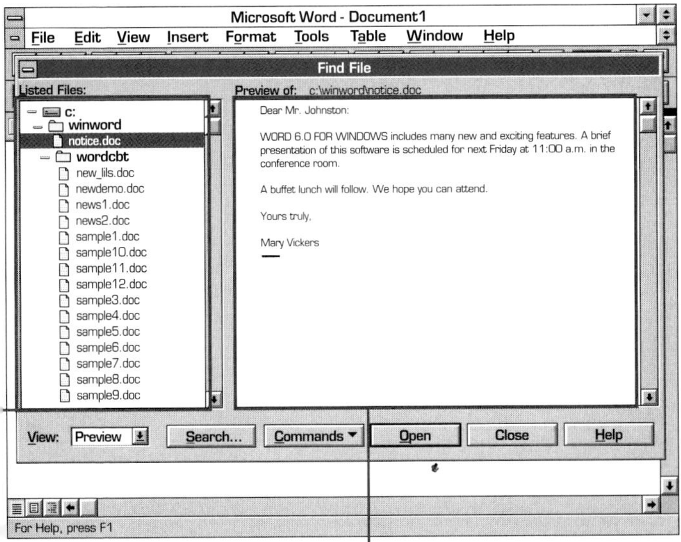

◆ After a few moments the **Find File** dialog box appears.

◆ This area displays the names of the files Word found.

◆ This area displays the contents of the highlighted file.

9 To display the contents of another file, press ↓ or ↑ on your keyboard.

CREATE A NEW DOCUMENT

You can create a document to start a new letter, report or memo. Word lets you have several documents open at the same time.

CREATE A NEW DOCUMENT

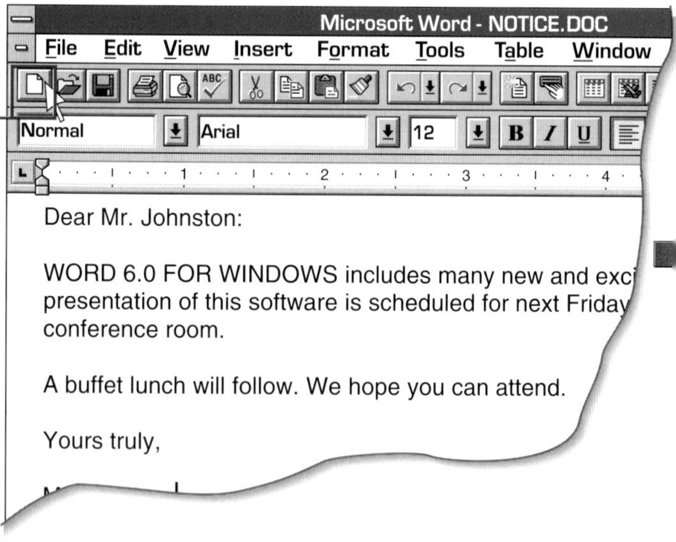
Microsoft Word - NOTICE.DOC
File Edit View Insert Format Tools Table Window
Normal
Arial
12
Dear Mr. Johnston:
WORD 6.0 FOR WINDOWS includes many new and exc
presentation of this software is scheduled for next Friday
conference room.
A buffet lunch will follow. We hope you can attend.
Yours truly,

1 Move the mouse over 🗋 and then press the left button.

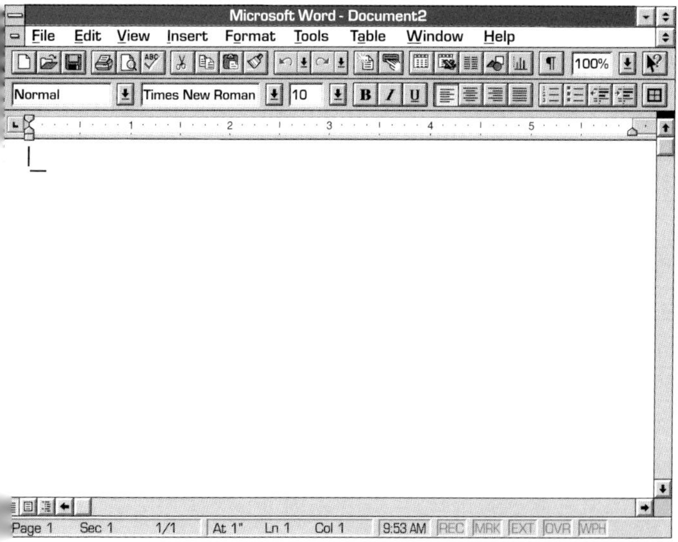

◆ A new document
ppears.

ote: The previous document is now idden behind the new document.

◆ Think of each document as a separate piece of paper. When you create a document, you are placing a new piece of paper on your screen.

ARRANGE OPEN DOCUMENTS

NOTICE.DOC
Dear Mr. Johnston:
WORD 6.0 FOR WINDOWS includes many new and exciting features. A brief presentation of this software is scheduled for next Friday at 11:00 a.m. in the conference room.

ARRANGE OPEN DOCUMENTS

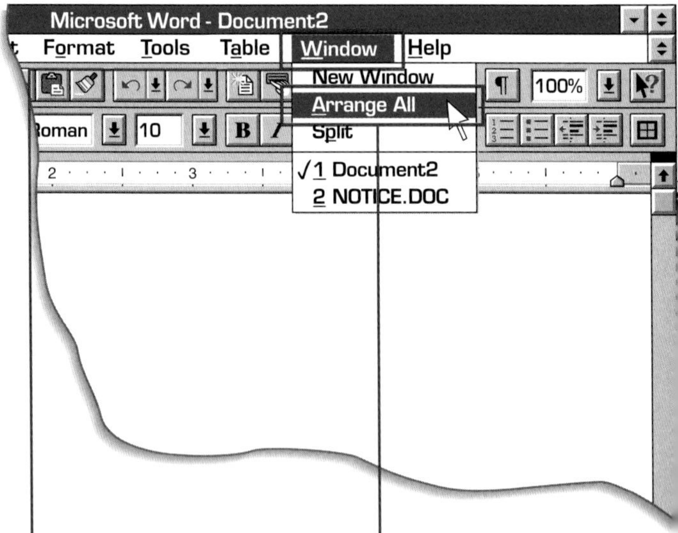
Microsoft Word - Document2
Format
Tools
Table
Window
Help
New Window
Arrange All
Split
✓1 Document2
2 NOTICE.DOC
100%
10

1 To arrange all of your open documents, move the mouse ⇖ over **Window** and then press the left button.

2 Move the mouse ⇖ over **Arrange All** and then press the left button.

If you have several documents open, some of them may be hidden from view. To view the contents of each document, you can use the Arrange All command.

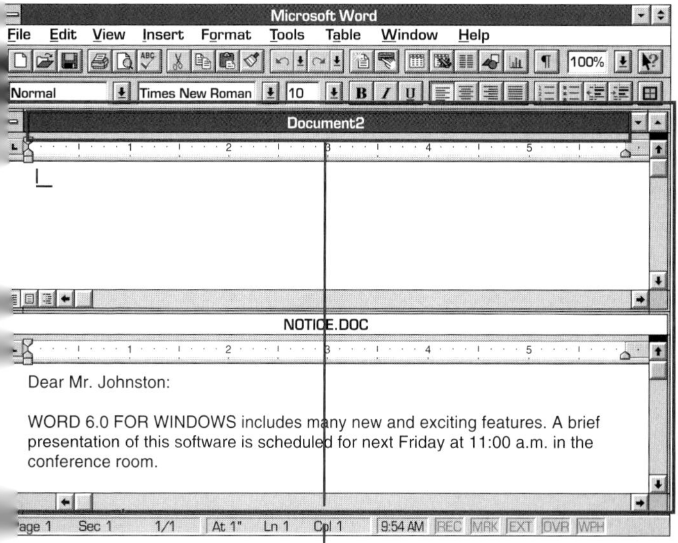

◆ You can now view e contents of all your ɔen documents at the me time.

◆ You can only work in the current document, which displays a highlighted title bar.

Note: To make another document current, move the mouse anywhere over the document and then press the left button.

COPY OR MOVE TEXT BETWEEN DOCUMENTS

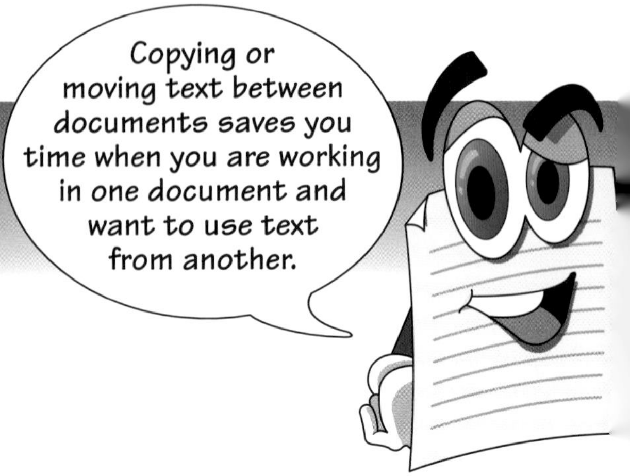

Copying or moving text between documents saves you time when you are working in one document and want to use text from another.

COPY OR MOVE TEXT BETWEEN DOCUMENTS

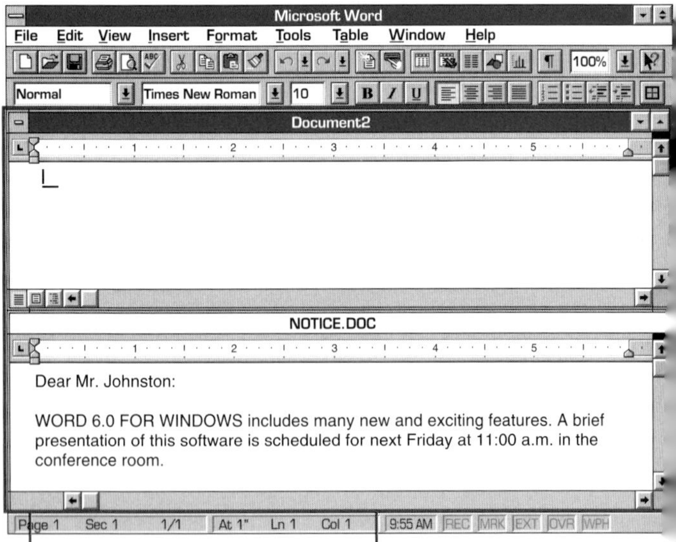

1 Open the documents you want to copy or move text between.

Note: To open a saved document, refer to page 106. To create a new document, refer to page 116.

2 Display the contents of both documents by using the **Arrange All** command.

*Note: For information on the **Arrange All** command, refer to page 118.*

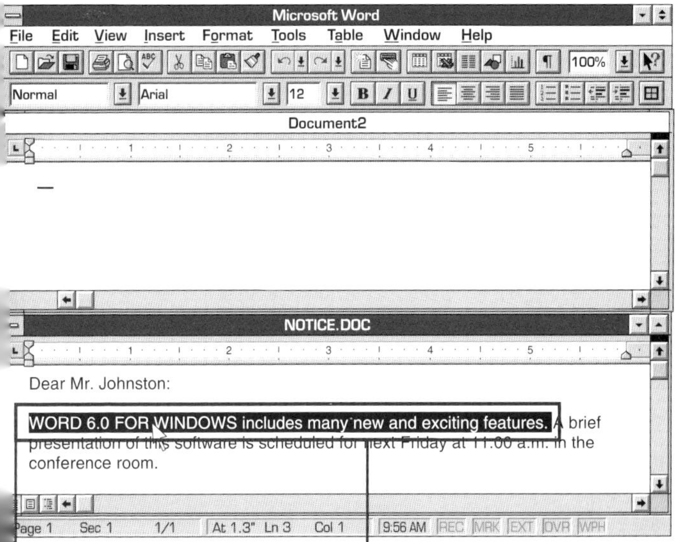

3 Select the text you
ant to copy or move to
nother document.

*te: To select text, refer to
ges 28 to 31.*

4 Move the mouse I anywhere over the selected text and I changes to ↖.

Note: To continue, refer to the next page.

COPY OR MOVE TEXT BETWEEN DOCUMENTS

COPY OR MOVE TEXT (Continued)

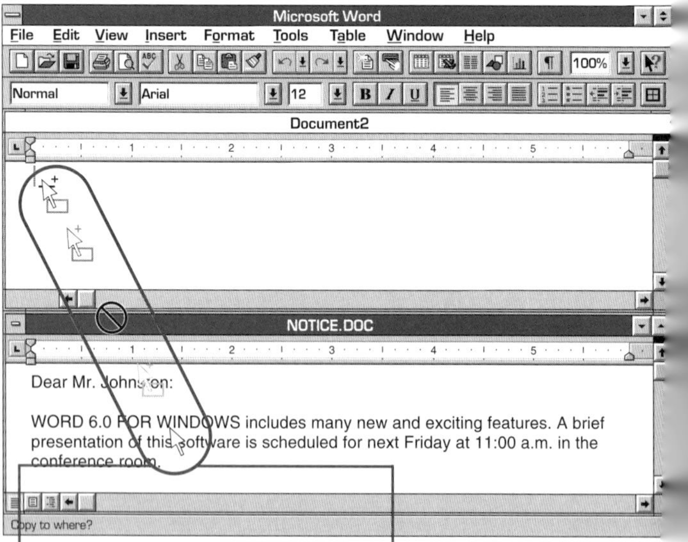
Microsoft Word
File Edit View Insert Format Tools Table Window Help
Normal
Arial
12
100%
Document2
NOTICE.DOC
Dear Mr. Johnston:
WORD 6.0 FOR WINDOWS includes many new and exciting features. A brief presentation of this software is scheduled for next Friday at 11:00 a.m. in the conference room.
Copy to where?

5 To copy the text, press and hold down Ctrl. Still holding down Ctrl, press and hold down the left button as you drag the mouse where you want to place the copy.

◆ To move the text, press and hold down the left button as you drag the mouse where you want to move the text.

COPY TEXT

When you copy text, Word *copies* the text and *pastes* the copy in a new location. The original text remains in its place.

MOVE TEXT

When you move text, Word *cuts* the text and *pastes* it in a new location. The original text disappears.

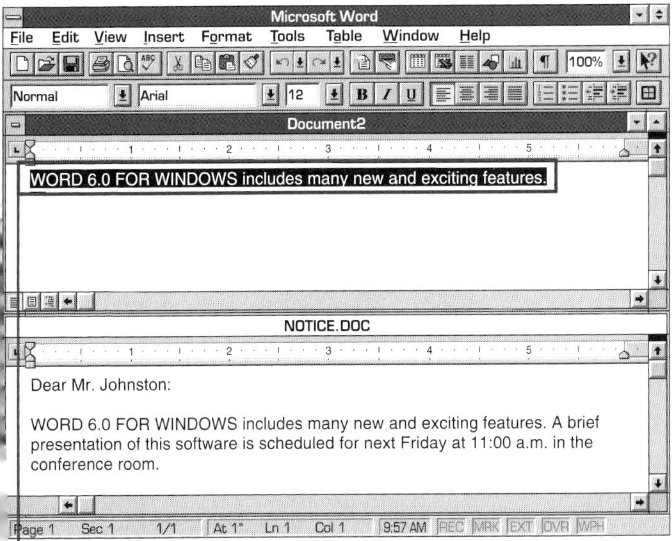
Microsoft Word
File Edit View Insert Format Tools Table Window Help
100%
Normal
Arial
12
Document2
WORD 6.0 FOR WINDOWS includes many new and exciting features.
NOTICE.DOC
Dear Mr. Johnston:
WORD 6.0 FOR WINDOWS includes many new and exciting features. A brief presentation of this software is scheduled for next Friday at 11:00 a.m. in the conference room.
Page 1 Sec 1 1/1 At 1" Ln 1 Col 1 9:57 AM REC MRK EXT OVR WPH

6 Release the button and he text appears in the new ocation.

MAXIMIZE A DOCUMENT

You can enlarge a document to fill your entire screen. This enables you to view more of its contents.

MAXIMIZE A DOCUMENT

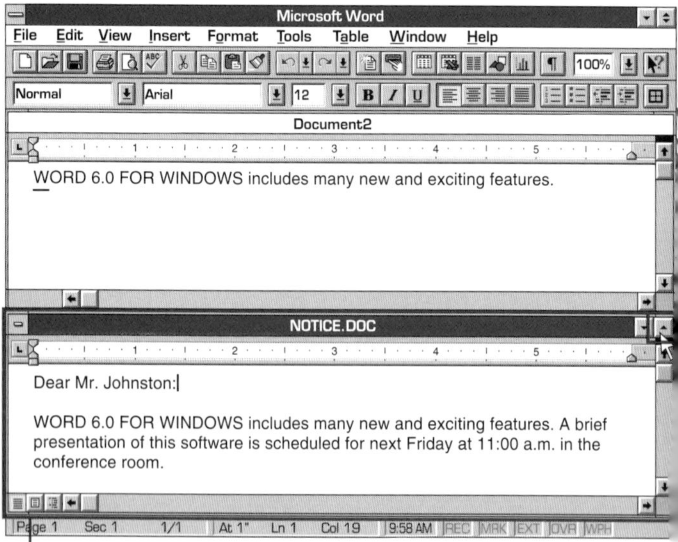
Microsoft Word
File Edit View Insert Format Tools Table Window Help
Normal
Arial
12
100%
Document2
WORD 6.0 FOR WINDOWS includes many new and exciting features.
NOTICE.DOC
Dear Mr. Johnston:
WORD 6.0 FOR WINDOWS includes many new and exciting features. A brief presentation of this software is scheduled for next Friday at 11:00 a.m. in the conference room.
Page 1 Sec 1 1/1 At 1" Ln 1 Col 19 9:58 AM REC MRK EXT OVR WPH

1 To select the document you want to maximize, move the mouse anywhere over the document and then press the left button.

2 Move the mouse over the document's **Maximize** button and then press the left button

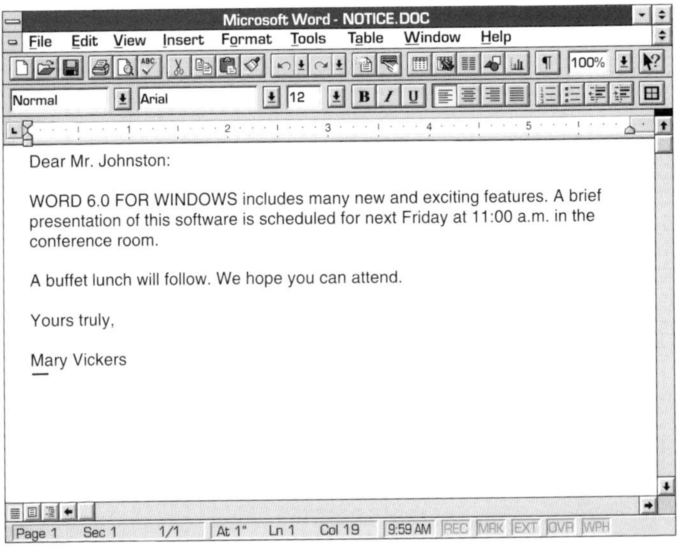
Microsoft Word - NOTICE.DOC
File Edit View Insert Format Tools Table Window Help
Normal
Arial
12
100%
Dear Mr. Johnston:
WORD 6.0 FOR WINDOWS includes many new and exciting features. A brief presentation of this software is scheduled for next Friday at 11:00 a.m. in the conference room.
A buffet lunch will follow. We hope you can attend.
Yours truly,
Mary Vickers
Page 1 Sec 1 1/1 At 1" Ln 1 Col 19 9:59 AM REC MRK EXT OVR WPH

◆ The document enlarges to fill your entire screen.

Note: The file you maximized covers all of your open documents.

SWITCH BETWEEN DOCUMENTS

SWITCH BETWEEN DOCUMENTS

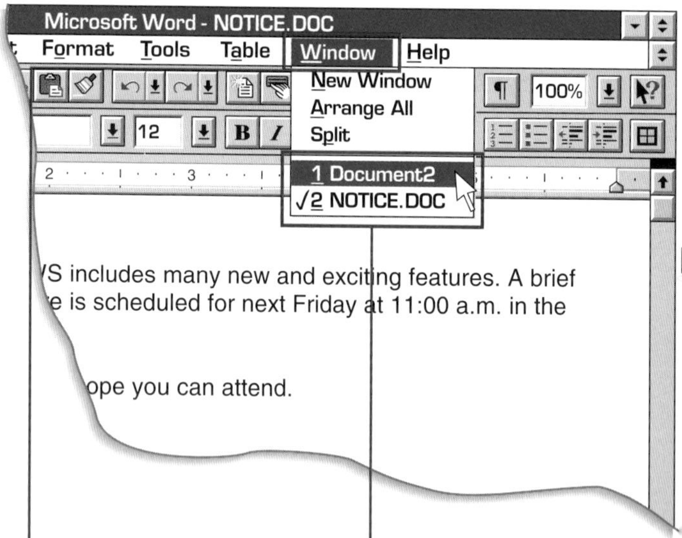
Microsoft Word - NOTICE.DOC
Format Tools Table Window Help
New Window
Arrange All
Split
1 Document2
√2 NOTICE.DOC
100%
12
/S includes many new and exciting features. A brief
e is scheduled for next Friday at 11:00 a.m. in the
ope you can attend.

1 To display a list of all your open documents, move the mouse ⇖ over **Window** and then press the left button.

2 Move the mouse ⇖ over the document you want to switch to and then press the left button.

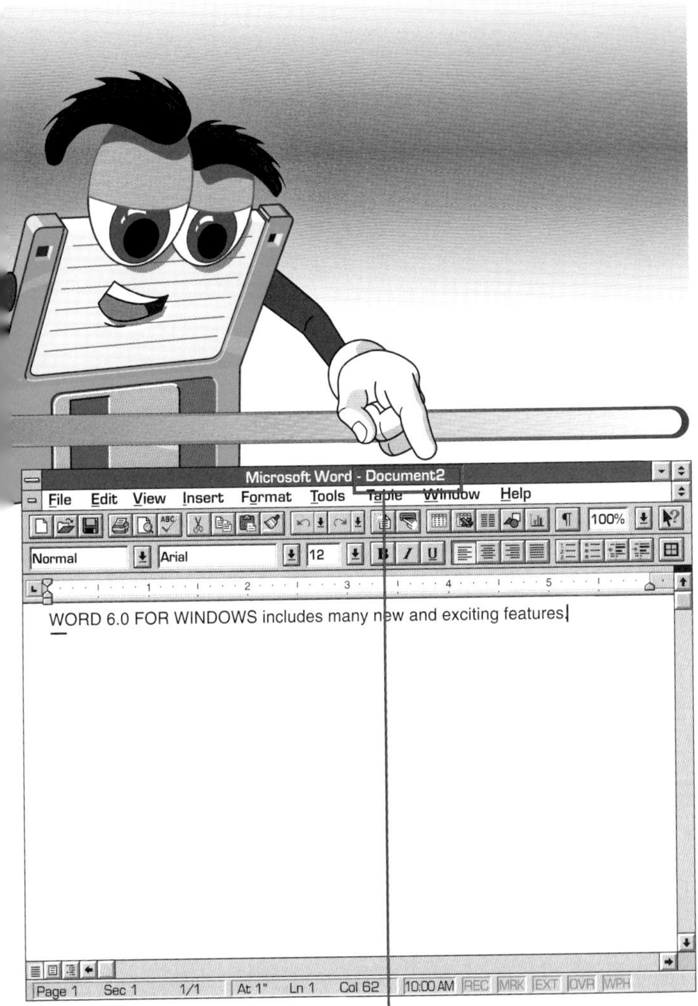

◆ The document appears.

◆ Word displays the name of the document at the top of your screen.

CLOSE A DOCUMENT

CLOSE A DOCUMENT

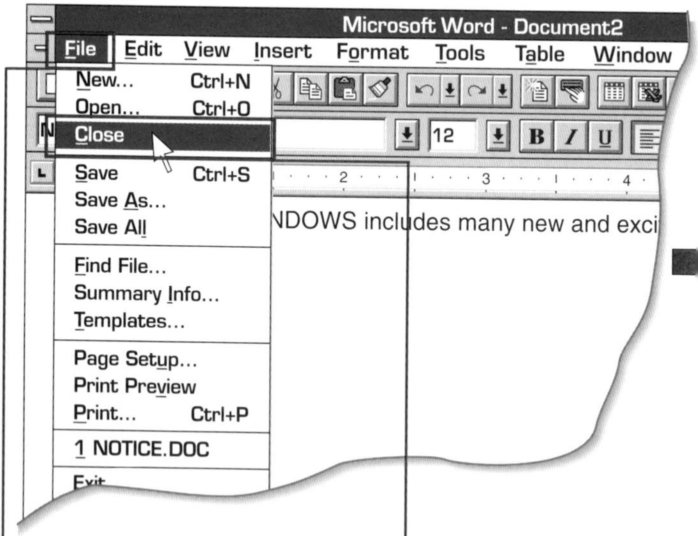

1 To close the document displayed on your screen, move the mouse over **File** and then press the left button.

2 Move the mouse over **Close** and then press the left button.

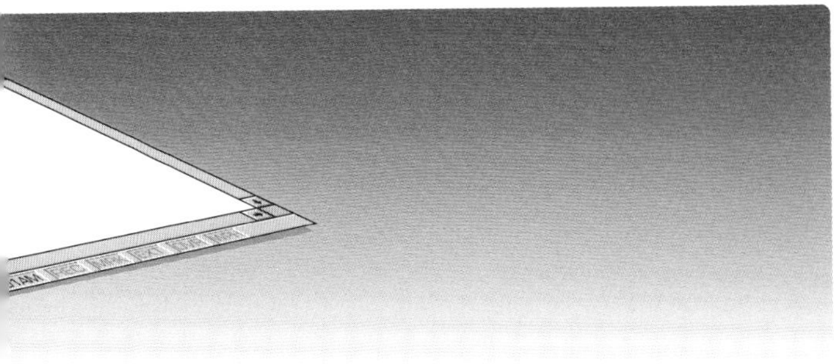

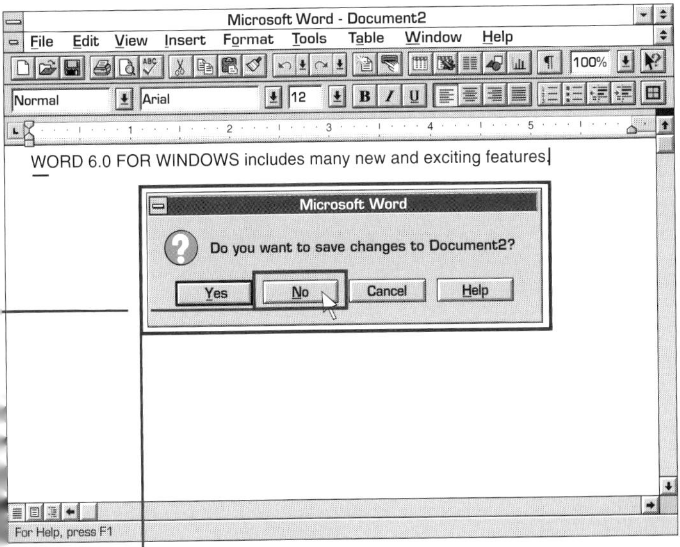

◆ This dialog box appears if you have not saved changes made to your document.

3 To close the document without saving the changes, move the mouse ⇖ over **No** and then press the left button.

◆ To save the changes, move the mouse ⇖ over **Yes** and then press the left button. For more information, refer to page 96.

Note: To continue, refer to the next page.

CLOSE A DOCUMENT

Closing a document removes it from your screen.

CLOSE A DOCUMENT (Continued)

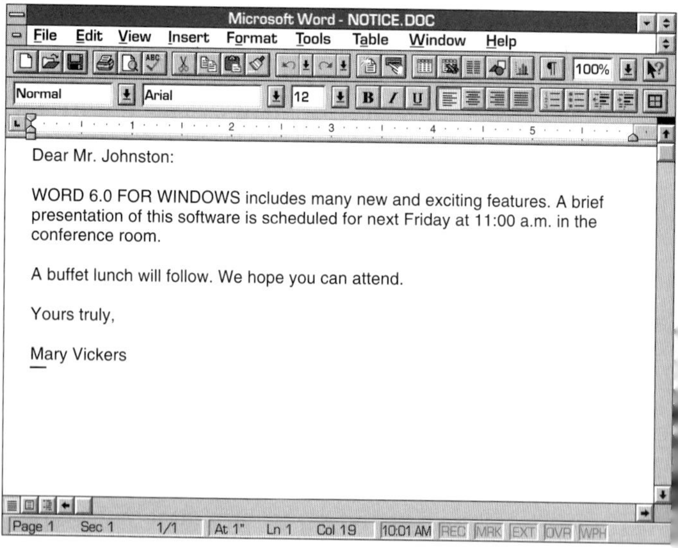
Microsoft Word - NOTICE.DOC
File Edit View Insert Format Tools Table Window Help
100%
Normal
Arial
12
Dear Mr. Johnston:
WORD 6.0 FOR WINDOWS includes many new and exciting features. A brief presentation of this software is scheduled for next Friday at 11:00 a.m. in the conference room.
A buffet lunch will follow. We hope you can attend.
Yours truly,
Mary Vickers
Page 1 Sec 1 1/1 At 1" Ln 1 Col 19 10:01 AM REC MRK EXT OVR WPH

◆ Word removes the document from your screen.

Note: If you had more than one document open, the second last document you worked on appears.

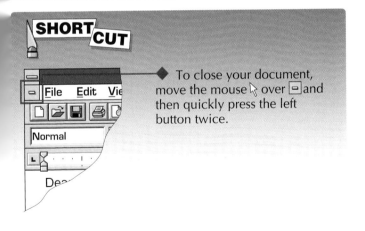

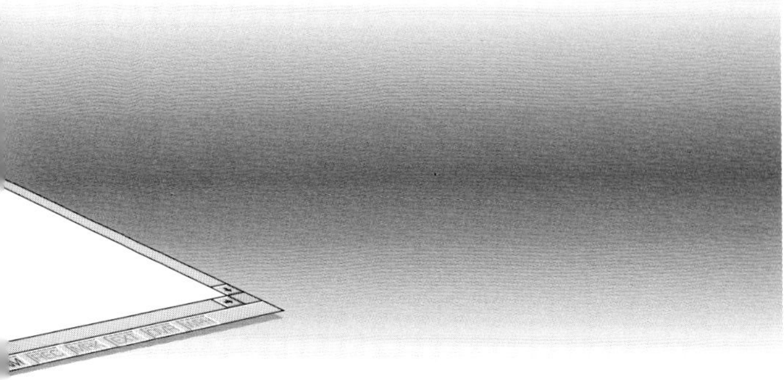

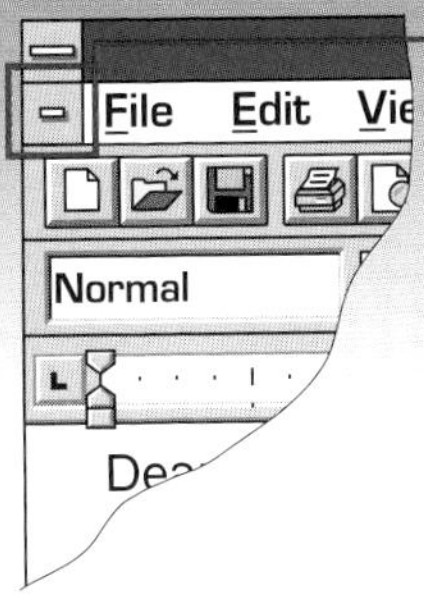

◆ To close your document, move the mouse ↖ over ⊟ and then quickly press the left button twice.

PREVIEW A DOCUMENT

PRINT

PREVIEW A DOCUMENT

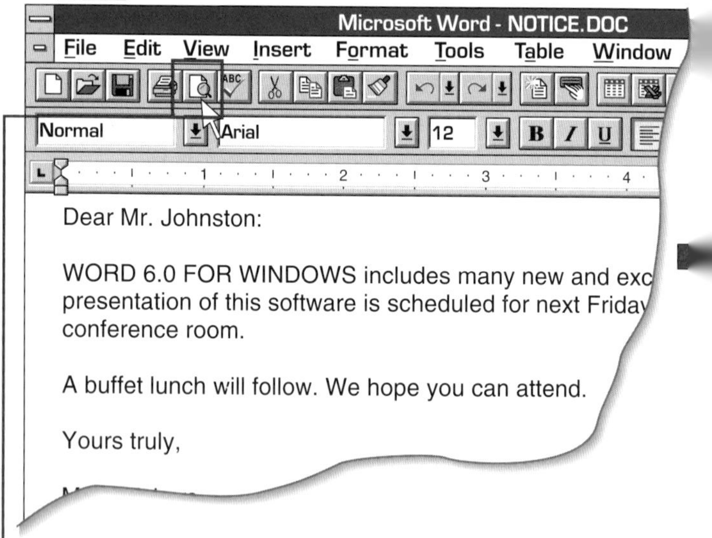

Microsoft Word - NOTICE.DOC
File Edit View Insert Format Tools Table Window
Normal
Arial
12
Dear Mr. Johnston:
WORD 6.0 FOR WINDOWS includes many new and exc
presentation of this software is scheduled for next Friday
conference room.
A buffet lunch will follow. We hope you can attend.
Yours truly,

1 Move the mouse over and then press the left button.

The Print Preview feature lets you see on screen what your document will look like when printed.

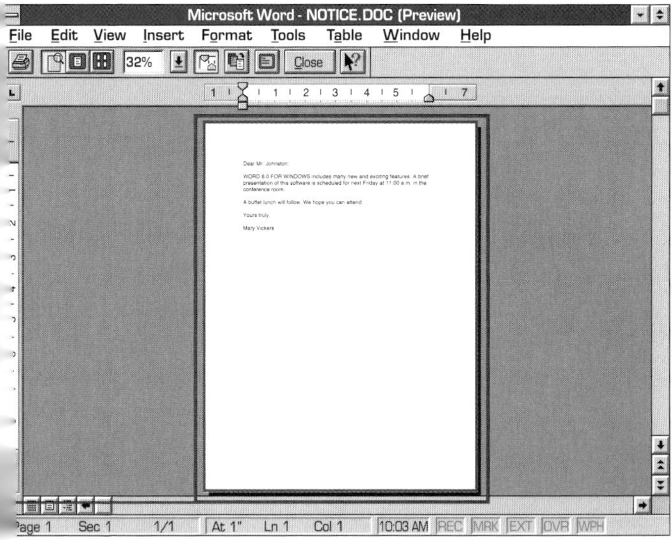

◆ The page you are currently working on appears in the Print Preview window.

◆ If your document contains more than one page, press **PageDown** on your keyboard to display the next page. Press **PageUp** to display the previous page.

PREVIEW A DOCUMENT

ZOOM IN OR OUT

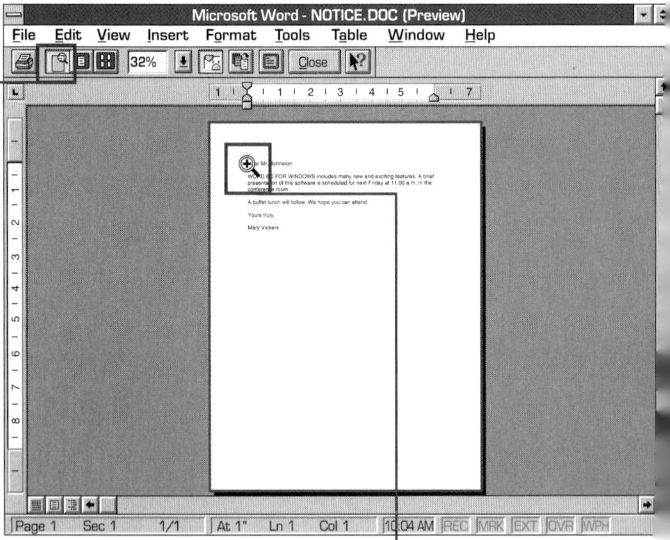

◆ If the mouse looks like I when over your document, you are in the editing mode.

1 To change to the zoom mode, move the mouse over and then press the left button (I changes to).

2 To magnify a section of the page, move the mouse over the sectio and then press the left button.

You can magnify a section of your document in Print Preview. This lets you make last minute changes before printing your document.

Note: To display your document in Print Preview, refer to page 132.

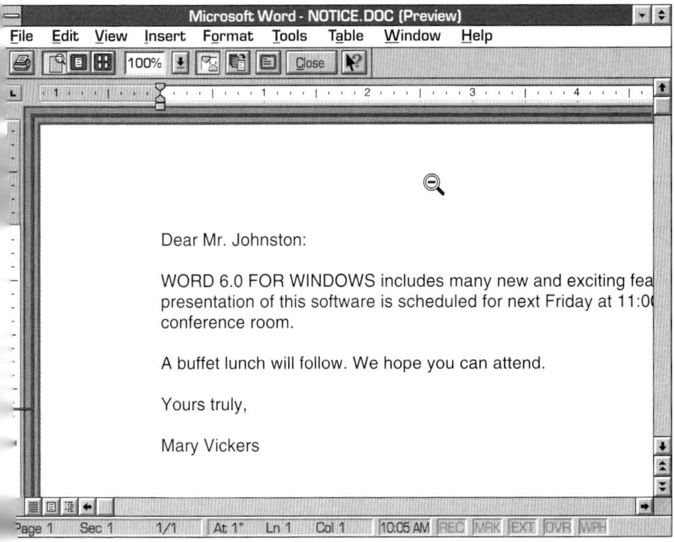
Microsoft Word - NOTICE.DOC (Preview)
File Edit View Insert Format Tools Table Window Help
100%
Close
Dear Mr. Johnston:
WORD 6.0 FOR WINDOWS includes many new and exciting fea
presentation of this software is scheduled for next Friday at 11:0
conference room.
A buffet lunch will follow. We hope you can attend.
Yours truly,
Mary Vickers
Page 1 Sec 1 1/1 At 1" Ln 1 Col 1 10:05 AM REC MRK EXT OVR WPH

A magnified view of e page appears and the ouse changes to .

te: To switch to the editing mode, peat step **1**.

3 To again display the entire page, move the mouse anywhere over the page and then press the left button.

PREVIEW A DOCUMENT

DISPLAY MULTIPLE PAGES

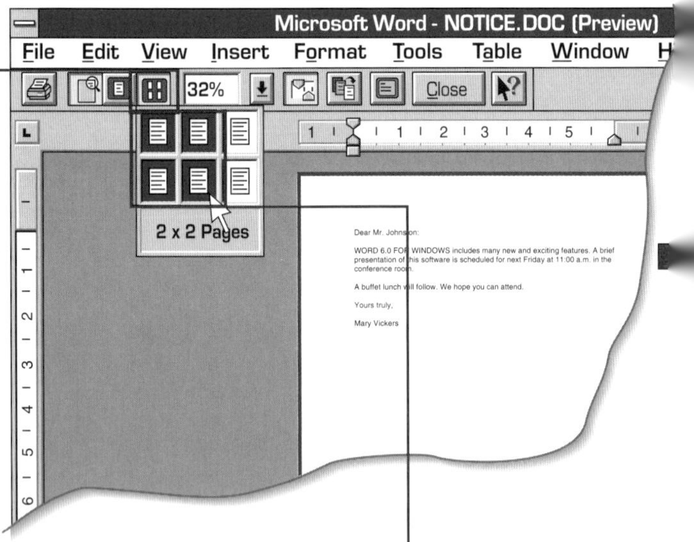

Microsoft Word - NOTICE.DOC (Preview)
File Edit View Insert Format Tools Table Window H
32%
Close
2 x 2 Pages
Dear Mr. Johnson:
WORD 6.0 FOR WINDOWS includes many new and exciting features. A brief presentation of this software is scheduled for next Friday at 11:00 a.m. in the conference room.
A buffet lunch will follow. We hope you can attend.
Yours truly,
Mary Vickers

1 Move the mouse over and then press and hold down the left button.

Note: To display your document in Print Preview, refer to page 132.

2 Still holding down th button, move the mouse over the number of page you want to display at once.

Note: If you drag the mouse dc or to the right, more options appe

In Print Preview, Word can display more than one page at a time. This lets you view the overall style of multiple pages at once.

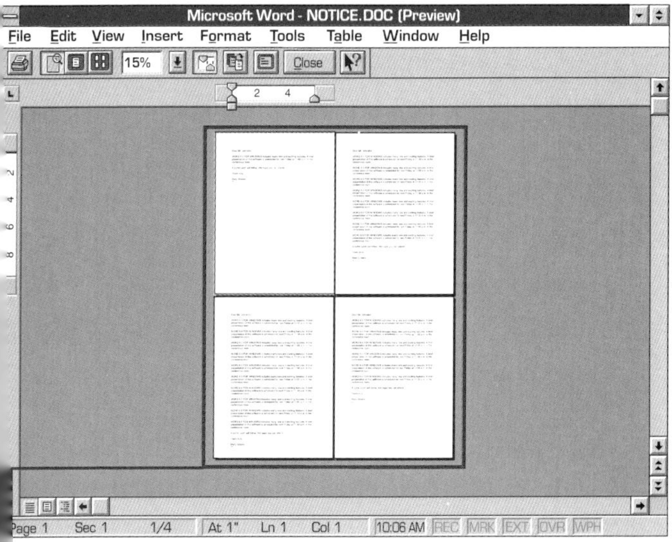

3 Release the button and the number of pages you specified appears on your screen.

Note: In this example, the document contains four pages.

PREVIEW A DOCUMENT

DISPLAY ONE PAGE

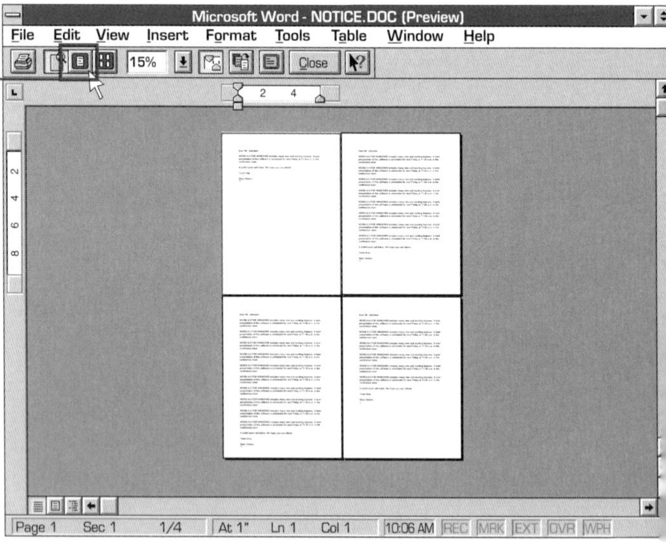

1 To display a single page, move the mouse over the one page button and then press the left button.

Note: To display your document Print Preview, refer to page 132.

SHRINK TO FIT

If the last page in your document has only a few lines of text, you can have Word fit the text on the second last page. This will remove one page from your document.

1 Move the mouse over the toolbar button on the Print Preview toolbar and then press the left button.

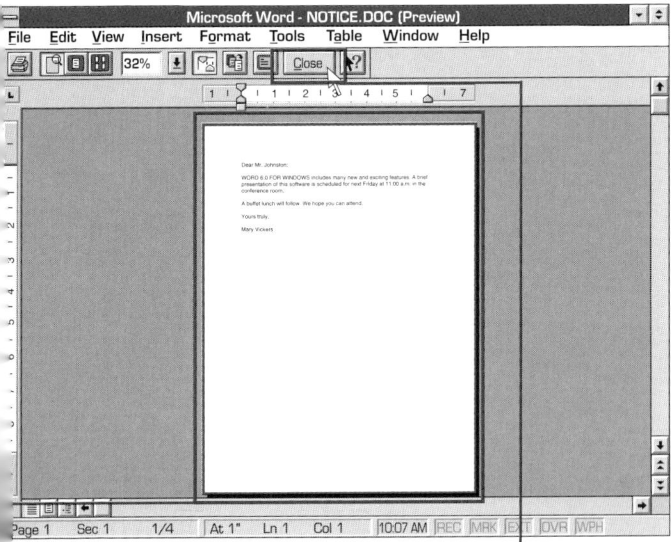

- A single page appears n your screen.
- Press **PageDown** on your ›yboard to display the ›xt page. Press **PageUp** to splay the previous page.

Close Print Preview

1 To close Print Preview and return to your document, move the mouse over **Close** and then press the left button.

PRINT A DOCUMENT

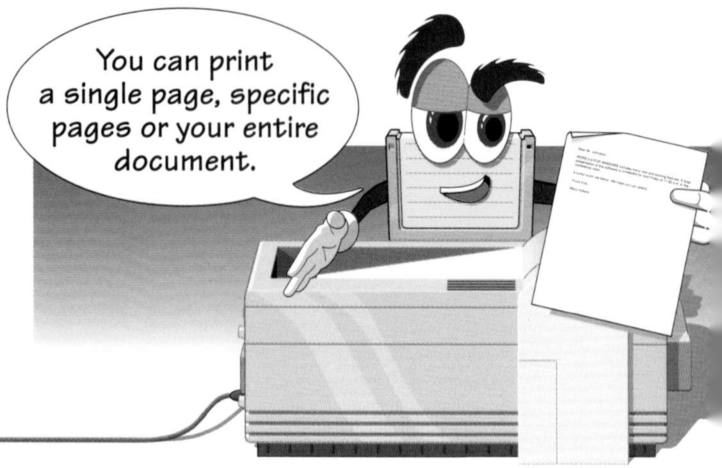
You can print a single page, specific pages or your entire document.

PRINT A DOCUMENT

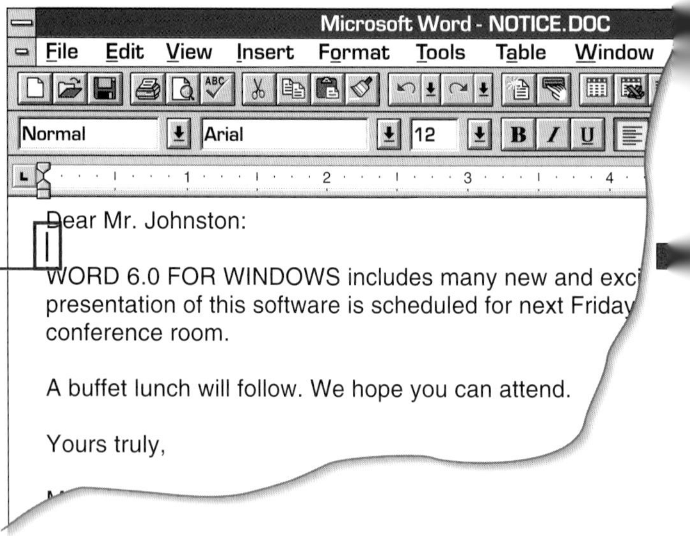
Microsoft Word - NOTICE.DOC
File Edit View Insert Format Tools Table Window
Normal
Arial
12
Dear Mr. Johnston:
WORD 6.0 FOR WINDOWS includes many new and exci
presentation of this software is scheduled for next Friday
conference room.
A buffet lunch will follow. We hope you can attend.
Yours truly,

1 To print a single page, position the insertion point anywhere on the page you want to print.

◆ To print your entire document or specific pages, position the insertion point anywhere in the document.

◆ To print a small section of text, select the text.

Note: To select text, refer to pages 28 to 31.

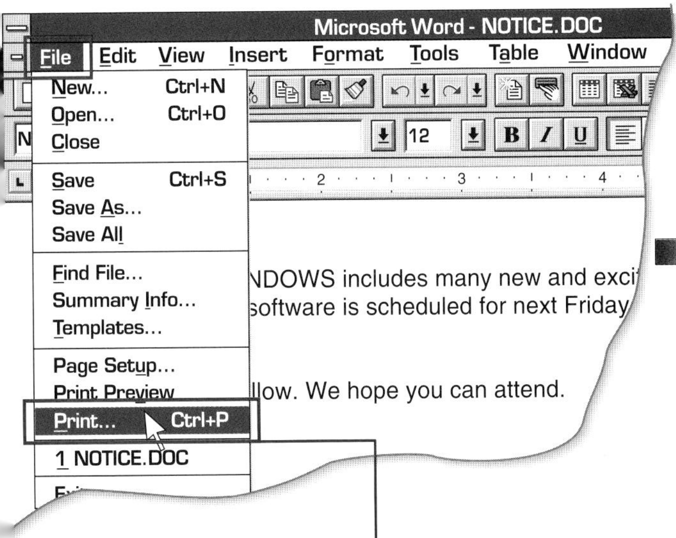
Microsoft Word - NOTICE.DOC
File
Edit
View
Insert
Format
Tools
Table
Window
New... Ctrl+N
Open... Ctrl+O
Close
Save Ctrl+S
Save As...
Save All
Find File...
Summary Info...
Templates...
Page Setup...
Print Preview
Print... Ctrl+P
1 NOTICE.DOC
12
B
I
U
NDOWS includes many new and exci
software is scheduled for next Friday
llow. We hope you can attend.

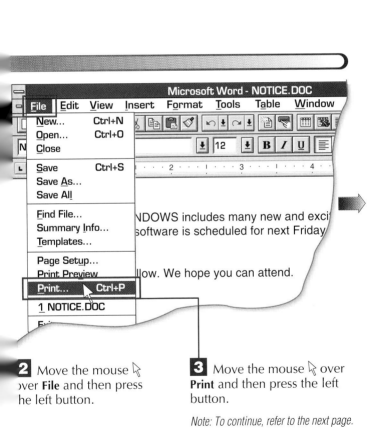

2 Move the mouse over **File** and then press the left button.

3 Move the mouse over **Print** and then press the left button.

Note: To continue, refer to the next page.

PRINT A DOCUMENT

Before printing your document, make sure your printer is on and it contains paper.

PRINT A DOCUMENT (Continued)

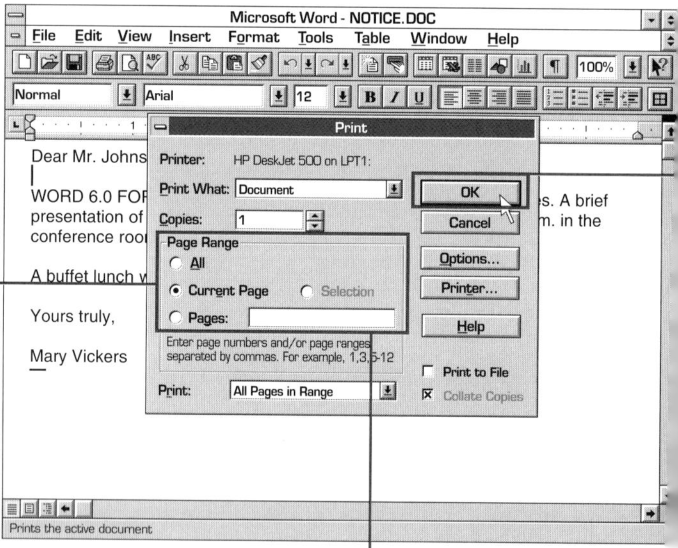

◆ The **Print** dialog box appears.

4 Move the mouse over the range you want to print (example: **Current Page**) and then press the left button.

◆ To print specific pages in your document, select **Pages** in step **4**. Then type the page numbers separated by commas (example: **1,3,5**) or type the first and last page numbers separated by a dash (example: **3-5**).

SHORT CUT

◆ To quickly print your entire document, move the mouse over and then press the left button.

Dear Mr. Johnston:

WORD 6.0 FOR WINDOWS includes many new and exciting features. A brief presentation of this software is scheduled for next Friday at 11:00 a.m. in the conference room.

A buffet lunch will follow. We hope you can attend.

Yours truly,

Mary Vickers

5 To print your document, move the mouse over **OK** and then press the left button.

CHANGE VIEWS

Word offers three basic views that you can use to display your document.
NORMAL VIEW

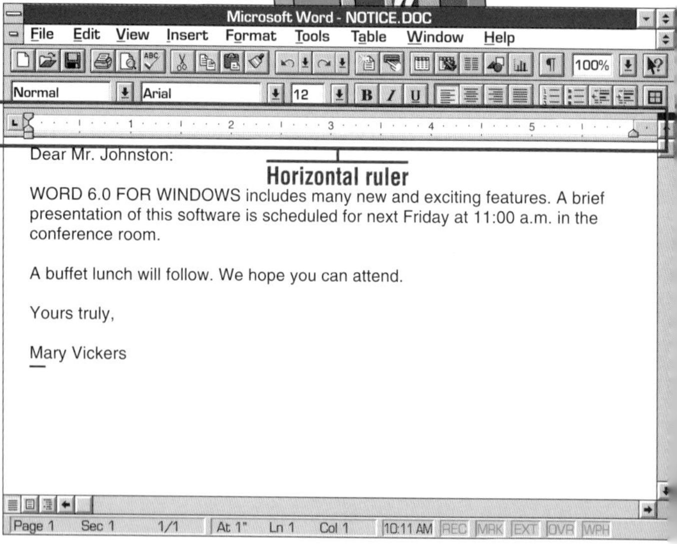
Microsoft Word - NOTICE.DOC
File Edit View Insert Format Tools Table Window Help
Normal
Arial
12
100%
Horizontal ruler
Dear Mr. Johnston:
WORD 6.0 FOR WINDOWS includes many new and exciting features. A brief presentation of this software is scheduled for next Friday at 11:00 a.m. in the conference room.
A buffet lunch will follow. We hope you can attend.
Yours truly,
Mary Vickers
Page 1 Sec 1 1/1 At 1" Ln 1 Col 1 10:11 AM REC MRK EXT OVR WPH

◆ The Normal view simplifies the page layout so you can type and edit the document quickly.

◆ This view does not display top or bottom margins, headers, footers or page numbers.

OUTLINE VIEW

◆ The Outline view lets you create an outline of your document, similar to a Table of Contents. You can display the headings and subheadings and hide the body text. This view helps you work more efficiently with longer documents.

PAGE LAYOUT VIEW

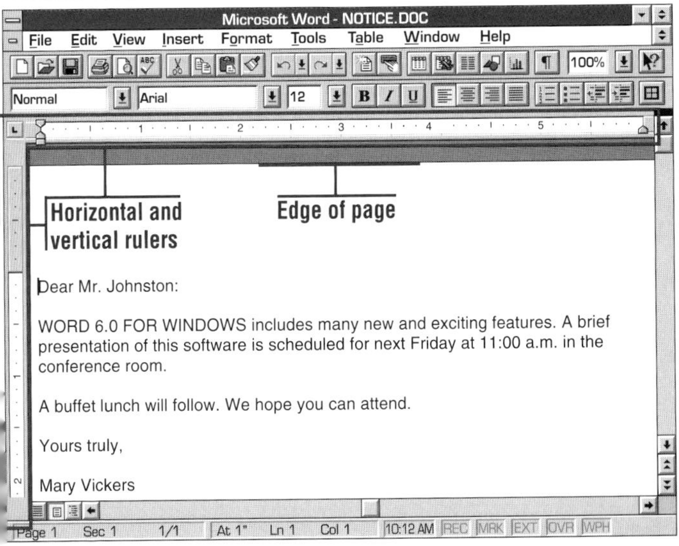
Microsoft Word - NOTICE.DOC
File Edit View Insert Format Tools Table Window Help
Normal
Arial
12
100%
Horizontal and vertical rulers
Edge of page
Dear Mr. Johnston:
WORD 6.0 FOR WINDOWS includes many new and exciting features. A brief presentation of this software is scheduled for next Friday at 11:00 a.m. in the conference room.
A buffet lunch will follow. We hope you can attend.
Yours truly,
Mary Vickers
Page 1 Sec 1 1/1 At 1" Ln 1 Col 1 10:12 AM REC MRK EXT OVR WPH

◆ The Page Layout view displays your document exactly the way it will appear on a printed page.

◆ This view displays all features in your document including top and bottom margins, headers, footers and page numbers.

CHANGE VIEWS

You can select a different view at any time to better suit your needs.
CHANGE VIEWS

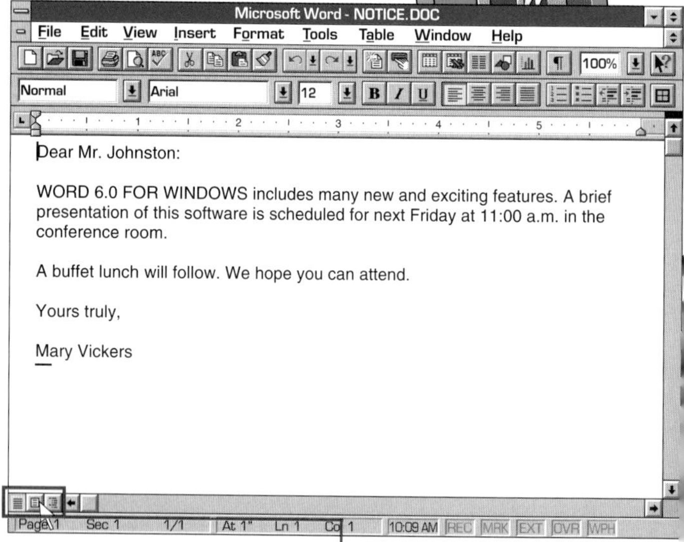
Microsoft Word - NOTICE.DOC
File Edit View Insert Format Tools Table Window Help
Normal
Arial
12
100%
Dear Mr. Johnston:
WORD 6.0 FOR WINDOWS includes many new and exciting features. A brief presentation of this software is scheduled for next Friday at 11:00 a.m. in the conference room.
A buffet lunch will follow. We hope you can attend.
Yours truly,
Mary Vickers
Page 1 Sec 1 1/1 At 1" Ln 1 Col 1 10:09 AM REC MRK EXT OVR WPH

When you first start Word, your document appears in the Normal view.

1 To change to another view, move the mouse over one of the options listed below (example:) and then press the left button.

- Normal View
- Page Layout View
- Outline View

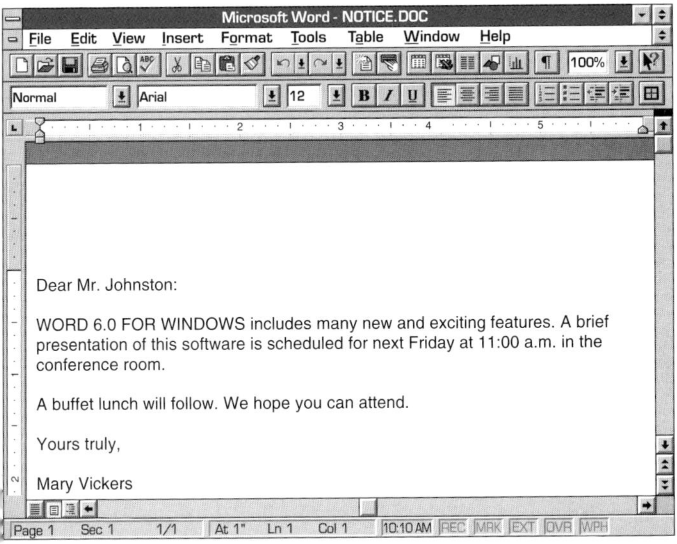
Microsoft Word - NOTICE.DOC
File Edit View Insert Format Tools Table Window Help
100%
Normal
Arial
12
Dear Mr. Johnston:
WORD 6.0 FOR WINDOWS includes many new and exciting features. A brief presentation of this software is scheduled for next Friday at 11:00 a.m. in the conference room.
A buffet lunch will follow. We hope you can attend.
Yours truly,
Mary Vickers
Page 1 Sec 1 1/1 At 1" Ln 1 Col 1 10:10 AM REC MRK EXT OVR WPH

◆ Your document appears in the new view (example: **Page Layout**).

DISPLAY OR HIDE TOOLBARS

Word offers eight different toolbars that you can display or hide at any time.

DISPLAY OR HIDE TOOLBARS

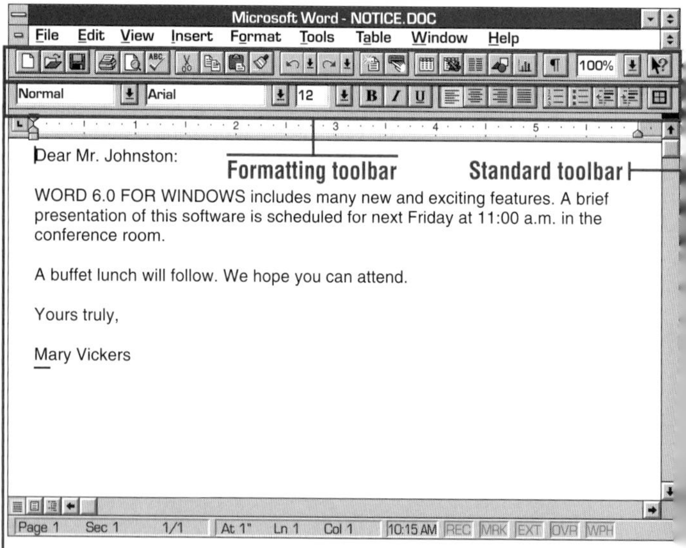

◆ When you first start Word, the Standard and Formatting toolbars appear on your screen.

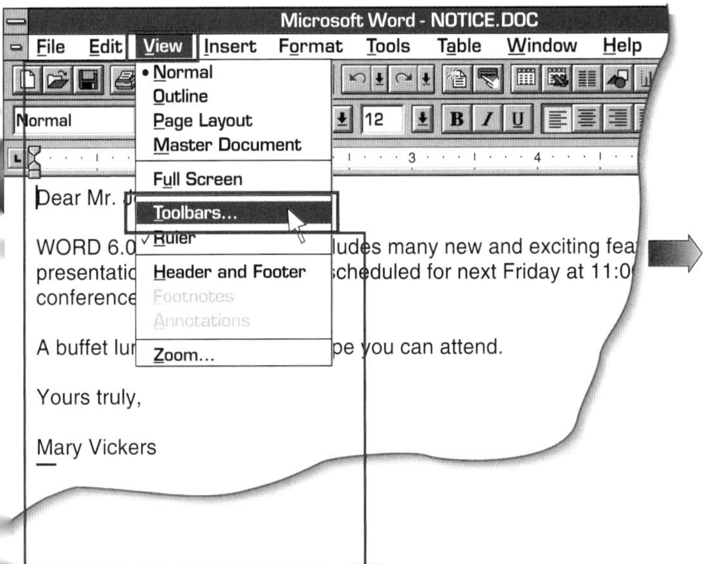

1 To display or hide a toolbar, move the mouse over **View** and then press the left button.

2 Move the mouse over **Toolbars** and then press the left button.

◆ The **Toolbars** dialog box appears.

Note: To continue, refer to the next page.

DISPLAY OR HIDE TOOLBARS

Each toolbar contains a series of buttons that let you quickly choose commands.

DISPLAY OR HIDE TOOLBARS (Continued)

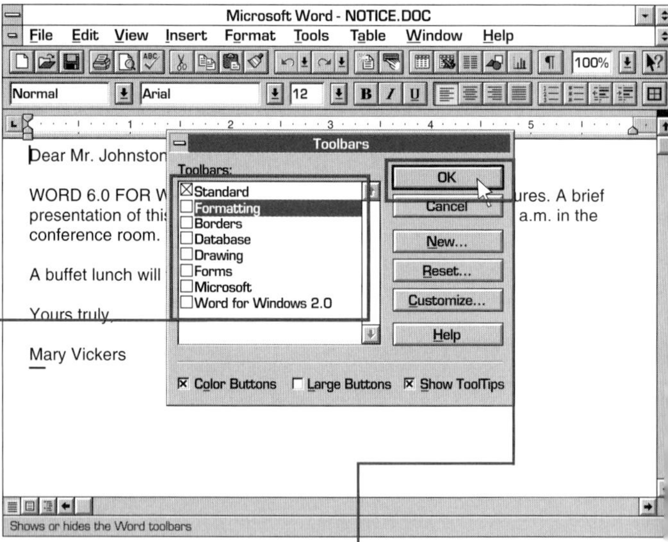

3 To hide a toolbar, move the mouse ⇖ over the toolbar name (example: **Formatting**) and then press the left button (☒ changes to ☐).

◆ To display a toolbar, move the mouse ⇖ over the toolbar name and then press the left button (☐ changes to ☒).

4 Repeat step **3** until you have selected all the toolbars you want to hide or display.

5 Move the mouse ⇖ over **OK** and then press the left button.

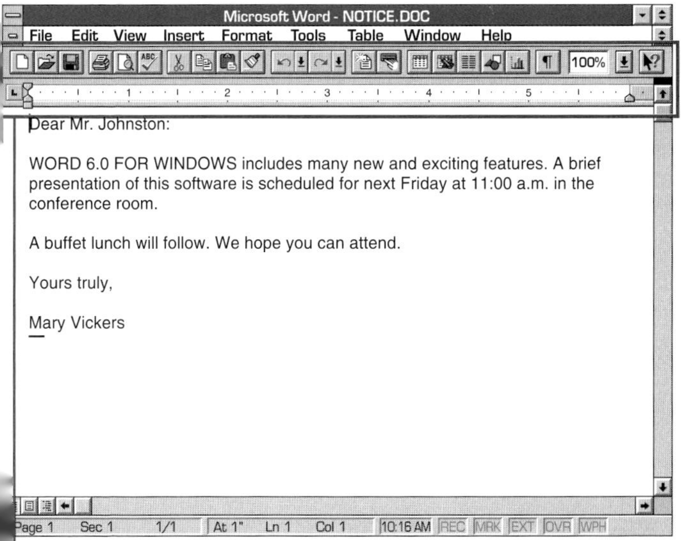

▶ The screen hides or displays the toolbar(s) you selected.

Note: A screen displaying fewer toolbars provides a larger and less cluttered working area.

DISPLAY OR HIDE TOOLBARS

You can quickly display or hide a toolbar by using the right button on your mouse.

QUICKLY DISPLAY OR HIDE A TOOLBAR

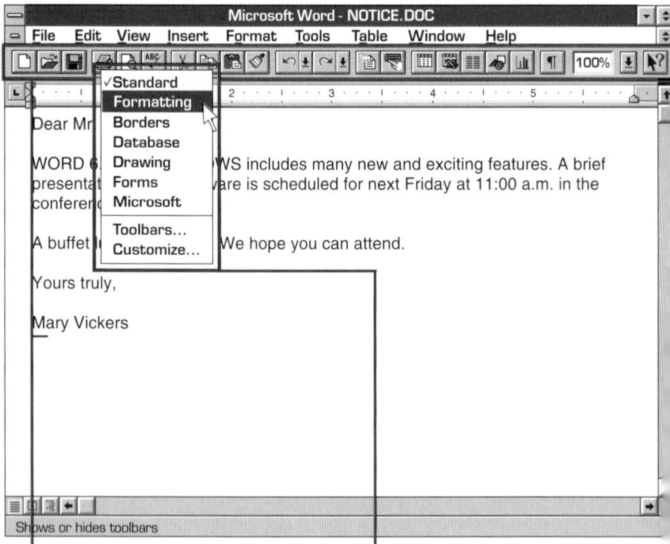
Microsoft Word - NOTICE.DOC
File Edit View Insert Format Tools Table Window Help
100%
√Standard
Formatting
Borders
Database
Drawing
Forms
Microsoft
Toolbars...
Customize...
Dear Mr
WORD 6 ... WS includes many new and exciting features. A brief
presenta... are is scheduled for next Friday at 11:00 a.m. in the
conferen
A buffet ... We hope you can attend.
Yours truly,
Mary Vickers
Shows or hides toolbars

1 Move the mouse anywhere over a toolbar displayed on your screen and then press the **right** mouse button.

◆ A list of the available toolbars appears.

2 Move the mouse over the toolbar you want to display or hide and then press the left button.

Note: A √ beside a toolbar name tells you the toolbar is currently displayed on your screen.

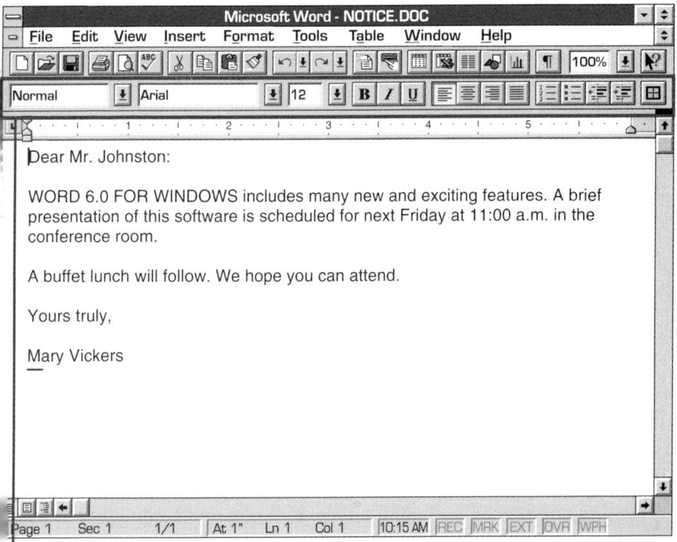
Microsoft Word - NOTICE.DOC
File Edit View Insert Format Tools Table Window Help
100%
Normal
Arial
12
Dear Mr. Johnston:
WORD 6.0 FOR WINDOWS includes many new and exciting features. A brief presentation of this software is scheduled for next Friday at 11:00 a.m. in the conference room.
A buffet lunch will follow. We hope you can attend.
Yours truly,
Mary Vickers
Page 1 Sec 1 1/1 At 1" Ln 1 Col 1 10:15 AM REC MRK EXT OVR WPH

◆ The screen displays
r hides the toolbar
ou selected.

DISPLAY OR HIDE THE RULER

The Ruler lets you indent paragraphs and change margin and tab settings. If you are not using the ruler, you can hide it to provide a larger and less cluttered working area.

DISPLAY OR HIDE THE RULER

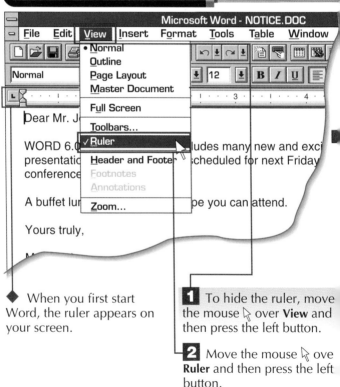

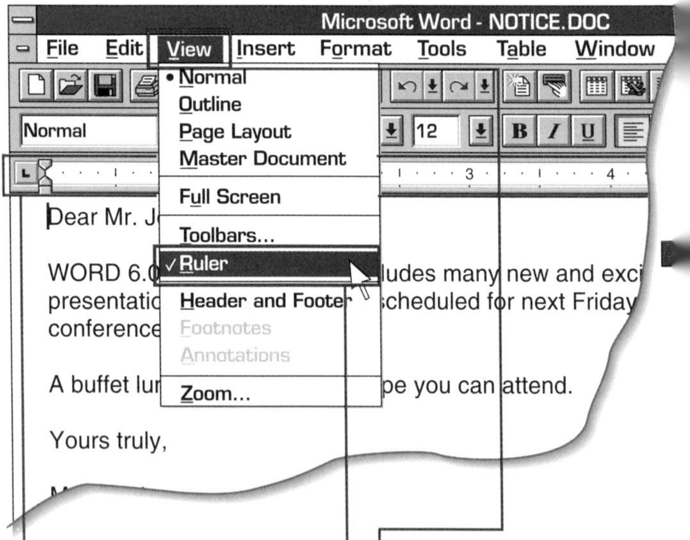

◆ When you first start Word, the ruler appears on your screen.

1 To hide the ruler, move the mouse over **View** and then press the left button.

2 Move the mouse ove **Ruler** and then press the left button.

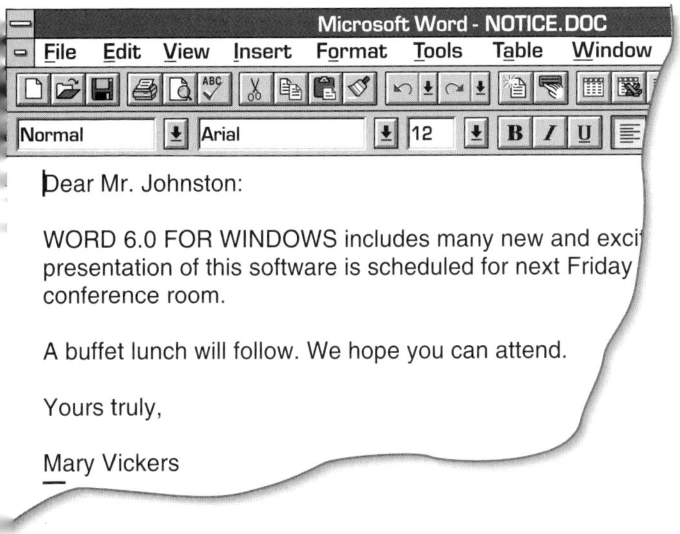
Microsoft Word - NOTICE.DOC
File Edit View Insert Format Tools Table Window
Normal
Arial
12
Dear Mr. Johnston:
WORD 6.0 FOR WINDOWS includes many new and exci
presentation of this software is scheduled for next Friday
conference room.
A buffet lunch will follow. We hope you can attend.
Yours truly,
Mary Vickers

The **Ruler** disappears om your screen.

To again display the ruler, repeat steps 1 and 2.

USING FULL SCREEN VIEW

USING FULL SCREEN VIEW

Microsoft Word - NOTICE.DOC

File   Edit   **View**   Insert   Format   Tools   Table   Window

- • Normal
- **O**utline
- **P**age Layout
- **M**aster Document

Full Screen

Toolbars...
✓ **R**uler

Header and Footer
Footnotes
Annotations

Zoom...

Normal   12   **B** *I* U

Dear Mr. J

WORD 6.0   ludes many new and exci
presentatio   scheduled for next Friday
conference

A buffet lu   pe you can attend.

Yours truly,

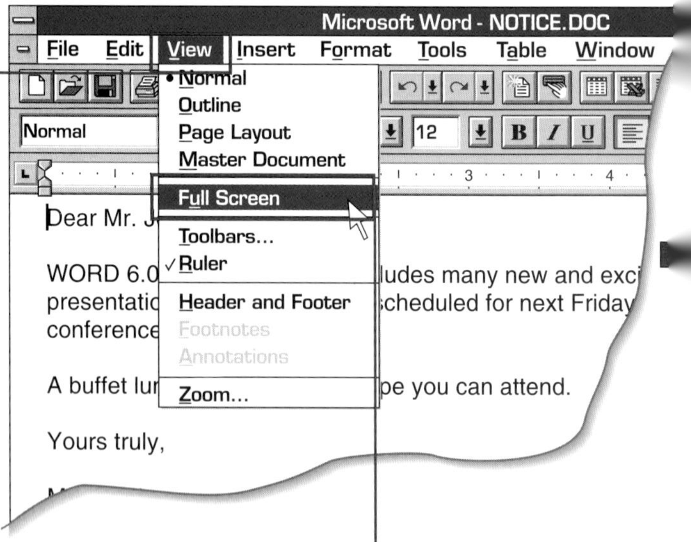

1 To use the Full Screen view, move the mouse ▷ over **View** and then press the left button.

2 Move the mouse ▷ over **Full Screen** and then press the left button.

You can use the Full Screen view to display more of your document. This will hide all screen elements such as the ruler, menu and toolbars to provide you with more working area.

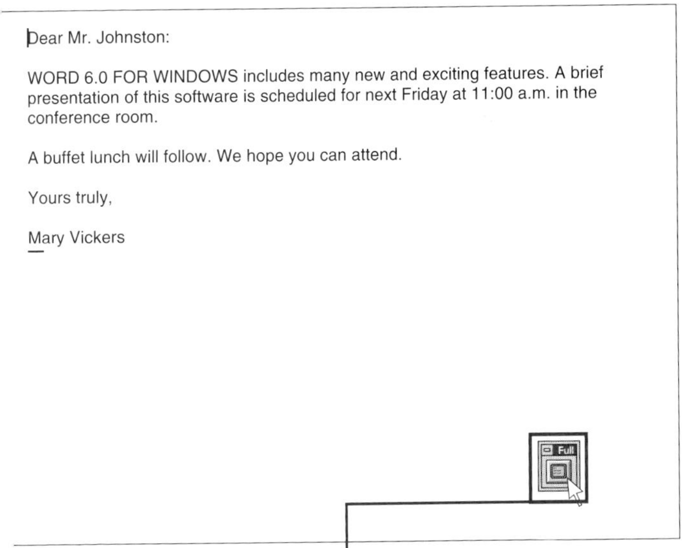
Dear Mr. Johnston:

WORD 6.0 FOR WINDOWS includes many new and exciting features. A brief presentation of this software is scheduled for next Friday at 11:00 a.m. in the conference room.

A buffet lunch will follow. We hope you can attend.

Yours truly,

Mary Vickers

◆ Word uses the entire creen to display the text n your document.

3 To return to the previous view, move the mouse over and then press the left button **or** press Alt, V, U.

BOLD, ITALICS AND UNDERLINE

bold
italic
underline

BOLD, ITALICIZE AND UNDERLINE TEXT

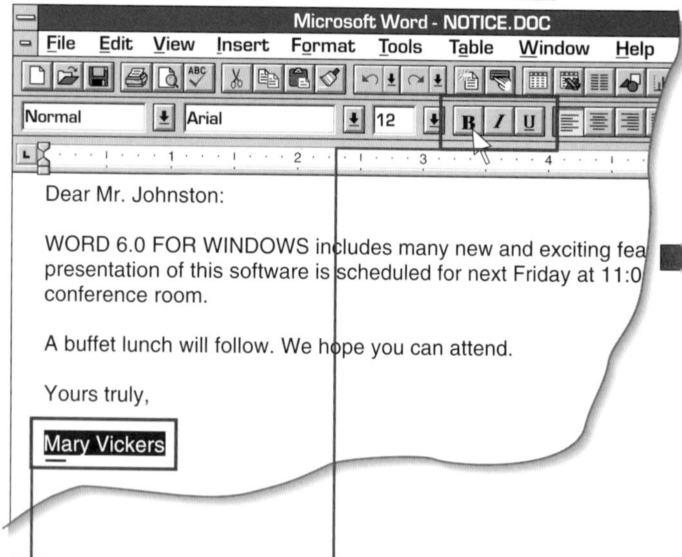
Microsoft Word - NOTICE.DOC
File Edit View Insert Format Tools Table Window Help
Normal
Arial
12
Dear Mr. Johnston:
WORD 6.0 FOR WINDOWS includes many new and exciting fea
presentation of this software is scheduled for next Friday at 11:0
conference room.
A buffet lunch will follow. We hope you can attend.
Yours truly,
Mary Vickers

1 Select the text you want to change.

Note: To select text, refer to pages 28 to 31.

2 Move the mouse over one of the following options and then press the left button.

- **B** Bold text
- *I* Italicize text
- U Underline text

You can use the Bold, Italic and Underline features to emphasize important information. This will improve the overall appearance of your document.

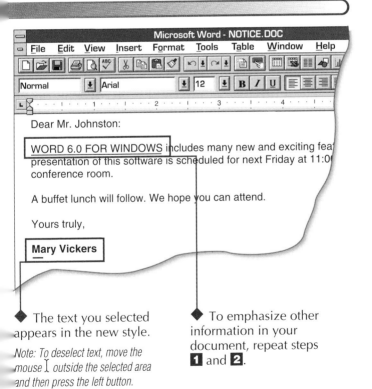

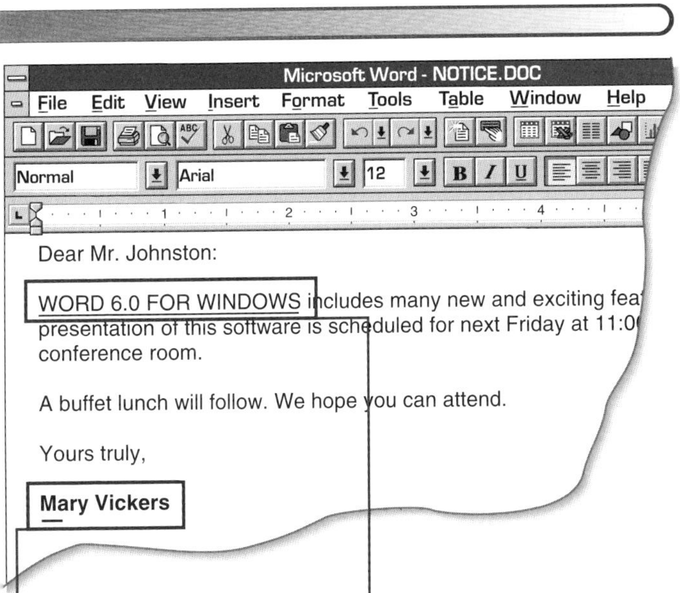
Microsoft Word - NOTICE.DOC
File Edit View Insert Format Tools Table Window Help
Normal
Arial
12
Dear Mr. Johnston:
WORD 6.0 FOR WINDOWS includes many new and exciting fea
presentation of this software is scheduled for next Friday at 11:0
conference room.
A buffet lunch will follow. We hope you can attend.
Yours truly,
Mary Vickers

◆ The text you selected appears in the new style.

Note: To deselect text, move the mouse I outside the selected area and then press the left button.

◆ To emphasize other information in your document, repeat steps **1** and **2**.

CHANGE FONTS

CHANGE FONTS

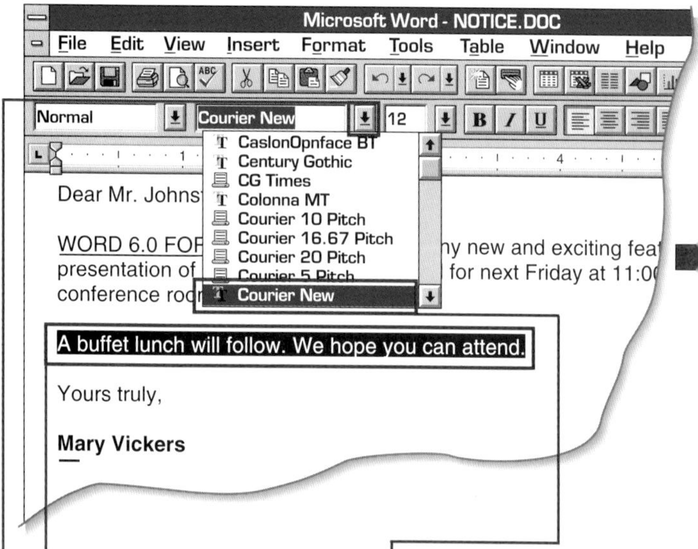

1 Select the text you want to change to a new font.

Note: To select text, refer to pages 28 to 31.

2 To display a list of the available fonts, move the mouse ⇖ over ⬇ beside the **Font** box and then press the left button.

3 Press ⬇ or ⬆ on your keyboard until you highlight the font you want to use (example: **Courier New**) and then press Enter.

You can change the design of characters in your document to emphasize headings and make text easier to read.

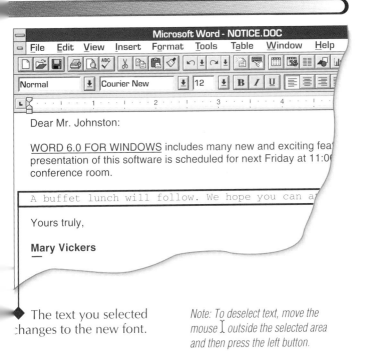

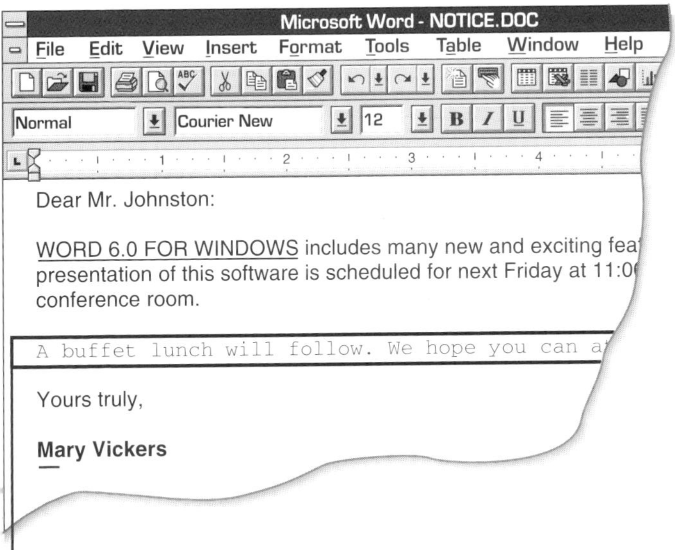

◆ The text you selected changes to the new font.

Note: To deselect text, move the mouse ⟂ outside the selected area and then press the left button.

CHANGE FONTS

You can increase or decrease the size of text in your document.

CHANGE FONT SIZE

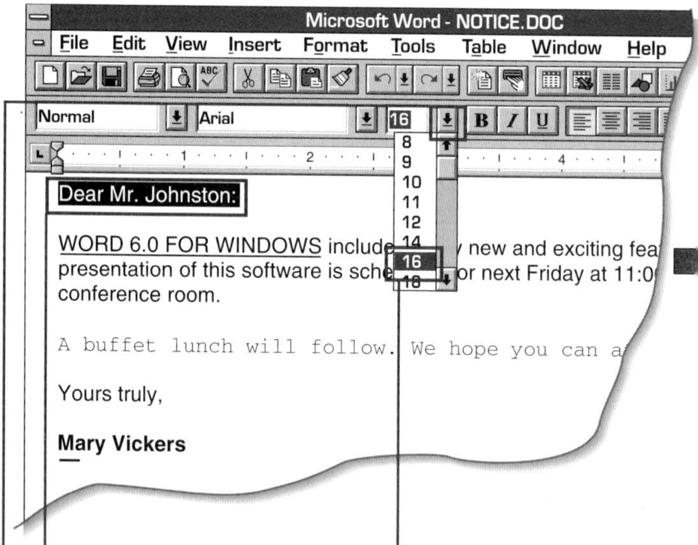

Microsoft Word - NOTICE.DOC
File Edit View Insert Format Tools Table Window Help
Normal
Arial
16
8
9
10
11
12
14
16
18
Dear Mr. Johnston:
WORD 6.0 FOR WINDOWS includ
new and exciting fea
presentation of this software is sch
or next Friday at 11:0
conference room.
A buffet lunch will follow. We hope you can a
Yours truly,
Mary Vickers

1 Select the text you want to change to a new font size.

Note: To select text, refer to pages 28 to 31.

2 To display a list of the available font sizes, move the mouse over ⬇ beside the **Font Size** box and then press the left button.

3 Press ↓ or ↑ on your keyboard until you highlight the font size you want to use (example: **16**) and then press Enter.

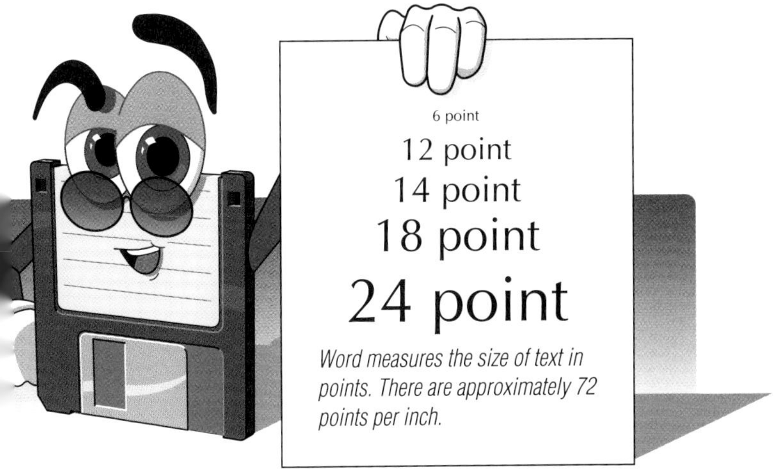
6 point
12 point
14 point
18 point
24 point

Word measures the size of text in points. There are approximately 72 points per inch.

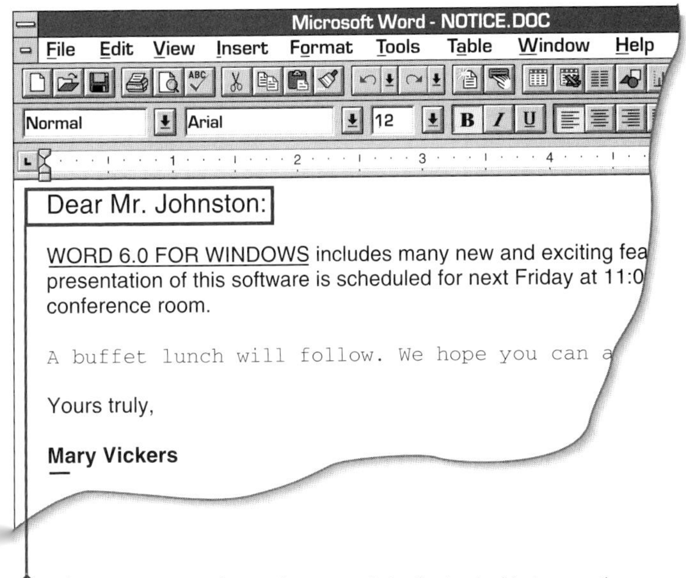
Microsoft Word - NOTICE.DOC
File Edit View Insert Format Tools Table Window Help
Normal
Arial
12
Dear Mr. Johnston:
WORD 6.0 FOR WINDOWS includes many new and exciting fea
presentation of this software is scheduled for next Friday at 11:0
conference room.
A buffet lunch will follow. We hope you can a
Yours truly,
Mary Vickers

◆ The text you selected changes to the new font size.

Note: To deselect text, move the mouse I outside the selected area and then press the left button.

CHANGE FONTS

CHANGE FONTS

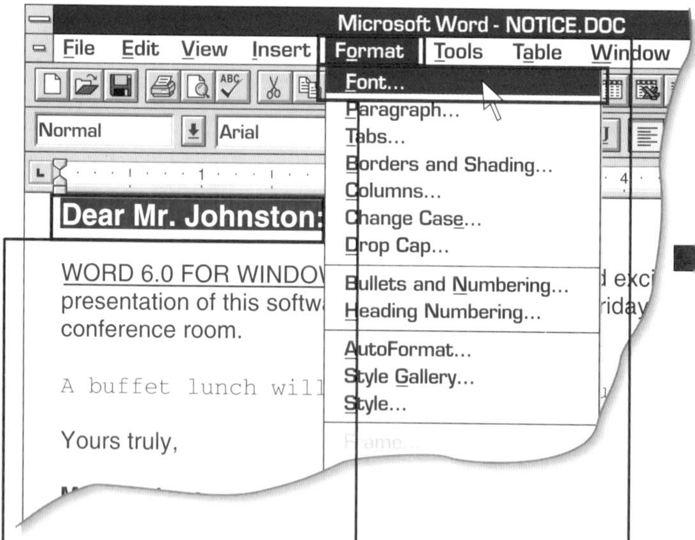

1 Select the text you want to change.

Note: To select text, refer to pages 28 to 31.

2 Move the mouse over **Format** and then press the left button.

3 Move the mouse over **Font** and then press the left button.

You can change the design and size of characters in your document at the same time by using the Font dialog box.

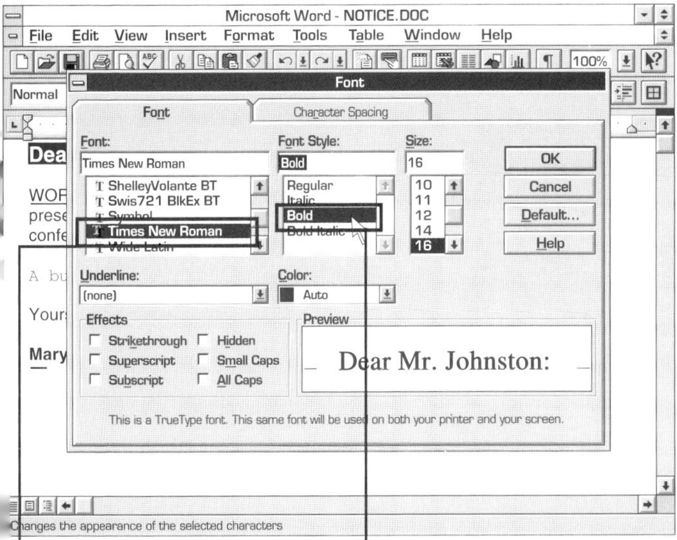

4 Move the mouse over he font you want to use example: **Times New Roman**) nd then press the left button.

'ote: To view all of the available font ptions, use the scroll bar. To use the croll bar, refer to page 26.

5 Move the mouse over the font style you want to use (example: **Bold**) and then press the left button.

Note: To continue, refer to the next page.

CHANGE FONTS (Continued)

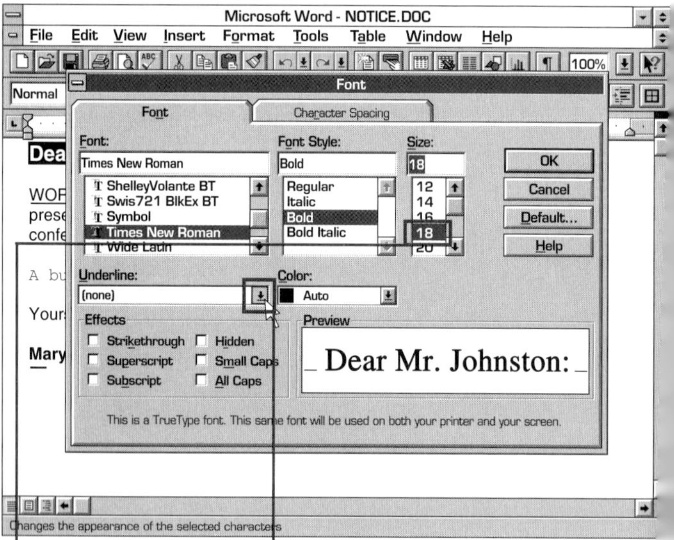

6 Move the mouse over the font size you want to use (example: **18**) and then press the left button.

7 To select an underline style, move the mouse over ⬇ in the **Underline:** box and then press the left button.

You can change the font of text to turn a dull, lifeless letter into an interesting, attractive document.

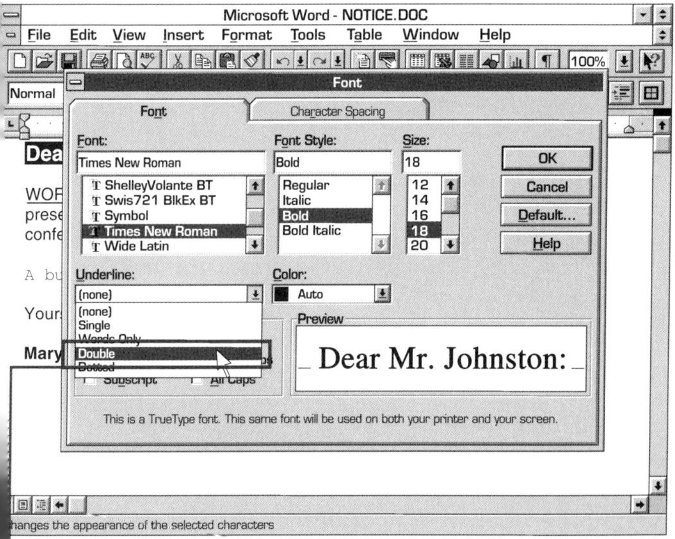

3 Move the mouse over the underline style you want to use (example: **Double**) and then press the left button.

Note: To continue, refer to the next page.

The Font dialog box offers several effects that you can apply to text in your document.

CHANGE FONTS (Continued)

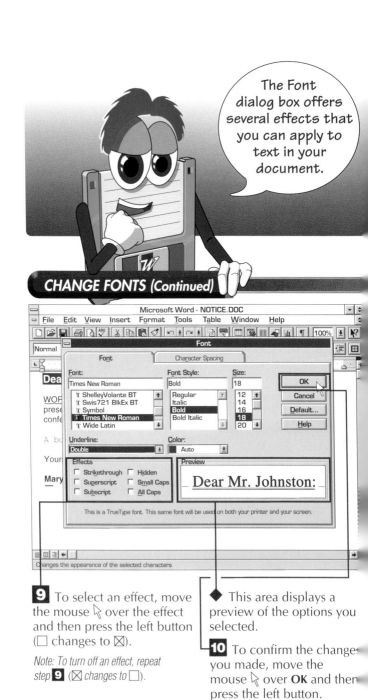

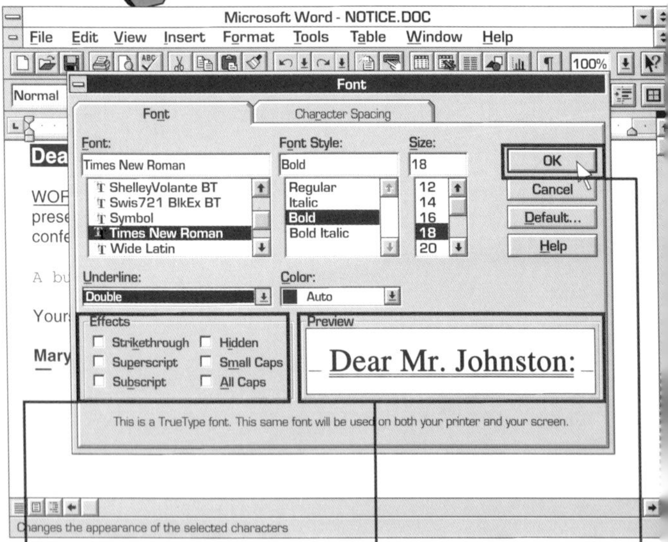

9 To select an effect, move the mouse ⇖ over the effect and then press the left button (☐ changes to ☒).

Note: To turn off an effect, repeat step **9** *(☒ changes to ☐).*

◆ This area displays a preview of the options you selected.

10 To confirm the changes you made, move the mouse ⇖ over **OK** and then press the left button.

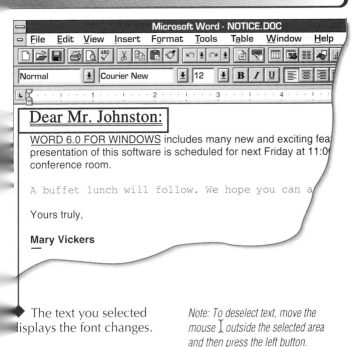

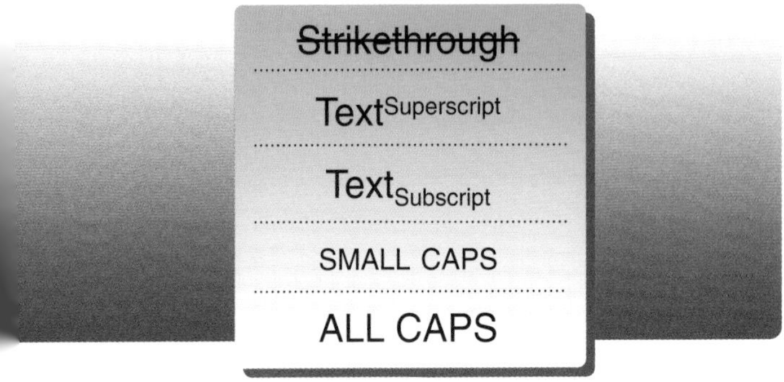
Strikethrough
TextSuperscript
TextSubscript
SMALL CAPS
ALL CAPS

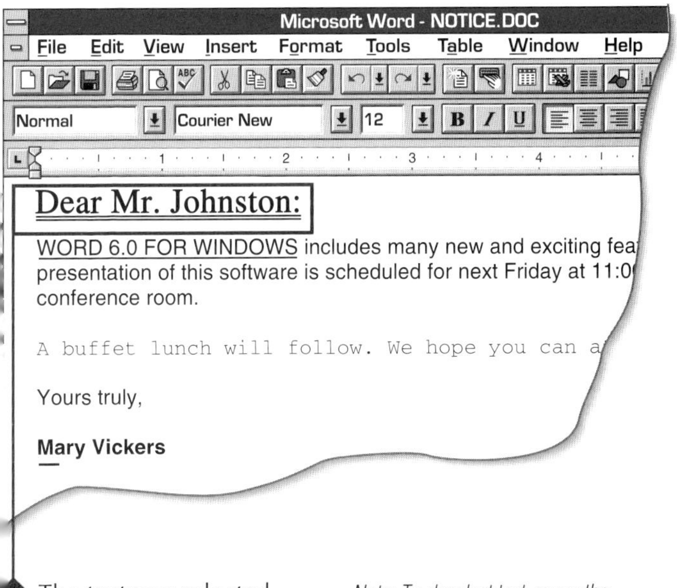
Microsoft Word - NOTICE.DOC
File Edit View Insert Format Tools Table Window Help
Normal
Courier New
12
Dear Mr. Johnston:
WORD 6.0 FOR WINDOWS includes many new and exciting fea
presentation of this software is scheduled for next Friday at 11:0
conference room.
A buffet lunch will follow. We hope you can a
Yours truly,
Mary Vickers

◆ The text you selected displays the font changes.

Note: To deselect text, move the mouse I outside the selected area and then press the left button.

INSERT A SYMBOL

TM

INSERT A SYMBOL

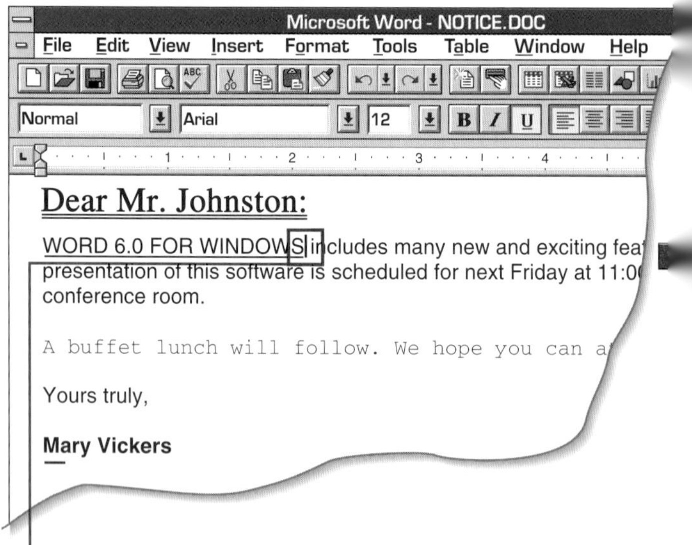
Microsoft Word - NOTICE.DOC
File Edit View Insert Format Tools Table Window Help
Normal
Arial
12
Dear Mr. Johnston:
WORD 6.0 FOR WINDOWS includes many new and exciting fea
presentation of this software is scheduled for next Friday at 11:0
conference room.
A buffet lunch will follow. We hope you can a
Yours truly,
Mary Vickers

1 Position the insertion point where you want a symbol to appear in your document.

Word lets you insert symbols into your document that are not displayed on your keyboard.

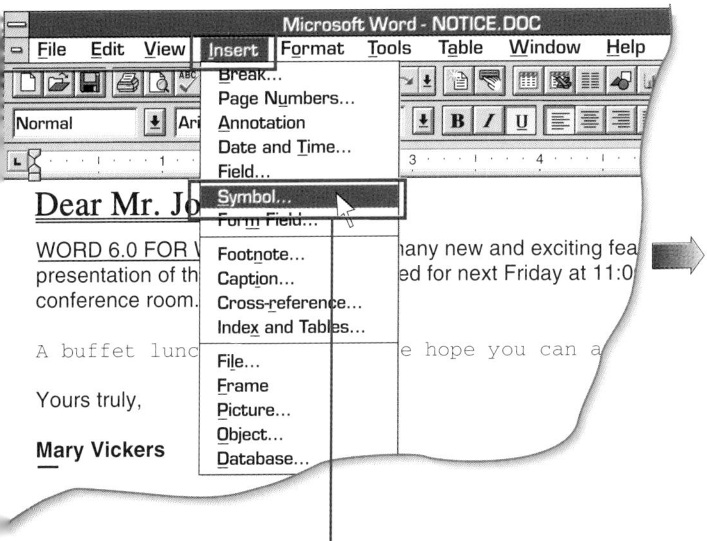

2 Move the mouse over **Insert** and then press the left button.

3 Move the mouse over **Symbol** and then press the left button.

Note: To continue, refer to the next page.

INSERT A SYMBOL (Continued)

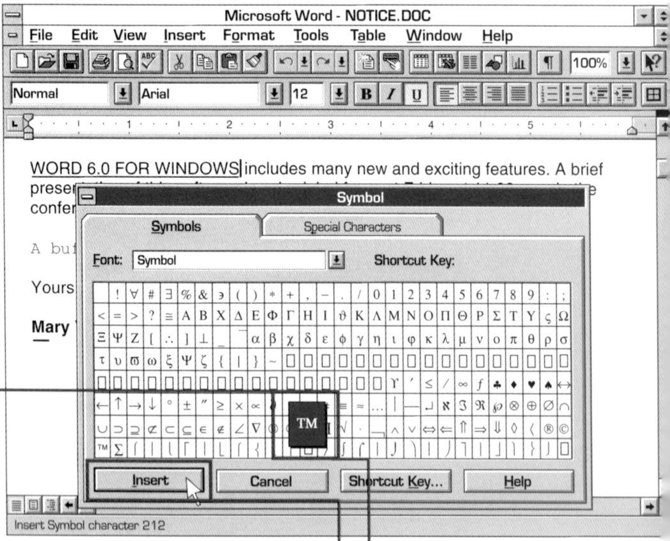

◆ The **Symbol** dialog box appears.

4 Move the mouse over the symbol you want to insert (example: **TM**) and then press the left button.

◆ An enlarged version of the symbol appears.

5 To insert the symbol into your document, move the mouse over **Insert** and then press the left button.

Word offers a wide selection of symbols. For example, you can insert the ™, ®, ♣, ∑, or © symbol into your document.

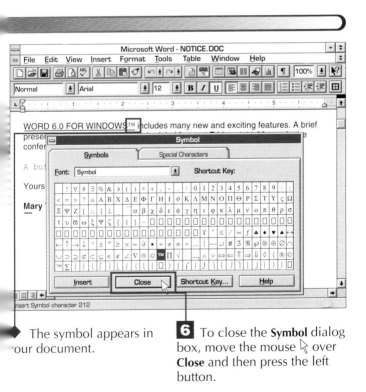

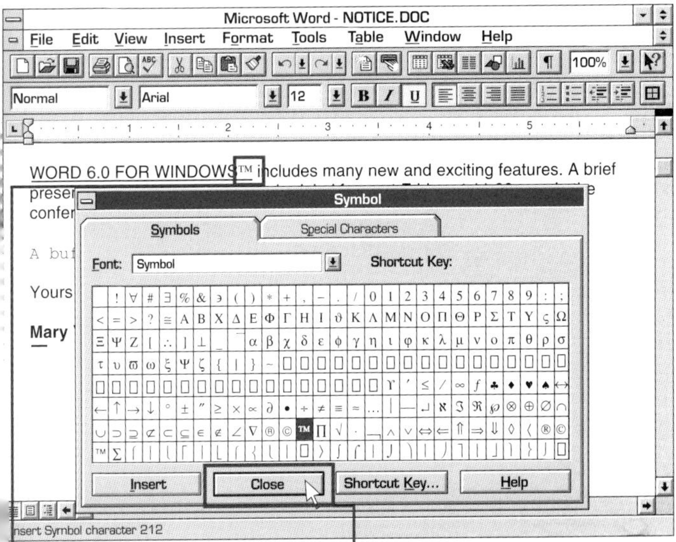

◆ The symbol appears in your document.

6 To close the **Symbol** dialog box, move the mouse over **Close** and then press the left button.

CHANGE PARAGRAPH ALIGNMENT

You can enhance the appearance of your document by aligning text in different ways. Word offers four alignment options.

CHANGE PARAGRAPH ALIGNMENT

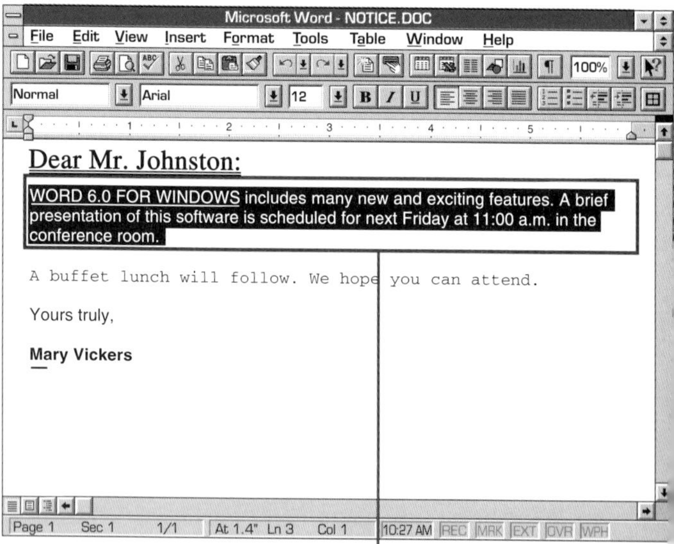
Microsoft Word - NOTICE.DOC
File Edit View Insert Format Tools Table Window Help
100%
Normal
Arial
12
Dear Mr. Johnston:
WORD 6.0 FOR WINDOWS includes many new and exciting features. A brief presentation of this software is scheduled for next Friday at 11:00 a.m. in the conference room.
A buffet lunch will follow. We hope you can attend.
Yours truly,
Mary Vickers
Page 1 Sec 1 1/1 At 1.4" Ln 3 Col 1 10:27 AM REC MRK EXT OVR WPH

Word automatically left aligns any text you type in your document.

1 Select the paragraph(s) you want to change.

Note: To select text, refer to pages 28 to 31.

Right
Center
Left
Full
FORMAT

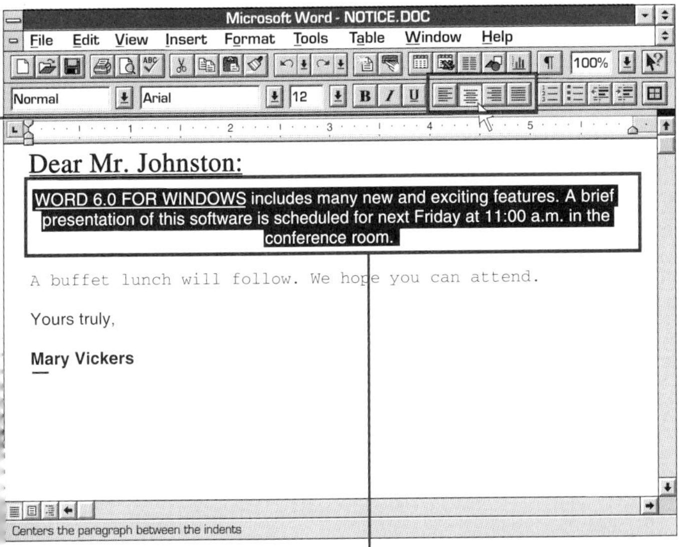
Microsoft Word - NOTICE.DOC
File Edit View Insert Format Tools Table Window Help
Normal
Arial
12
100%
Dear Mr. Johnston:
WORD 6.0 FOR WINDOWS includes many new and exciting features. A brief presentation of this software is scheduled for next Friday at 11:00 a.m. in the conference room.
A buffet lunch will follow. We hope you can attend.
Yours truly,
Mary Vickers
Centers the paragraph between the indents

2 Move the mouse over one of the following options and then press the left button.

- Left align paragraph
- Center paragraph
- Right align paragraph
- Fully align paragraph

◆ Word changes the alignment of the paragraph(s) you selected.

CHANGE LINE SPACING

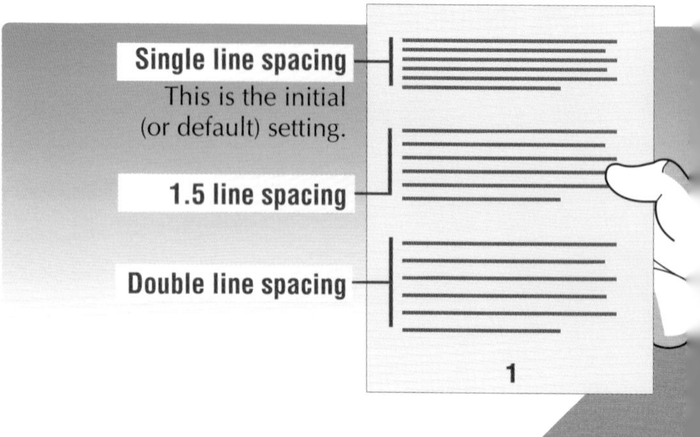

Single line spacing
This is the initial (or default) setting.
1.5 line spacing
Double line spacing
1

CHANGE LINE SPACING

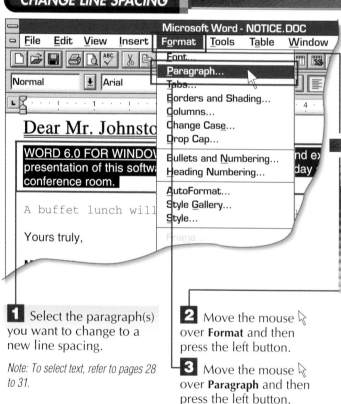

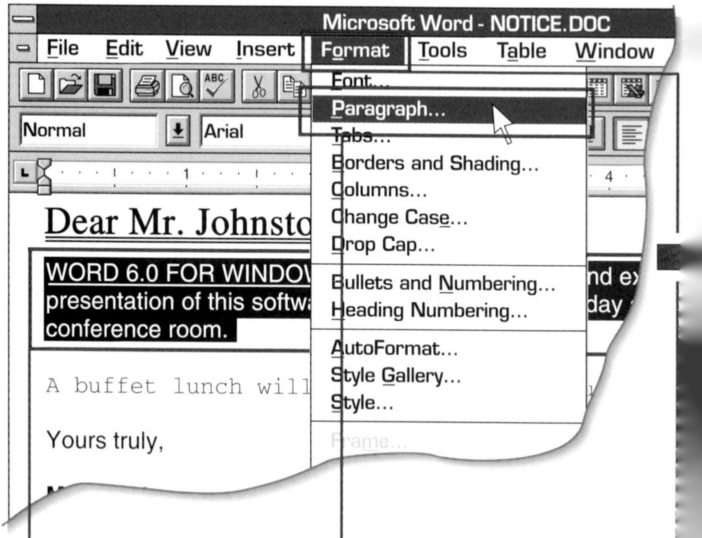

Microsoft Word - NOTICE.DOC
File Edit View Insert Format Tools Table Window
Normal
Arial
Font...
Paragraph...
Tabs...
Borders and Shading...
Columns...
Change Case...
Drop Cap...
Bullets and Numbering...
Heading Numbering...
AutoFormat...
Style Gallery...
Style...
Frame...
Dear Mr. Johnsto
WORD 6.0 FOR WINDO
presentation of this softw
conference room.
A buffet lunch will
Yours truly,

1 Select the paragraph(s) you want to change to a new line spacing.

Note: To select text, refer to pages 28 to 31.

2 Move the mouse over **Format** and then press the left button.

3 Move the mouse over **Paragraph** and then press the left button.

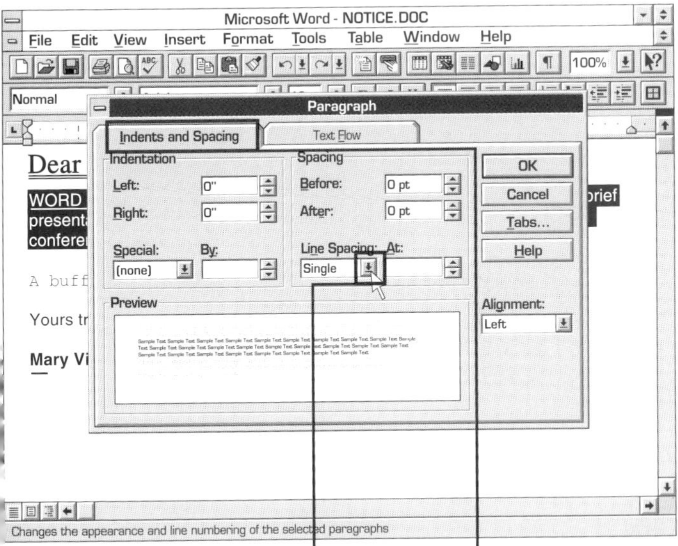

◆ The **Paragraph** dialog box appears.

4 Move the mouse over the **Indents and Spacing** tab and then press the left button.

5 Move the mouse over in the **Line Spacing:** box and then press the left button.

Note: To continue, refer to the next page.

CHANGE LINE SPACING

CHANGE LINE SPACING (Continued)

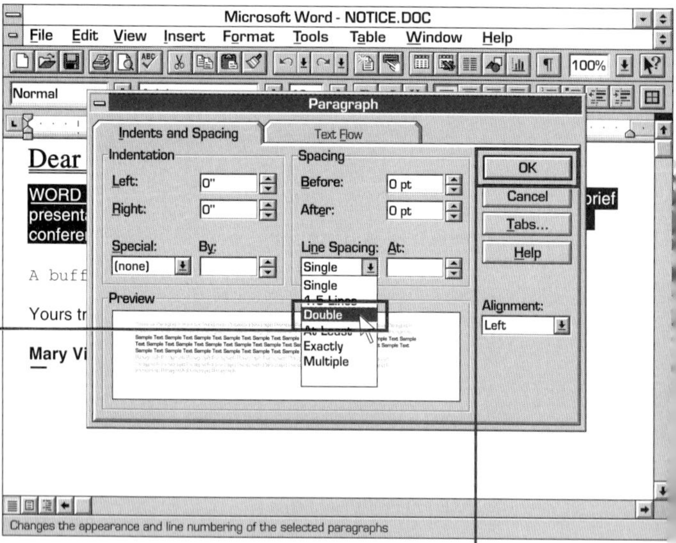

◆ A list of the available line spacing options appears.

6 Move the mouse over the line spacing you want to use (example: **Double**) and then press the left button.

7 Move the mouse over **OK** and then press the left button.

You can make
your document
easier to read by
changing the line
spacing.

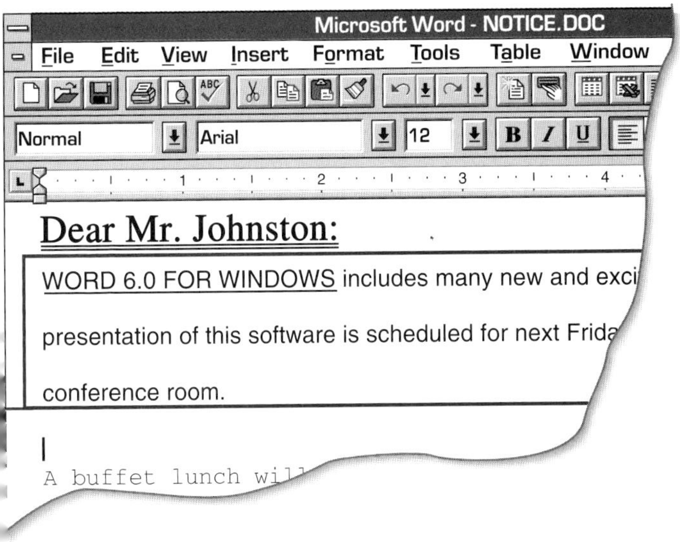
Microsoft Word - NOTICE.DOC
File Edit View Insert Format Tools Table Window
Normal
Arial
12
Dear Mr. Johnston:
WORD 6.0 FOR WINDOWS includes many new and exci
presentation of this software is scheduled for next Frida
conference room.
A buffet lunch wil

◆ Word changes the line spacing of the paragraph(s) you selected.

Note: To deselect text, move the mouse I outside the selected area and then press the left button.

ADD A TAB STOP

You can use tabs to line up columns of information in your document. Word offers four types of tabs.

ADD A TAB STOP

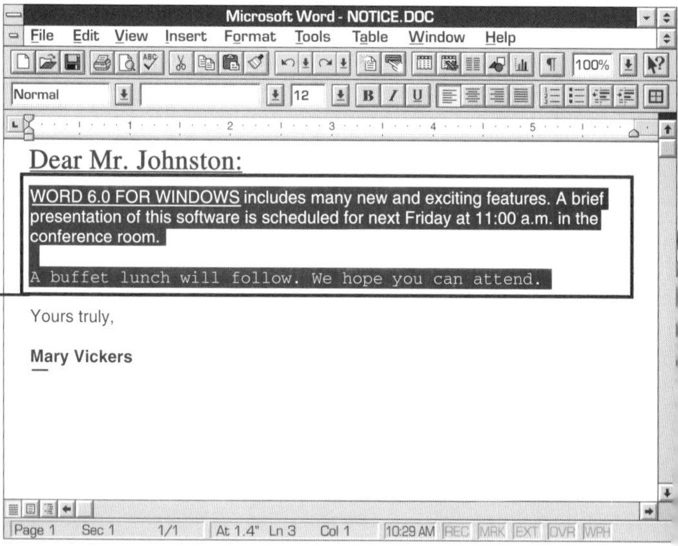

Microsoft Word - NOTICE.DOC
File Edit View Insert Format Tools Table Window Help
100%
Normal
12
Dear Mr. Johnston:
WORD 6.0 FOR WINDOWS includes many new and exciting features. A brief presentation of this software is scheduled for next Friday at 11:00 a.m. in the conference room.
A buffet lunch will follow. We hope you can attend.
Yours truly,
Mary Vickers
Page 1 Sec 1 1/1 At 1.4" Ln 3 Col 1 10:29 AM REC MRK EXT OVR WPH

1 Select the paragraph(s) you want to contain the new tab stops.

Note: To select text, refer to pages 28 to 31.

◆ To add tab stops to text you are about to type, position the insertion point where you want to begin typing the text.

Left tab

Right tab
Center tab
123.45 (Decimal tab)

Tab stop position

Microsoft Word - NOTICE.DOC

File Edit View Insert Format Tools Table Window

Normal   12   **B** *I* U

Dear Mr. Johnston:

WORD 6.0 FOR WINDOWS includes many new and exci
presentation of this software is scheduled for next Friday
conference room.

A buffet lunch will follow. We hope you

Yours truly,

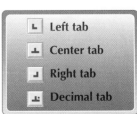

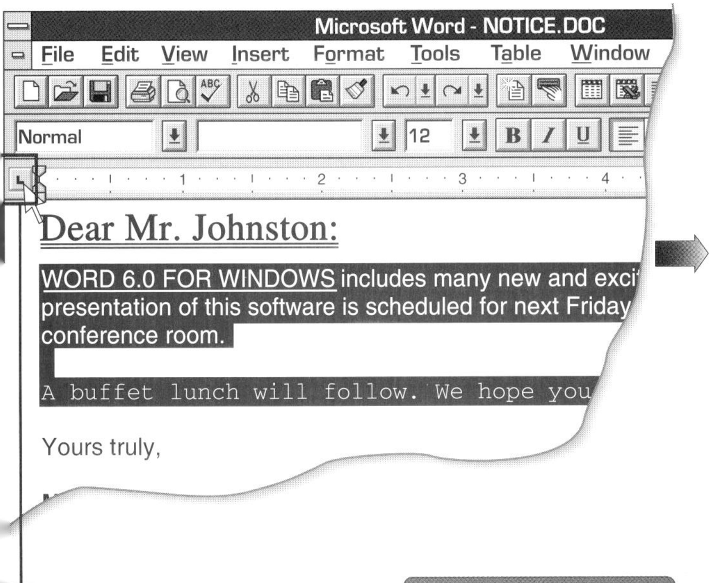

2 Move the mouse ⌖ over
this box and then press the left
button. Repeat this step until
the type of tab you want to add
appears (example: ⌊).

*Note: If the ruler is not displayed on your
screen, refer to page 154.*

⌊	Left tab
⌊	Center tab
⌊	Right tab
⌊	Decimal tab

*Note: To continue, refer to
the next page.*

ADD A TAB STOP

Make sure you use tabs rather than spaces to line up columns of text. This will ensure your document prints correctly.
FORMAT

ADD A TAB STOP (Continued)

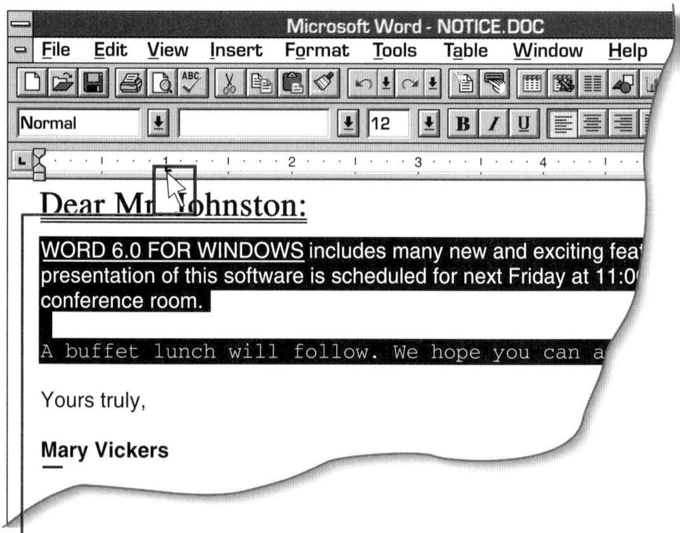

3 Move the mouse over the position on the ruler where you want to add the tab stop and then press the left button.

Note: Make sure you position the mouse over the lower half of the ruler.

◆ The new tab stop appears on the ruler.

Last Name First Name Address City State Zip Code
Appleton Jill 456 John Street Portland OR 97526
DeVries Monica 12 Willow Avenue Los Angeles CA 90032
Grossi Rob 23 Riverbead Road Seattle WA 98109
Knill Mark 97 Speers Road Denver CO 80207
Justin 15 Lakeshore Drive Atlanta GA 30367
Jennifer 34 Kerr Street Provo UT 84604
56 Devon Road Dallas TX 75236
Last Name First Name Address City State Zip Code
Appleton Jill 456 John Street Portland OR 97526
DeVries Monica 12 Willow Avenue Los Angeles CA 90032
Grossi Rob 23 Riverbead Road Seattle WA 98109
Knill Mark 97 Speers Road Denver CO 80207
Leung Justin 15 Lakeshore Drive Atlanta GA 30367
Matwey Jennifer 34 Kerr Street Provo UT 84604
mith Albert 56 Devon Road Dallas TX 75236
nith Betty 111 Linton Street Los Angeles CA 90071
nith Carol 36 Ford Drive Santa Clara CA 95054
nderson David 55 Kennedy Road Buffalo NY 14213

◆ In this example, spaces were used to line up columns.

◆ In this example, tabs were used to line up columns.

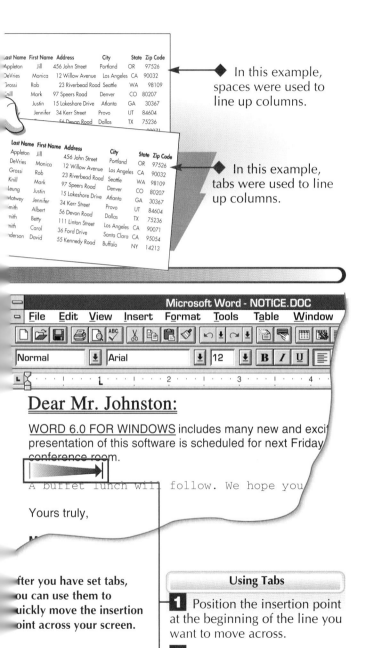

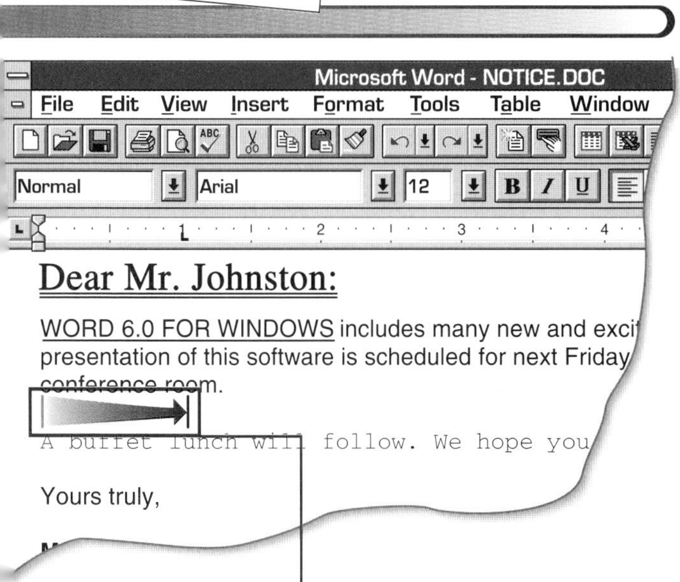
Microsoft Word - NOTICE.DOC
File Edit View Insert Format Tools Table Window
Normal
Arial
12
Dear Mr. Johnston:
WORD 6.0 FOR WINDOWS includes many new and exci
presentation of this software is scheduled for next Friday
conference room.
A buffet lunch will follow. We hope you
Yours truly,

fter you have set tabs, ou can use them to uickly move the insertion oint across your screen.

Using Tabs

1 Position the insertion point at the beginning of the line you want to move across.

2 Press Tab . The insertion point and any text that follows moves to the first tab stop.

MOVE A TAB STOP

You can easily move a tab stop to a different location on the ruler.
File Edit View Insert Format
Normal
12
Dear Mr. Johnston:
WORD 6.0 FOR WINDOWS includes many new and exciting features. A brief presentation of this software is scheduled for next Friday at 11:00 a.m. in the conference room.

MOVE A TAB STOP

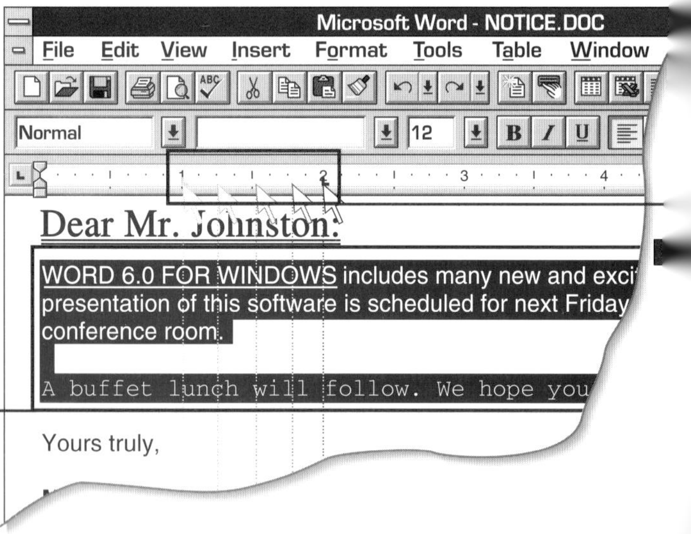
Microsoft Word - NOTICE.DOC
File Edit View Insert Format Tools Table Window
Normal
12
Dear Mr. Johnston:
WORD 6.0 FOR WINDOWS includes many new and exci
presentation of this software is scheduled for next Friday
conference room.
A buffet lunch will follow. We hope you
Yours truly,

1 Select the paragraph(s) containing the tab stop you want to move.

2 Move the mouse over the tab stop and then press and hold down the left button as you drag the tab stop to a new position.

◆ A dotted line indicates the new tab stop position.

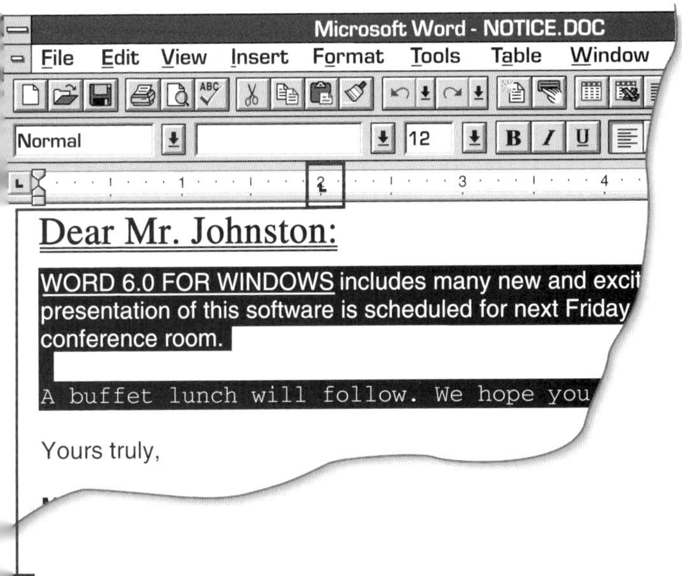
Microsoft Word - NOTICE.DOC
File Edit View Insert Format Tools Table Window
Normal
12
Dear Mr. Johnston:
WORD 6.0 FOR WINDOWS includes many new and excit
presentation of this software is scheduled for next Friday
conference room.
A buffet lunch will follow. We hope you
Yours truly,

3 Release the button and ıe tab stop moves to the ew position.

REMOVE A TAB STOP

Word lets you remove a tab stop from the ruler.
Microsoft Wo
File Edit View Insert Format Tools
Normal
12
Dear Mr. Johnston:
WORD 6.0 FOR WINDOWS includes many new and exciting features. A brief presentation of this software is scheduled for next Friday at 11:00 a.m. in the conference room.

REMOVE A TAB STOP

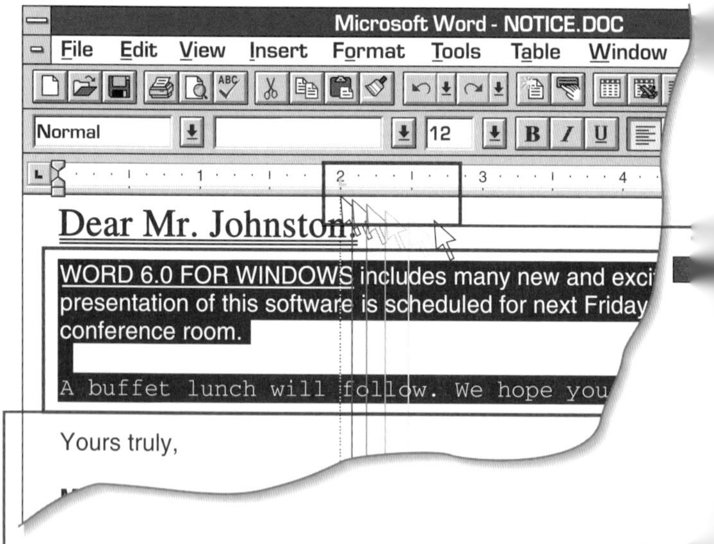

Microsoft Word - NOTICE.DOC
File Edit View Insert Format Tools Table Window
Normal
12
Dear Mr. Johnston:
WORD 6.0 FOR WINDOWS includes many new and exci
presentation of this software is scheduled for next Friday
conference room.
A buffet lunch will follow. We hope you
Yours truly,

1 Select the paragraph(s) containing the tab stop you want to remove.

2 Move the mouse over the tab stop and then press and hold down the left button as you drag the tab stop downward off the ruler.

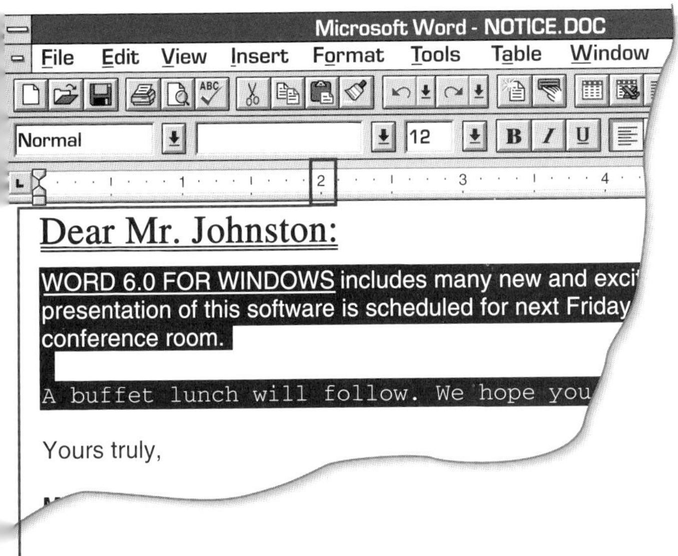
Microsoft Word - NOTICE.DOC
File Edit View Insert Format Tools Table Window
Normal
12
B I U
Dear Mr. Johnston:
WORD 6.0 FOR WINDOWS includes many new and exci
presentation of this software is scheduled for next Friday
conference room.
A buffet lunch will follow. We hope you
Yours truly,

3 Release the button and
ne tab stop disappears.

INDENT PARAGRAPHS

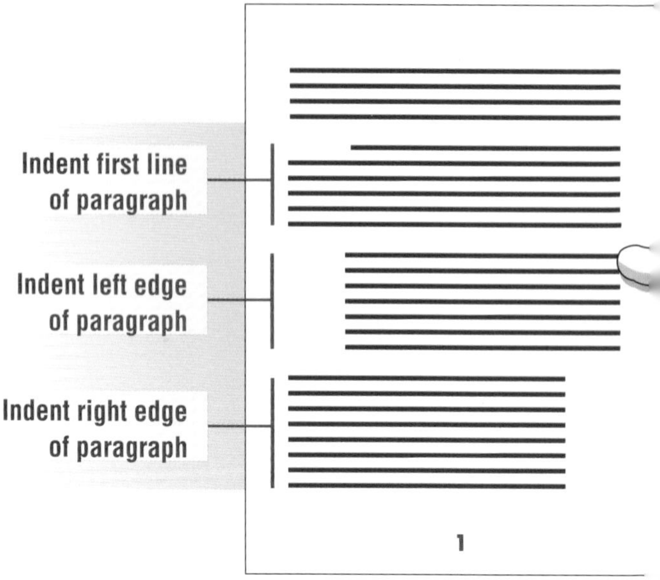

INDENT PARAGRAPHS

You can move these symbols on the ruler to indent paragraphs in your document.

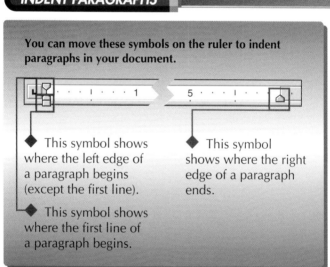

◆ This symbol shows where the left edge of a paragraph begins (except the first line).

◆ This symbol shows where the first line of a paragraph begins.

◆ This symbol shows where the right edge of a paragraph ends.

You can use the Indent feature to emphasize paragraphs in your document. Word offers several indent options.

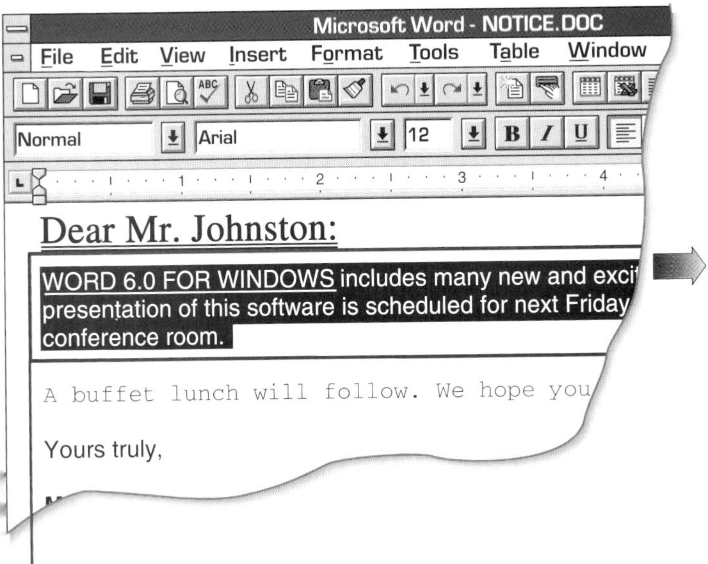
Microsoft Word - NOTICE.DOC
File Edit View Insert Format Tools Table Window
Normal
Arial
12
Dear Mr. Johnston:
WORD 6.0 FOR WINDOWS includes many new and exci
presentation of this software is scheduled for next Friday
conference room.
A buffet lunch will follow. We hope you
Yours truly,

1 Select the paragraph(s) you want to indent.

Note: To select text, refer to pages 28 to 31.

Note: To continue, refer to the next page.

INDENT PARAGRAPHS

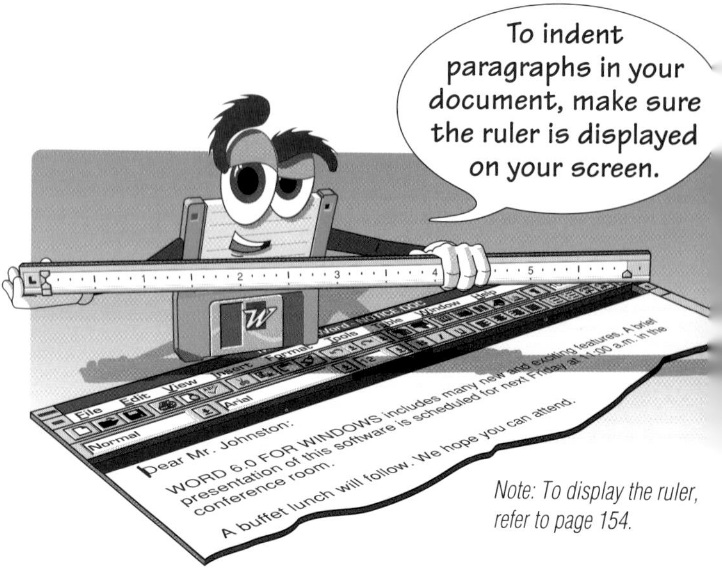

To indent paragraphs in your document, make sure the ruler is displayed on your screen.

Note: To display the ruler, refer to page 154.

INDENT PARAGRAPHS (Continued)

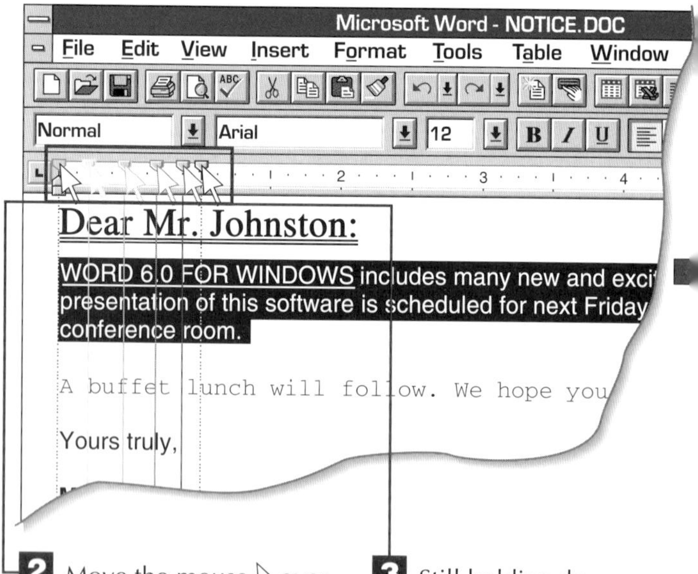

2 Move the mouse over the symbol you want to move (example:) and then press and hold down the left button.

3 Still holding down the button, move the mouse where you want to position the symbol.

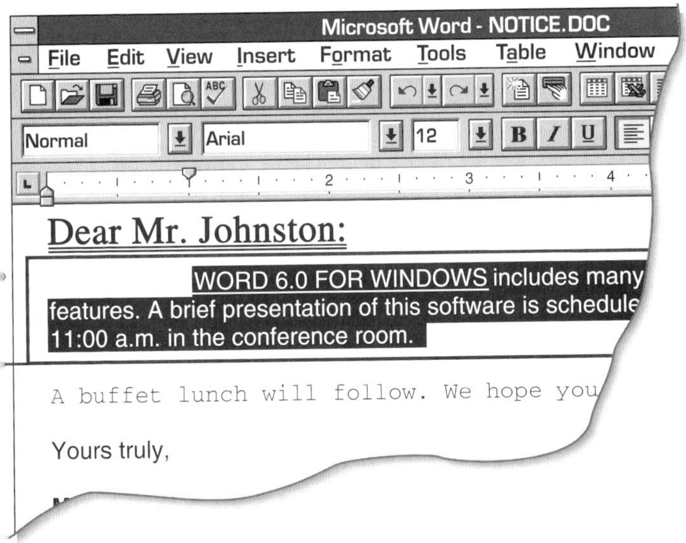

Microsoft Word - NOTICE.DOC
File Edit View Insert Format Tools Table Window
Normal
Arial
12
Dear Mr. Johnston:
WORD 6.0 FOR WINDOWS includes many
features. A brief presentation of this software is schedule
11:00 a.m. in the conference room.
A buffet lunch will follow. We hope you
Yours truly,

4 Release the button and Word indents the paragraph(s) you selected.

CREATE NUMBERED AND BULLETED LISTS

You can emphasize text in a list by beginning each item with a bullet or number.

CREATE NUMBERED AND BULLETED LISTS

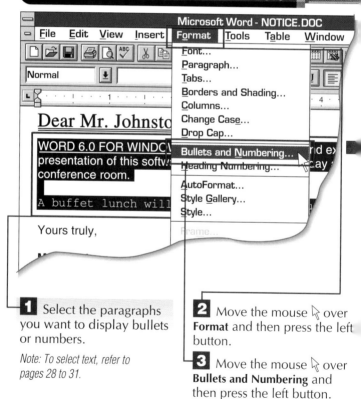

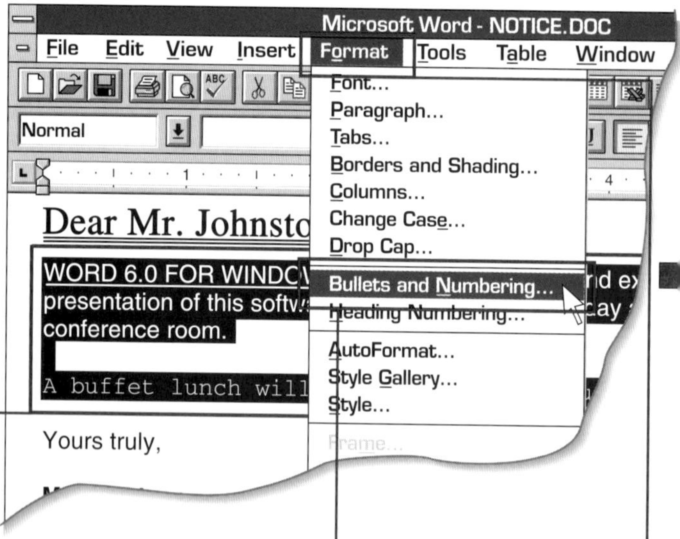

1 Select the paragraphs you want to display bullets or numbers.

Note: To select text, refer to pages 28 to 31.

2 Move the mouse over **Format** and then press the left button.

3 Move the mouse over **Bullets and Numbering** and then press the left button.

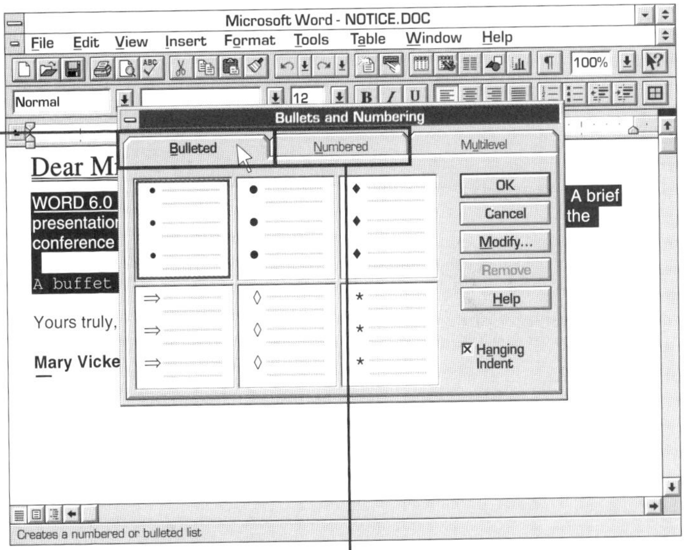

◆ The **Bullets and Numbering** dialog box appears.

4 To create a bulleted list, move the mouse ⇖ over the **Bulleted** tab and then press the left button.

◆ To create a numbered list, move the mouse ⇖ over the **Numbered** tab and then press the left button.

Note: To continue, refer to the next page.

CREATE NUMBERED AND BULLETED LISTS

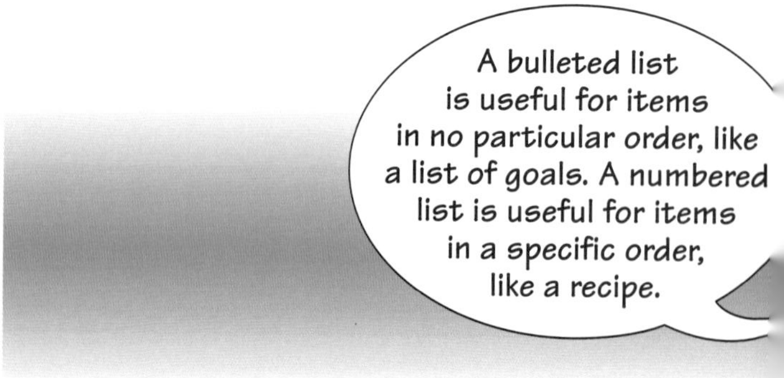
A bulleted list is useful for items in no particular order, like a list of goals. A numbered list is useful for items in a specific order, like a recipe.

CREATE NUMBERED AND BULLETED LISTS (Continued)

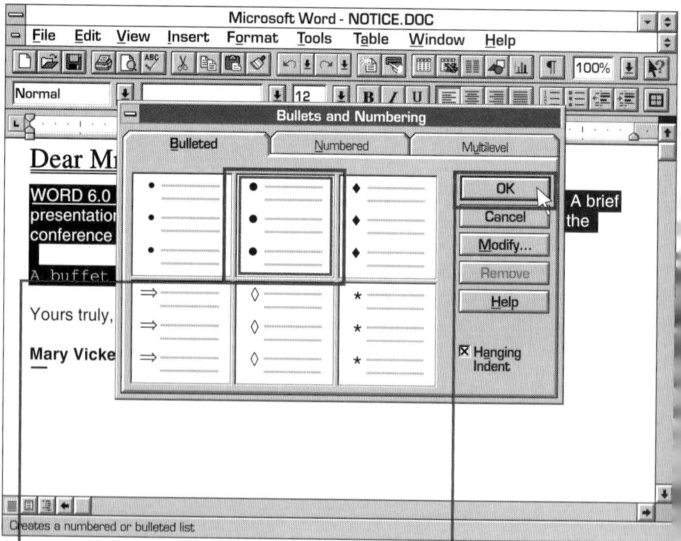

5 Move the mouse over the style you want to use and then press the left button.

6 Move the mouse over **OK** and then press the left button.

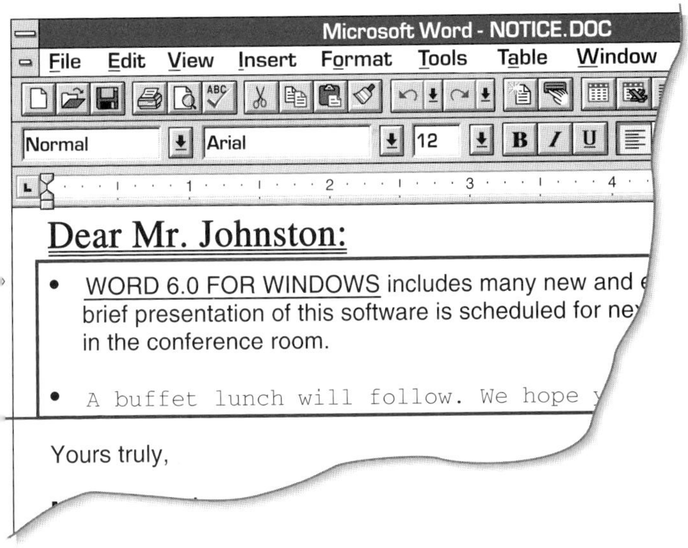

◆ The bullets or numbers appear in your document.

Note: To deselect text, move the mouse I outside the selected area and then press the left button.

INSERT A PAGE BREAK

If you want to start a new page at a specific place in your document, you can insert a page break.

INSERT A PAGE BREAK

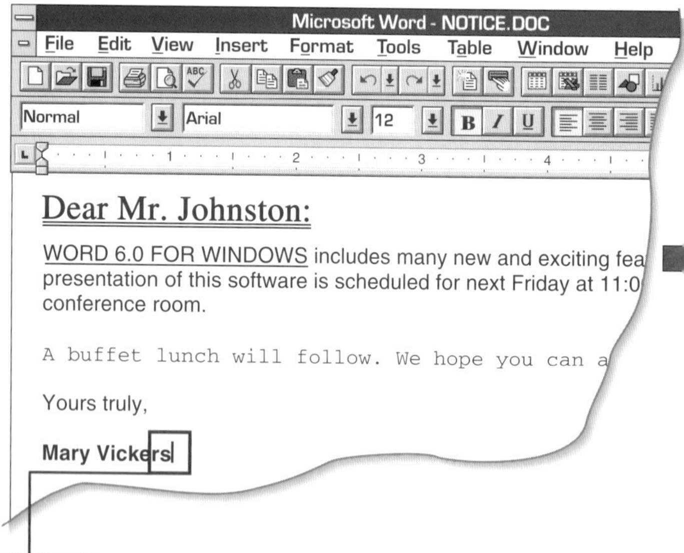
Microsoft Word - NOTICE.DOC
File Edit View Insert Format Tools Table Window Help
Normal
Arial
12
Dear Mr. Johnston:
WORD 6.0 FOR WINDOWS includes many new and exciting fea
presentation of this software is scheduled for next Friday at 11:0
conference room.
A buffet lunch will follow. We hope you can a
Yours truly,
Mary Vickers

1 Position the insertion point where you want to start a new page.

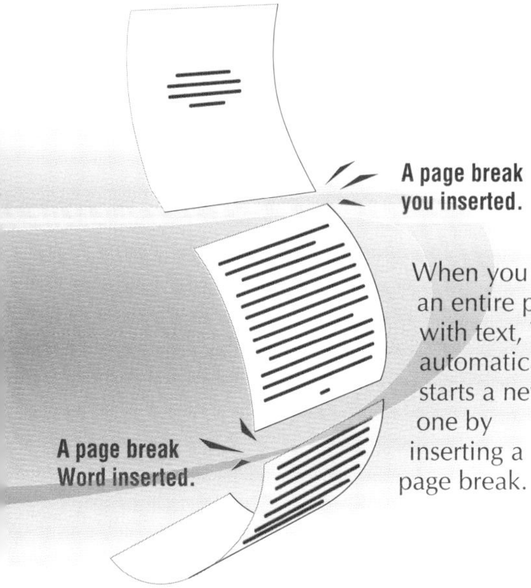

A page break you inserted.
A page break Word inserted.

When you fill an entire page with text, Word automatically starts a new one by inserting a page break.

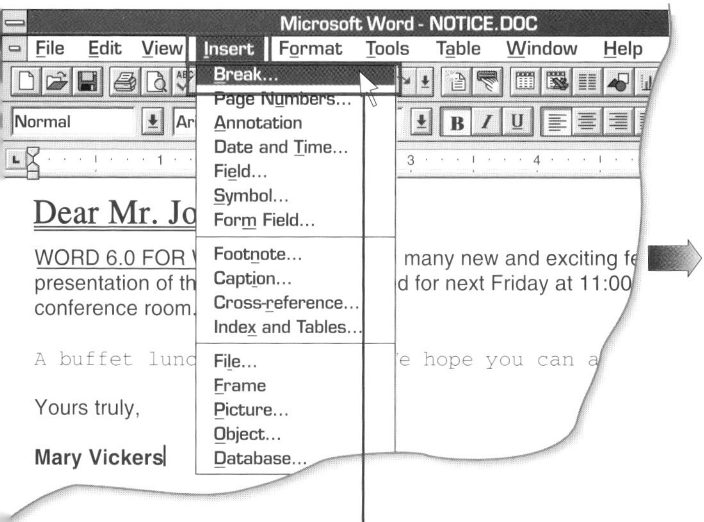

2 Move the mouse over **Insert** and then press the left button.

3 Move the mouse over **Break** and then press the left button.

Note: To continue, refer to the next page.

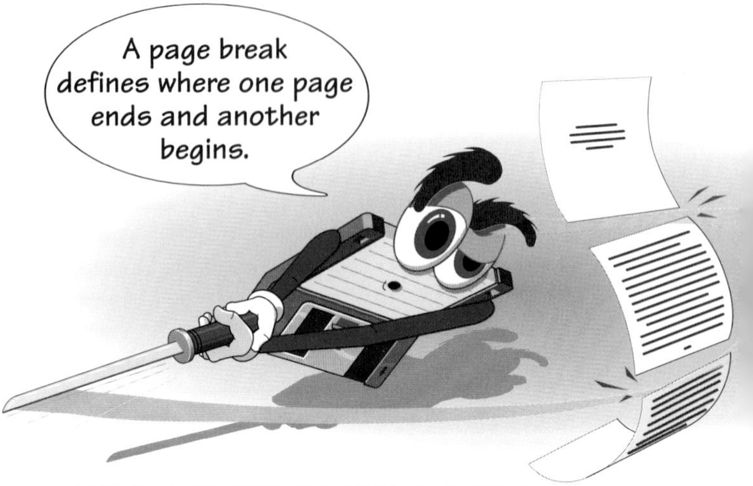

INSERT A PAGE BREAK

A page break defines where one page ends and another begins.

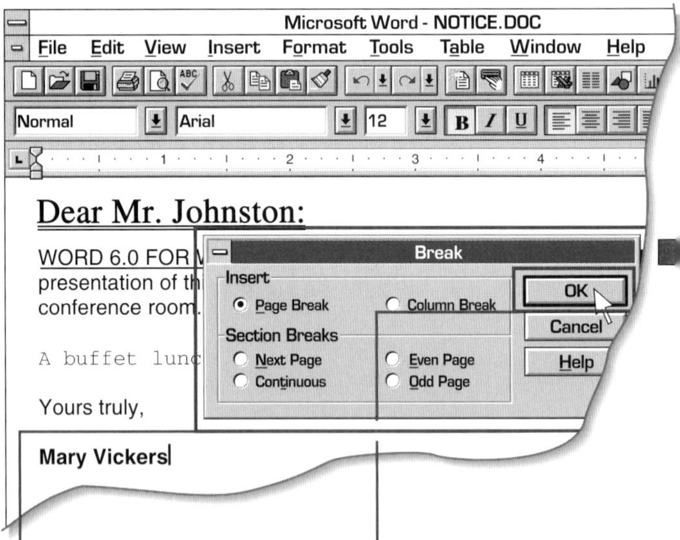

◆ The **Break** dialog box appears.

4 Move the mouse ℜ over **OK** and then press the left button.

SHORT CUT

To quickly insert a page break:

1 Position the insertion point where you want to start a new page.

2 Press Ctrl + Enter .

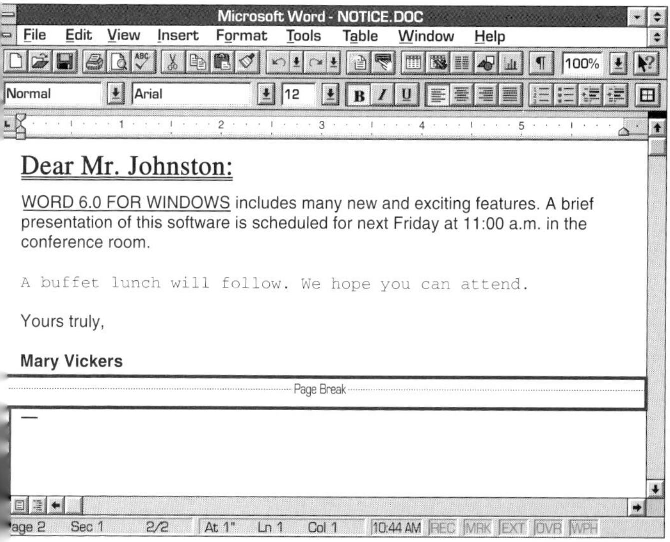
Microsoft Word - NOTICE.DOC
File Edit View Insert Format Tools Table Window Help
Normal
Arial
12
100%
Dear Mr. Johnston:
WORD 6.0 FOR WINDOWS includes many new and exciting features. A brief presentation of this software is scheduled for next Friday at 11:00 a.m. in the conference room.
A buffet lunch will follow. We hope you can attend.
Yours truly,
Mary Vickers
Page Break
'age 2 Sec 1 2/2 At 1" Ln 1 Col 1 10:44 AM REC MRK EXT OVR WPH

If your document is in ıe Normal view, a dotted ıe with the words **Page** **reak** appears across your :reen. This line defines here one page ends and ıother begins.

Note: The ***Page Break*** *line will not appear when you print your document.*

DELETE A PAGE BREAK

After you insert a page break, you can remove it at any time.
DELETE A PAGE BREAK

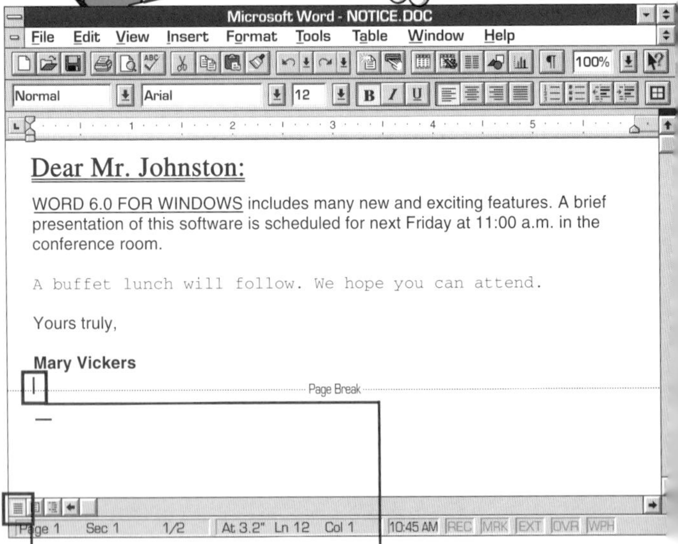
Microsoft Word - NOTICE.DOC
File Edit View Insert Format Tools Table Window Help
Normal
Arial
12
100%
Dear Mr. Johnston:
WORD 6.0 FOR WINDOWS includes many new and exciting features. A brief presentation of this software is scheduled for next Friday at 11:00 a.m. in the conference room.
A buffet lunch will follow. We hope you can attend.
Yours truly,
Mary Vickers
Page Break
Page 1 Sec 1 1/2 At 3.2" Ln 12 Col 1 10:45 AM REC MRK EXT OVR WPH

1 To display your document in the Normal view, move the mouse over ▤ and then press the left button.

2 Position the insertion point on the **Page Break** line and then press **Delete**.

Microsoft Word - NOTICE.DOC
File Edit View Insert Format Tools Table Window Help
100%
Normal
Arial
12
Dear Mr. Johnston:
WORD 6.0 FOR WINDOWS includes many new and exciting features. A brief presentation of this software is scheduled for next Friday at 11:00 a.m. in the conference room.
A buffet lunch will follow. We hope you can attend.
Yours truly,
Mary Vickers
Page 1 Sec 1 1/1 At 3" Ln 11 Col 13 10:45 AM REC MRK EXT OVR WPH

The **Page Break** line disappears.

CHANGE MARGINS

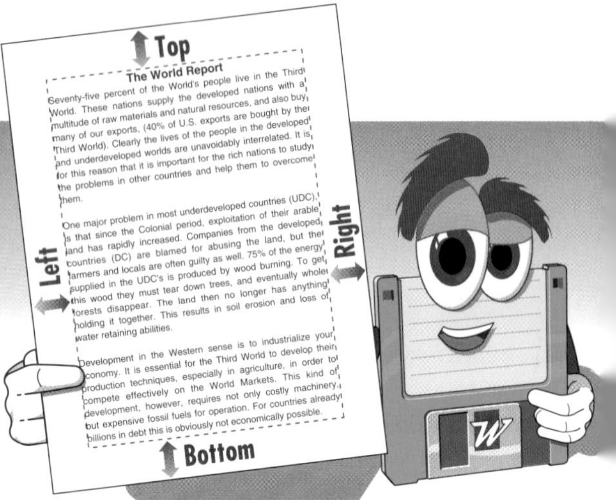

CHANGE MARGINS

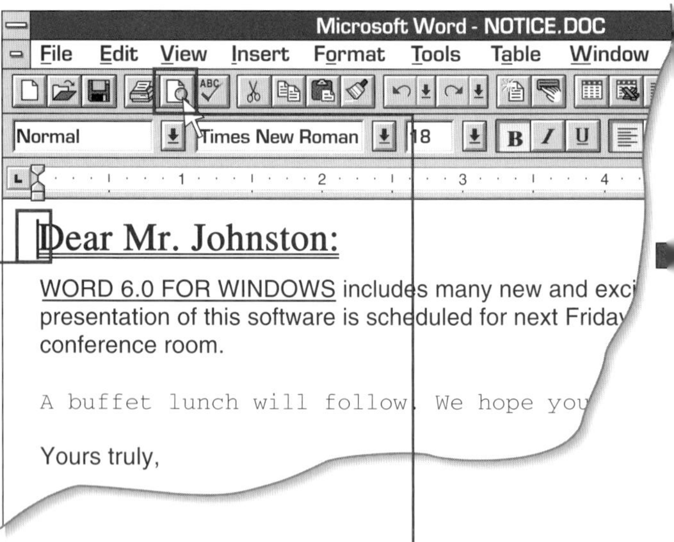

1 To change the margins for your entire document, position the insertion point anywhere in the document.

2 Move the mouse ⌖ over 🔍 and then press the left button.

A margin is the amount of space between the text and the edges of your paper.

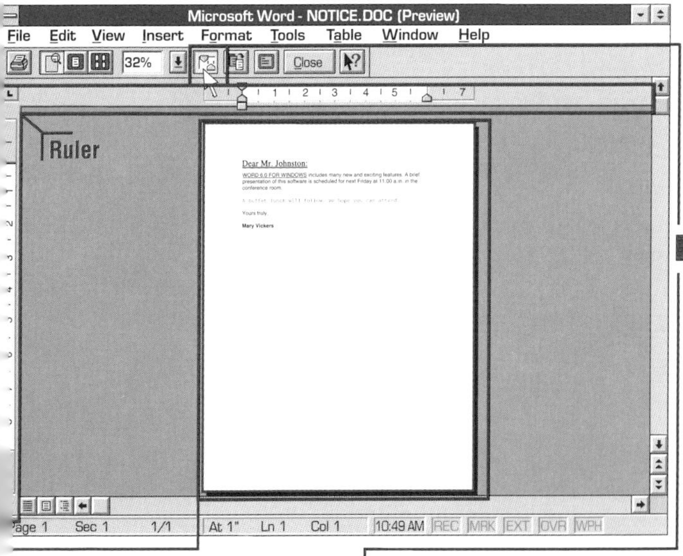

The page you were orking on appears in the int Preview window.

te: For more information on ing Print Preview, refer to ges 132 to 139.

3 If the ruler is not displayed, move the mouse over and then press the left button.

Note: To continue, refer to the next page.

CHANGE MARGINS

When you create a document, the top and bottom margins are set at 1 inch. The left and right margins are set at 1.25 inches. You can easily change these settings.

Microsoft Word - NOTICE.DOC (Preview)

File   Edit   View   Insert   Format   Tools   Table   Window   Help

32%   Close

Left Margin ——— 1 | 2 | 3 | 4 | 5 — Right Margin

Top Margin

Bottom Margin

Page 1   Sec 1   1/1   At 1"   Ln 1   Col 1   10:50 AM   REC   MRK   EXT   OVR   WPH

Dear Mr. Johnston:

WORD 6.0 FOR WINDOWS includes many new and exciting features. A brief presentation of this software is scheduled for next Friday at 11:00 a.m. in the Conference room.

A buffet lunch will follow. We hope you can attend.

Yours truly,

Mary Vickers

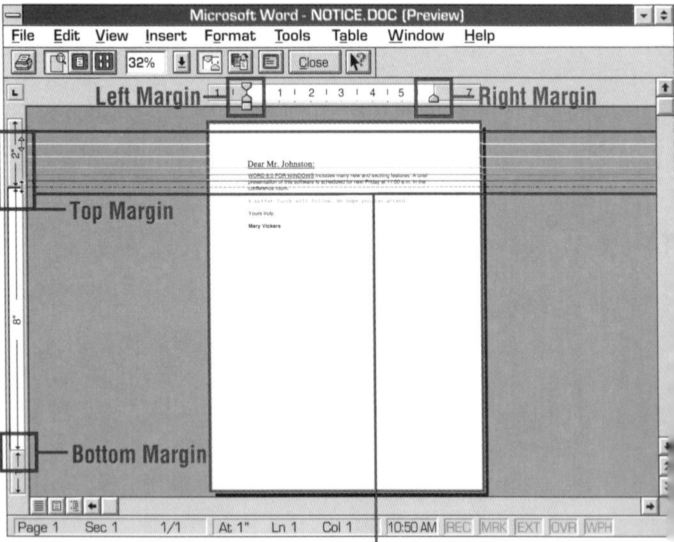

4 Move the mouse ⬦ over the margin boundary you want to move and ⬦ changes to ↕ or ↔.

5 To display the page measurements as you drag the margin boundary, press and hold down Alt.

6 Still holding down Alt, press and hold down the left button as you drag the margin boundary to a new location. A dotted line shows the location of the new margin.

TIP

If you only want to change the left and right margins for a part of your document, it is much easier to change the indentation.

Note: To indent paragraphs, refer to page 188.

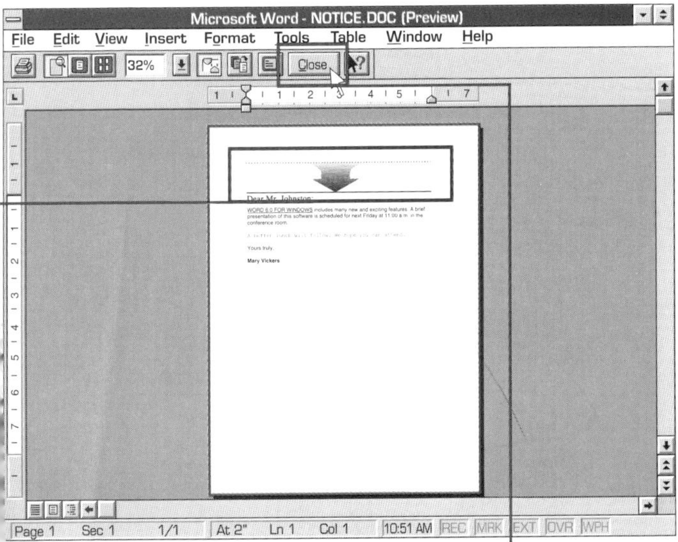

7 Release the button and then Alt to display the margin changes.

8 Repeat steps **4** to **7** for each margin you want to change.

9 To close Print Preview and return to your document, move the mouse over **Close** and then press the left button.

Note: The top and bottom margins are not visible on your screen when in the Normal view.

ADD HEADERS OR FOOTERS

Headers display information at the top of each page. Footers display information at the bottom of each page. They may include the title of your document, the date or your company name.

ADD HEADERS OR FOOTERS

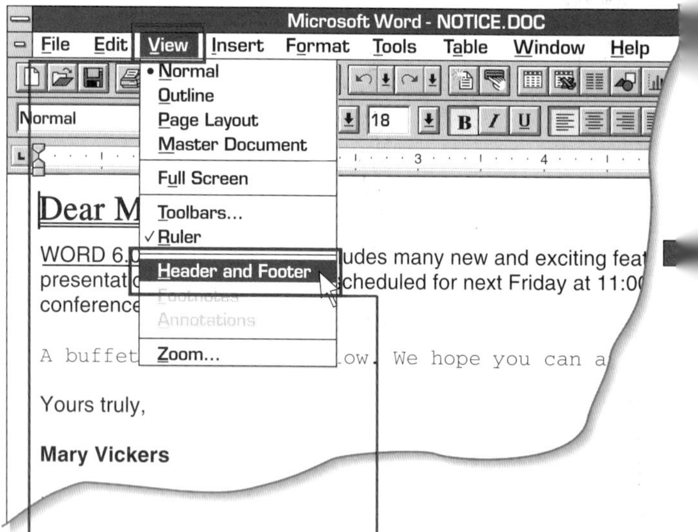

1 To add a header or footer to every page in your document, move the mouse over **View** and then press the left button.

2 Move the mouse over **Header and Footer** and then press the left button.

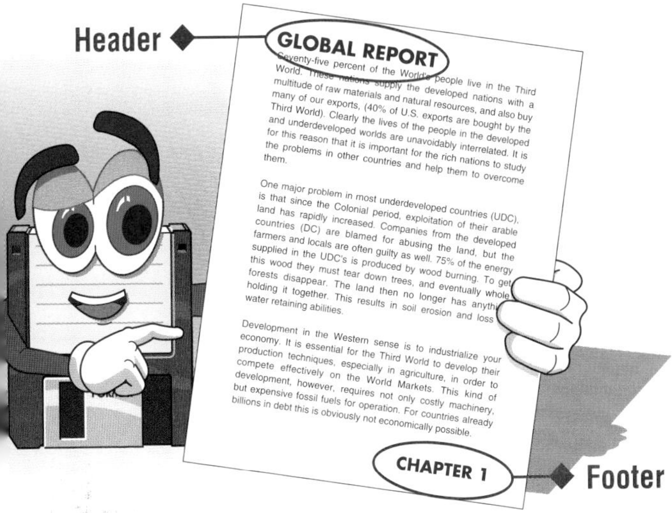

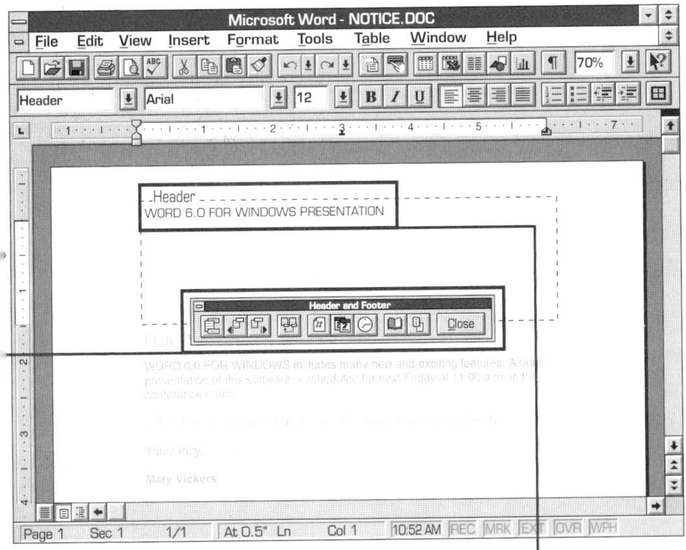

◆ The text in your document appears dimmed.

◆ The **Header and Footer** toolbar appears.

3 To create a header, type the header text. You can format the header text as you would any text in your document.

Note: To continue, refer to the next page.

ADD HEADERS OR FOOTERS

Headers and footers will not appear on your screen if you are in the Normal view.

GLOBAL REPORT

Seventy-five percent of the World's people live in the Third World. These nations supply the developed nations with a multitude of raw materials and natural resources, and many of our exports, (40% of U.S. exports are bought by the Third World). Clearly the lives of the people in the developed and underdeveloped worlds are unavoidably interrelated. It is for this reason that it is important for the rich nations to solve the problems in other countries and help them to overcome them.

One major problem in most underdeveloped countries is that since the Colonial period, exploitation of their land has rapidly increased. Companies from the developed countries (DC) are blamed for abusing the land, but farmers and locals are often guilty as well. 75% of the energy supplied in the UDC's is produced by wood burning. To get this wood they must tear down trees, and eventually whole forests disappear. The land then no longer has anything holding it together. This results in soil erosion and loss of water retaining abilities.

Development in the Western sense is to industrialize your economy. It is essential for the Third World to develop their production techniques, especially in agriculture, in order to compete effectively on the World Markets. This kind of development, however, requires not only costly machinery, but expensive fossil fuels for operation. For countries already billions in debt this is obviously not economically possible.

CHAPTER 1

ADD HEADERS OR FOOTERS (Continued)

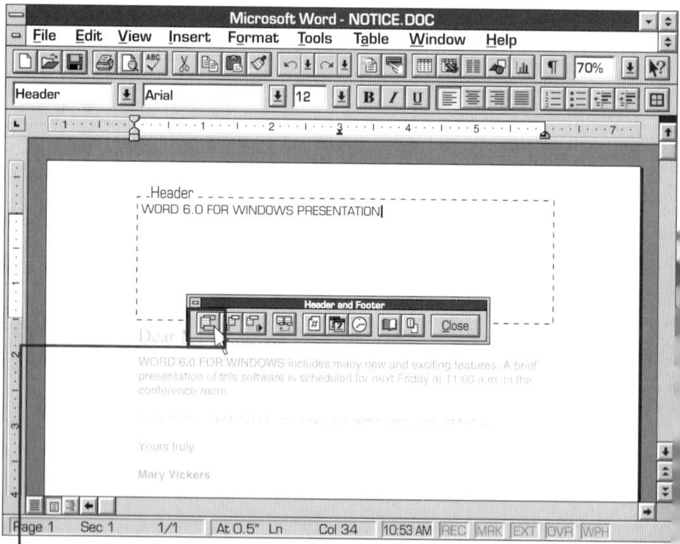

4 To create a footer, move the mouse ⌖ over 🗐 and then press the left button.

Note: You can return to the header area at any time by repeating step **4**.

TIP

To view headers or footers, move the mouse over and then press the left button.

Note: For more information on Print Preview, refer to pages 132 to 139.

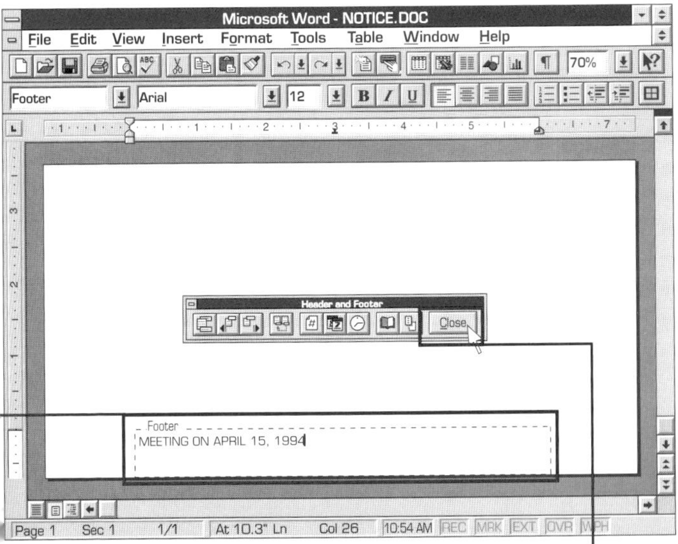

◆ The **Footer** area appears.

5 Type the footer text. You can format the footer text as you would any text in your document.

6 To return to your document, move the mouse over **Close** and then press the left button.

ADD PAGE NUMBERS

You can have Word automatically number the pages in your document.
FORMAT
42

ADD PAGE NUMBERS

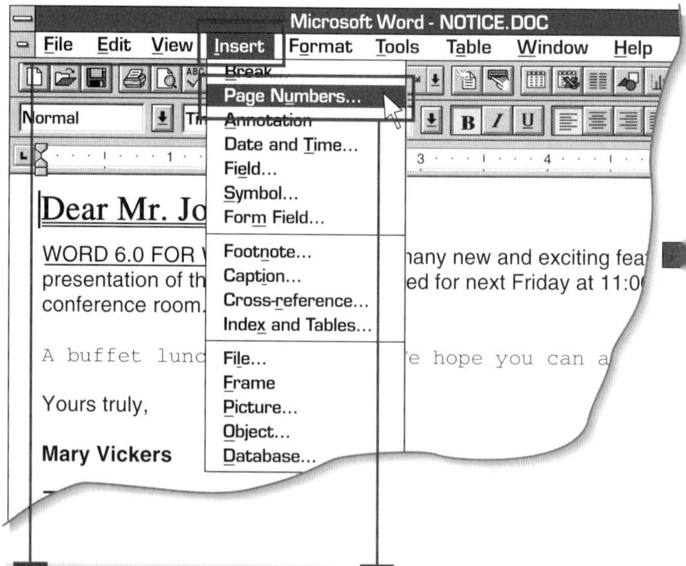

1 Move the mouse over **Insert** and then press the left button.

2 Move the mouse over **Page Numbers** and then press the left button.

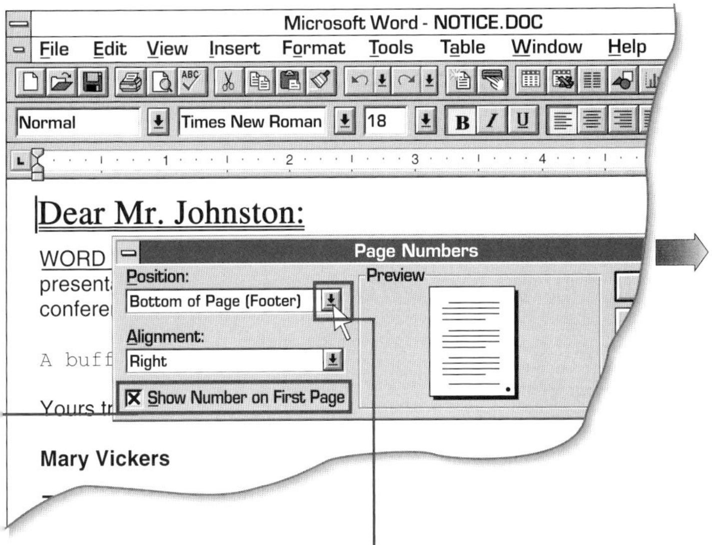

◆ The **Page Numbers** dialog box appears.

◆ To hide the page number on the first page of your document, move the mouse over **Show Number on First Page** and then press the left button (☒ changes to ☐).

3 To select a position for the page numbers, move the mouse over ⬇ in the **Position:** box and then press the left button.

Note: To continue, refer to the next page.

ADD PAGE NUMBERS

Page numbers will not appear on your screen if you are in the Normal view.
FORMAT
42

ADD PAGE NUMBERS (Continued)

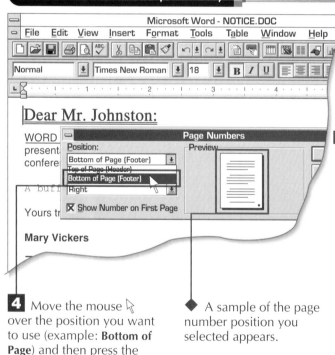

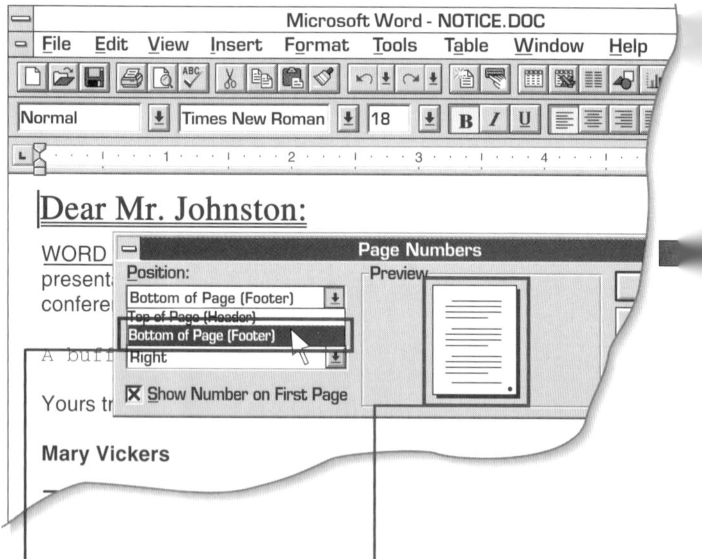
Microsoft Word - NOTICE.DOC
File Edit View Insert Format Tools Table Window Help
Normal
Times New Roman
18
Dear Mr. Johnston:
WORD
present
confere
A buff
Yours tr
Mary Vickers
Page Numbers
Position:
Bottom of Page (Footer)
Top of Page (Header)
Bottom of Page (Footer)
Right
Show Number on First Page
Preview

4 Move the mouse over the position you want to use (example: **Bottom of Page**) and then press the left button.

◆ A sample of the page number position you selected appears.

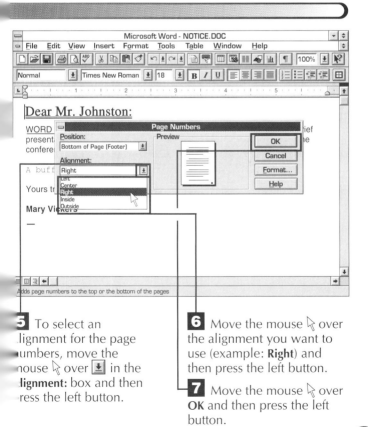

TIP

To view page numbers, move the mouse over and then press the left button.

Note: For more information on Print Preview, refer to pages 132 to 139.

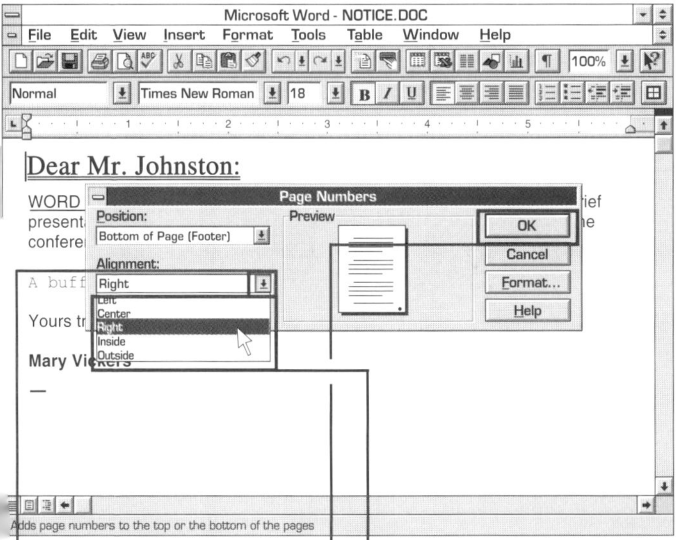

5 To select an lignment for the page umbers, move the nouse over in the **lignment:** box and then ress the left button.

6 Move the mouse over the alignment you want to use (example: **Right**) and then press the left button.

7 Move the mouse over **OK** and then press the left button.

CENTER A PAGE

FORMAT
Dear Mr. Johnston:
WORD 6.0 FOR WINDOWS includes many new and exciting features. A brief presentation of this software is scheduled for next Friday at 11:00 a.m. in the conference room.
A buffet lunch will follow. We hope you can attend.
Yours truly,
Mary Vickers

CENTER A PAGE

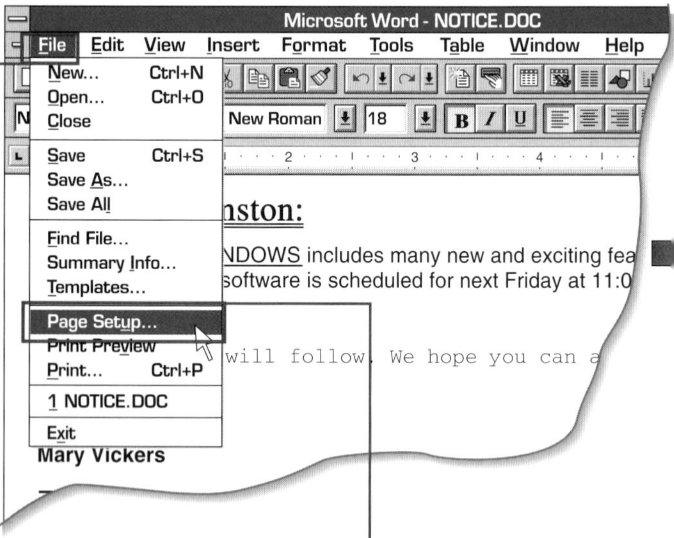
Microsoft Word - NOTICE.DOC
File Edit View Insert Format Tools Table Window Help
New... Ctrl+N
Open... Ctrl+O
Close
Save Ctrl+S
Save As...
Save All
Find File...
Summary Info...
Templates...
Page Setup...
Print Preview
Print... Ctrl+P
1 NOTICE.DOC
Exit
New Roman
18
nston:
NDOWS includes many new and exciting fea
software is scheduled for next Friday at 11:0
will follow. We hope you can a
Mary Vickers

1 Move the mouse over **File** and then press the left button.

2 Move the mouse over **Page Setup** and then press the left button.

You can vertically center text on a page. This is useful when creating title pages or short memos.

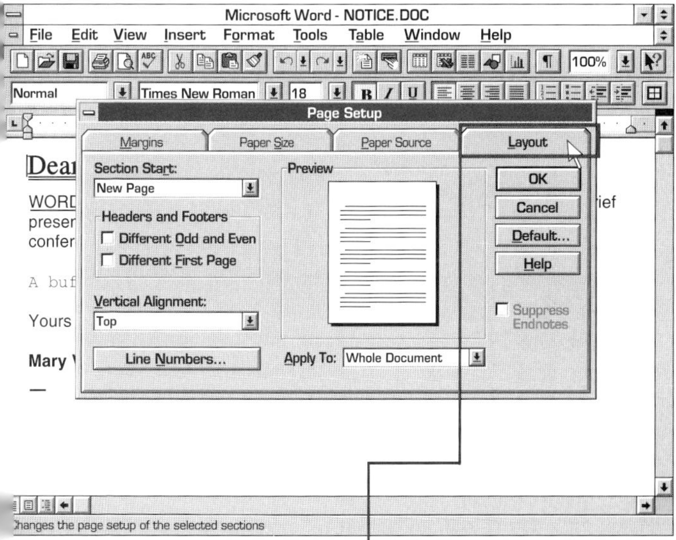

◆ The **Page Setup** dialog box appears.

3 Move the mouse over the **Layout** tab and then press the left button.

Note: To continue, refer to the next page.

CENTER A PAGE

CENTER A PAGE (Continued)

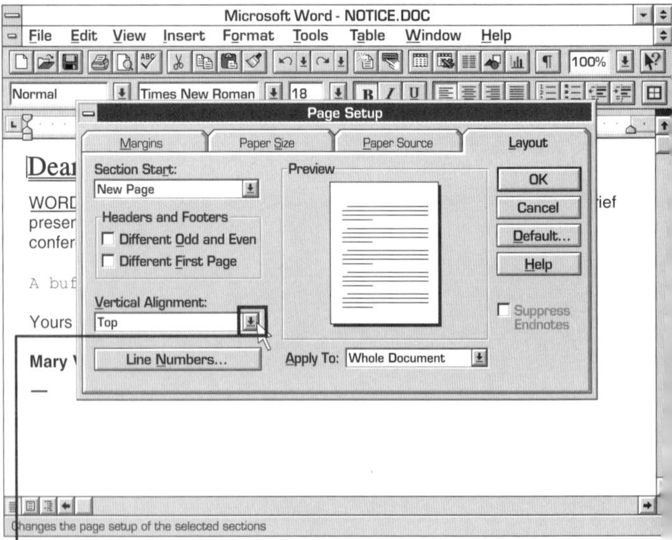

4 Move the mouse over ⬇ in the **Vertical Alignment**: box and then press the left button.

To view the text centered on a page, move the mouse ⌖ over 🔍 and then press the left button.

Note: For more information on Print Preview, refer to pages 132 to 139.

Microsoft Word - NOTICE.DOC

File　Edit　View　Insert　Format　Tools　Table　Window　Help

Normal ⬇ Times New Roman ⬇ 18 ⬇ **B** *I* U

Page Setup

Margins　Paper Size　Paper Source　Layout

Section Start:
New Page ⬇

Headers and Footers
☐ Different Odd and Even
☐ Different First Page

Vertical Alignment:
Top ⬇
　Top
　Center
　Justified

Preview

Apply To: Whole Document ⬇

OK
Cancel
Default...
Help

☐ Suppress Endnotes

Dea

WORD
presen
confer

A buf

Yours

Mary

Changes the page setup of the selected sections

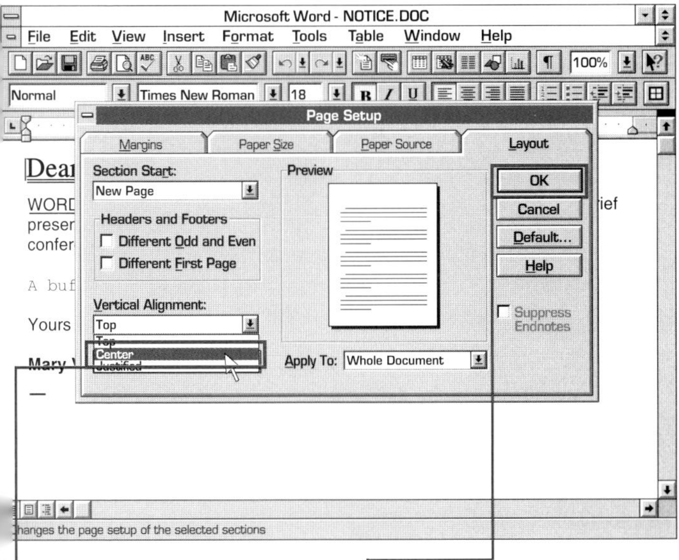

5 Move the mouse ⌖ over **Center** and then press the left button.

6 Move the mouse ⌖ over **OK** and then press the left button.

CREATE A TABLE

Tap
Tap
Tap

CREATE A TABLE

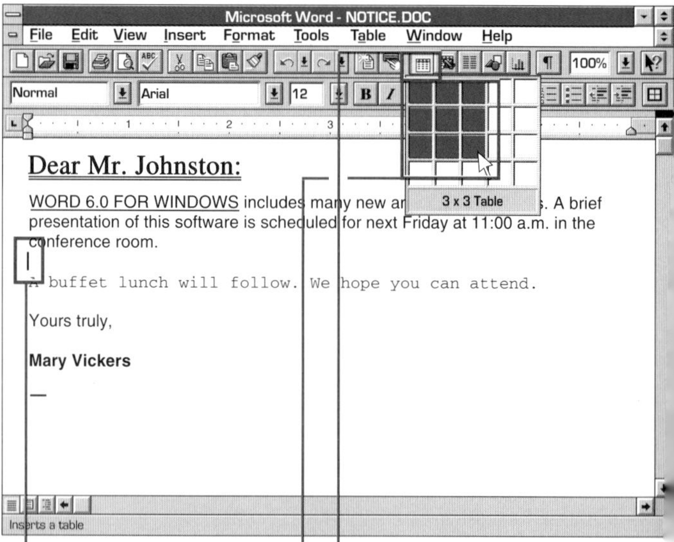
Microsoft Word - NOTICE.DOC
File Edit View Insert Format Tools Table Window Help
100%
Normal
Arial
12
3 x 3 Table
Dear Mr. Johnston:
WORD 6.0 FOR WINDOWS includes many new ar . A brief presentation of this software is scheduled for next Friday at 11:00 a.m. in the conference room.
A buffet lunch will follow. We hope you can attend.
Yours truly,
Mary Vickers
Inserts a table

1 To create a table, position the insertion point where you want the table to appear in your document.

2 Move the mouse over

3 Press and hold down the left button as you move the mouse over the number of rows and columns you want in your table (example: **3 x 3**).

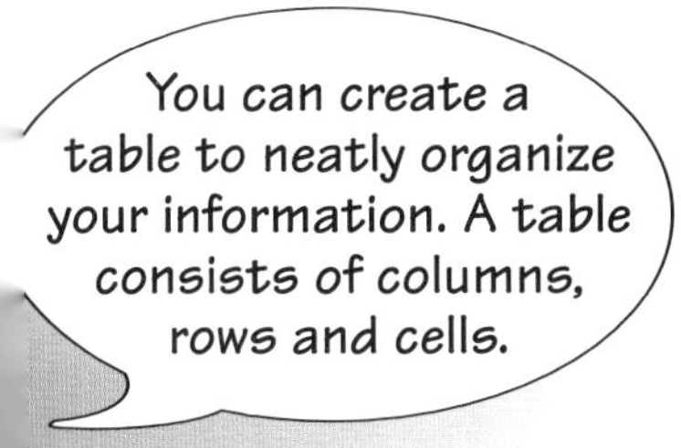

You can create a table to neatly organize your information. A table consists of columns, rows and cells.

- A **column** is a vertical line of boxes.
- A **row** is a horizontal line of boxes.
- A **cell** is the area where a row and column intersect.

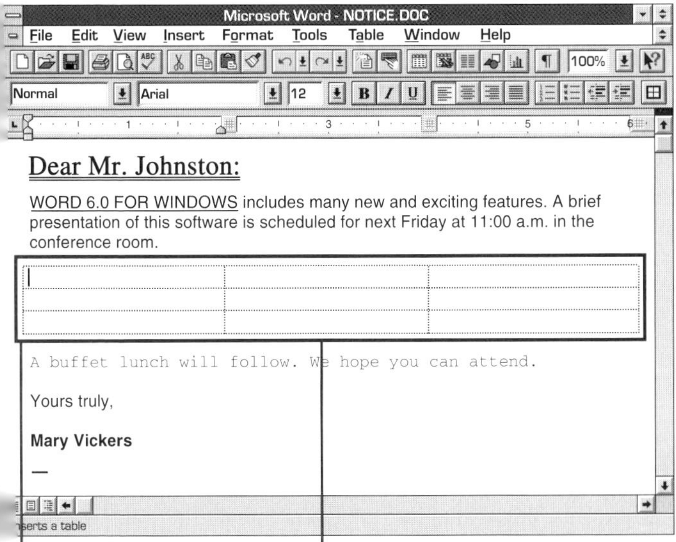

4 Release the button and the table appears.

- The dotted lines around the cells in the table will not appear when you print your document. To print table lines, you must add borders. For more information, refer to page 234.

TYPE TEXT IN A TABLE

When typing text in a table, you can use thes keys to quickly move between cells.

TYPE TEXT IN A TABLE

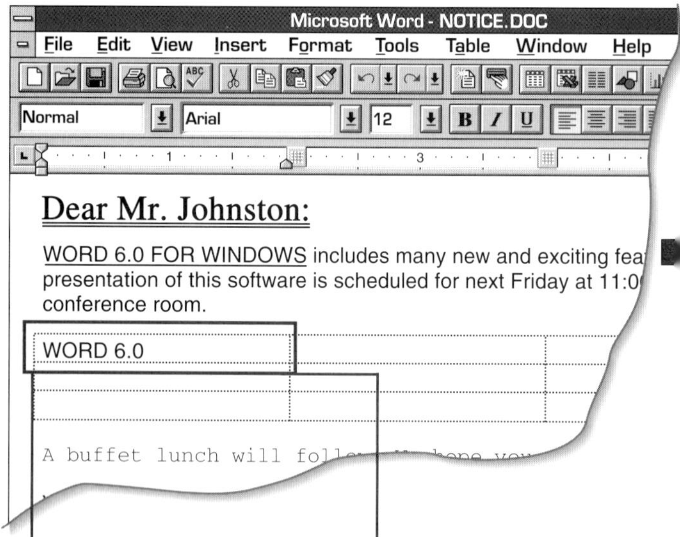
Microsoft Word - NOTICE.DOC
File Edit View Insert Format Tools Table Window Help
Normal
Arial
12
Dear Mr. Johnston:
WORD 6.0 FOR WINDOWS includes many new and exciting fea
presentation of this software is scheduled for next Friday at 11:0
conference room.
WORD 6.0
A buffet lunch will fo

1 Move the mouse over a cell where you want to type text and then press the left button.

2 Type the text.

Note: If the text you type is too long to fit on one line in the cell, Word wraps the text to the next line. To keep the te on the same line, refer to page 230 to change the column width.

Press this key to move **down** one cell.

Press this key to move **up** one cell.

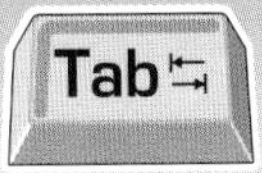
Tab

Press this key to move **right** one cell.

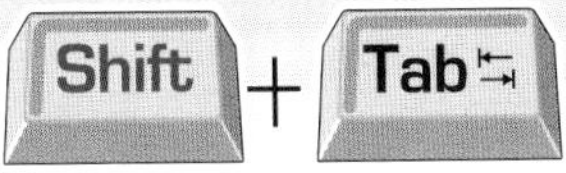
Shift
+
Tab

Press these keys to move **left** one cell.

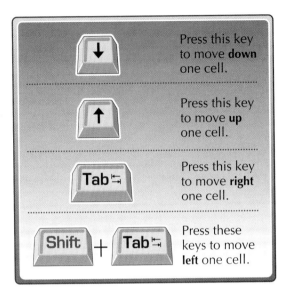

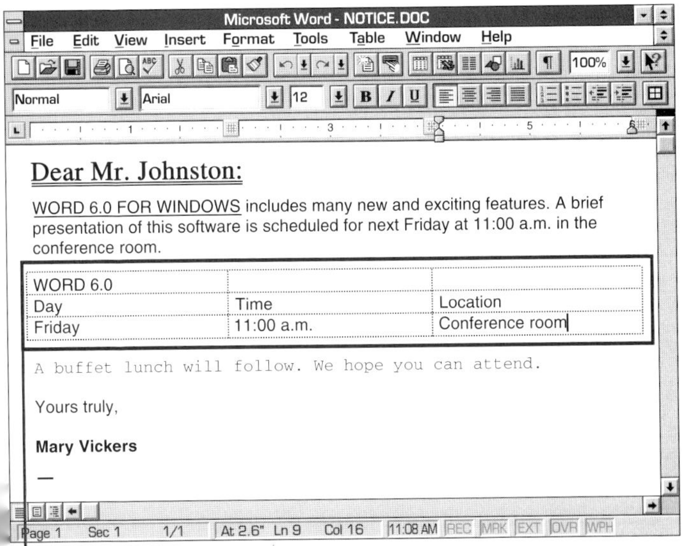
Microsoft Word - NOTICE.DOC
File Edit View Insert Format Tools Table Window Help
100%
Normal
Arial
12
Dear Mr. Johnston:
WORD 6.0 FOR WINDOWS includes many new and exciting features. A brief presentation of this software is scheduled for next Friday at 11:00 a.m. in the conference room.
WORD 6.0
Day
Time
Location
Friday
11:00 a.m.
Conference room
A buffet lunch will follow. We hope you can attend.
Yours truly,
Mary Vickers
Page 1 Sec 1 1/1 At 2.6" Ln 9 Col 16 11:08 AM REC MRK EXT OVR WPH

3 Repeat steps **1** and **2** until you have typed all the text.

◆ Pressing **Enter** after typing text in a cell will begin a new line and increase the row height. If you accidentally press **Enter**, immediately press **←Backspace** to cancel the action.

ADD A ROW

You can add a
row to your table if you
want to insert new
information.

ADD A ROW

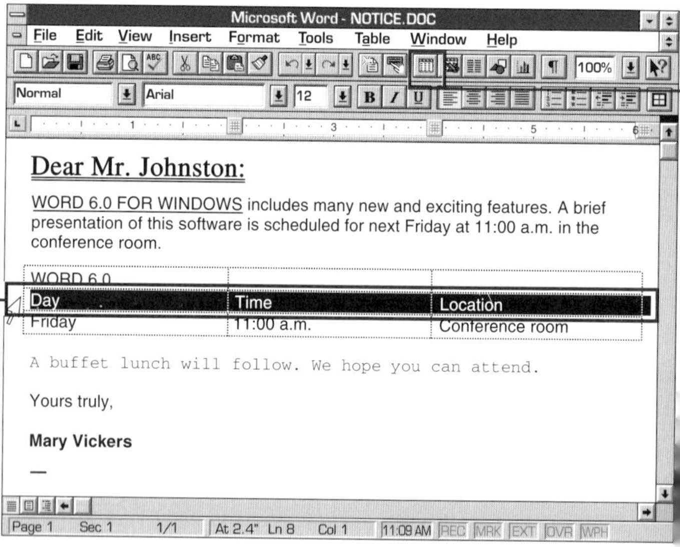

**Word adds a row above the
row you select.**

1 To select a row, move the
mouse I to the left edge of
the row (I changes to ⤢) and
then press the left button.

2 Move the mouse ⬚
over ⊞ and then press
the left button.

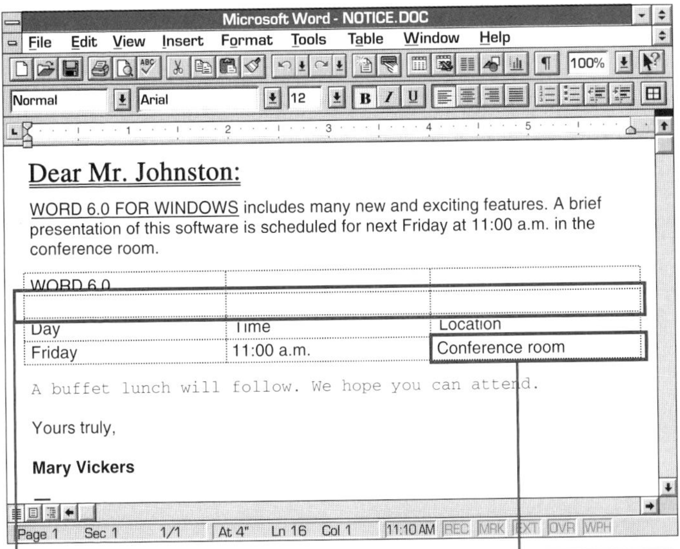
Microsoft Word - NOTICE.DOC
File Edit View Insert Format Tools Table Window Help
100%
Normal
Arial
12
Dear Mr. Johnston:
WORD 6.0 FOR WINDOWS includes many new and exciting features. A brief presentation of this software is scheduled for next Friday at 11:00 a.m. in the conference room.
WORD 6.0
Day
Time
Location
Friday
11:00 a.m.
Conference room
A buffet lunch will follow. We hope you can attend.
Yours truly,
Mary Vickers
Page 1 Sec 1 1/1 At 4" Ln 16 Col 1 11:10 AM REC MRK EXT OVR WPH

◆ The new row appears.

Note: To deselect a row, move the mouse I outside the table and then press the left button.

To add a row to the bottom of your table:

1 Position the insertion point in the bottom right cell of your table.

2 Press Tab and the new row appears.

ADD A COLUMN

You can add a column to your table at any time. The existing columns shift to make room for the new column.

ADD A COLUMN

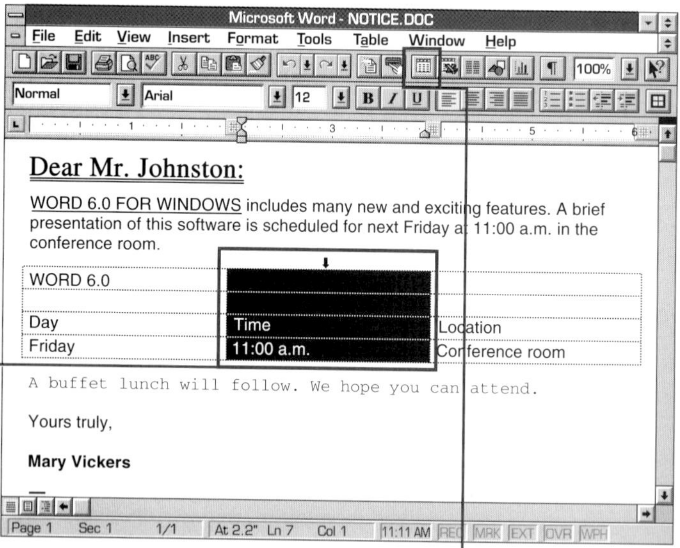

Word adds a column to the left of the column you select.

1 To select a column, move the mouse I to the top edge of the column (I changes to ↓) and then press the left button.

2 Move the mouse ⬚ over 🖩 and then press the left button.

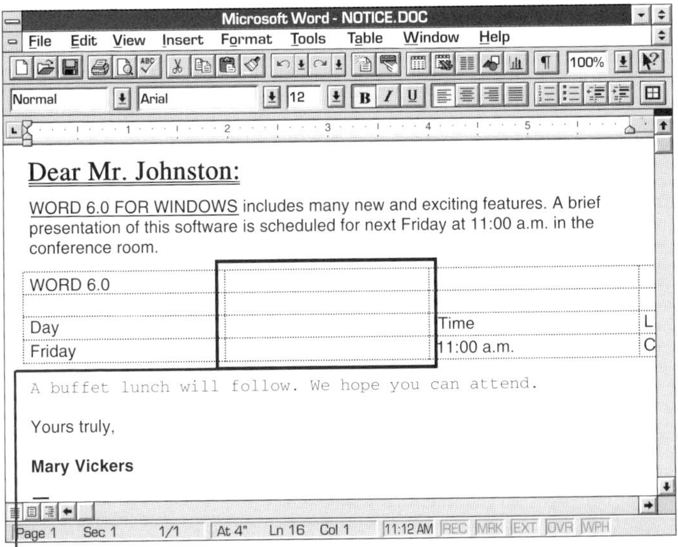
Microsoft Word - NOTICE.DOC
File Edit View Insert Format Tools Table Window Help
Normal
Arial
12
100%
Dear Mr. Johnston:
WORD 6.0 FOR WINDOWS includes many new and exciting features. A brief presentation of this software is scheduled for next Friday at 11:00 a.m. in the conference room.
WORD 6.0
Day
Friday
Time
11:00 a.m.
A buffet lunch will follow. We hope you can attend.
Yours truly,
Mary Vickers
Page 1 Sec 1 1/1 At 4" Ln 16 Col 1 11:12 AM REC MRK EXT OVR WPH

◆ The new column appears.

Note: To deselect a column, move the mouse I outside the table and then press the left button.

DELETE A ROW

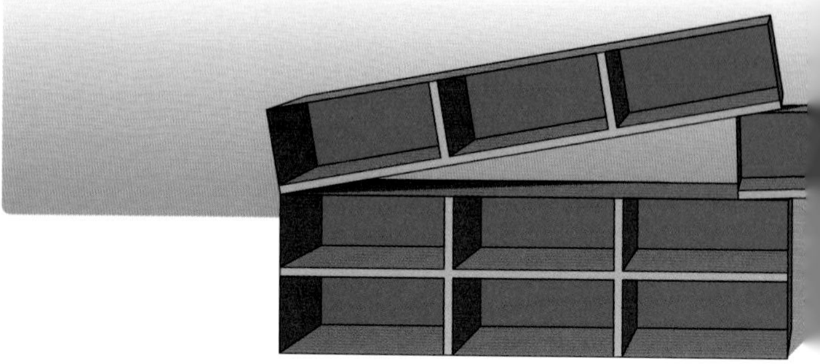

DELETE A ROW

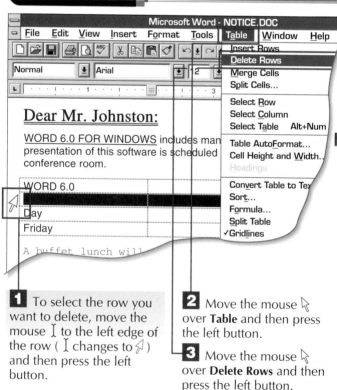

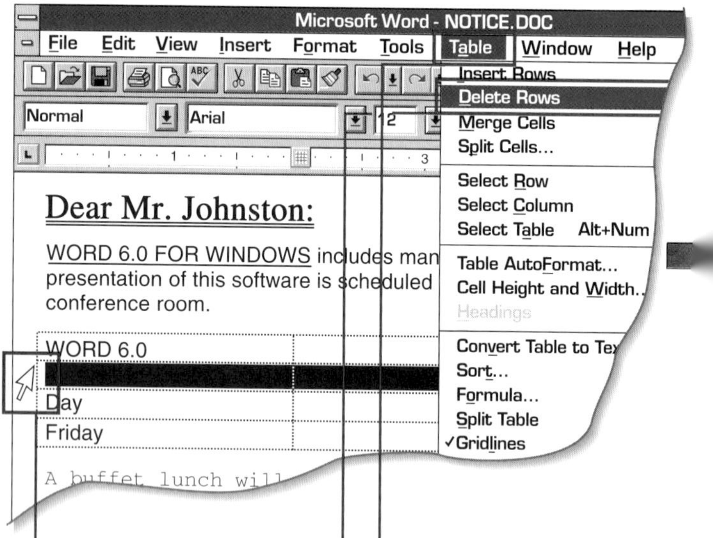

1 To select the row you want to delete, move the mouse I to the left edge of the row (I changes to ↖) and then press the left button.

2 Move the mouse ↖ over **Table** and then press the left button.

3 Move the mouse ↖ over **Delete Rows** and then press the left button.

You can delete a row from your table to remove information or extra cells you no longer need.
Tables

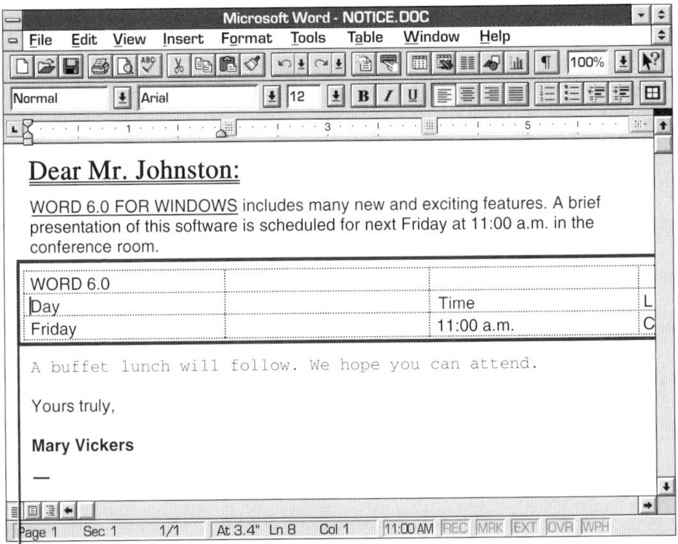
Microsoft Word - NOTICE.DOC
File Edit View Insert Format Tools Table Window Help
Normal
Arial
12
100%
Dear Mr. Johnston:
WORD 6.0 FOR WINDOWS includes many new and exciting features. A brief presentation of this software is scheduled for next Friday at 11:00 a.m. in the conference room.
WORD 6.0
Day
Time
Friday
11:00 a.m.
A buffet lunch will follow. We hope you can attend.
Yours truly,
Mary Vickers
Page 1 Sec 1 1/1 At 3.4" Ln 8 Col 1 11:00 AM REC MRK EXT OVR WPH

◆ The row disappears from your table.

DELETE A COLUMN

DELETE A COLUMN

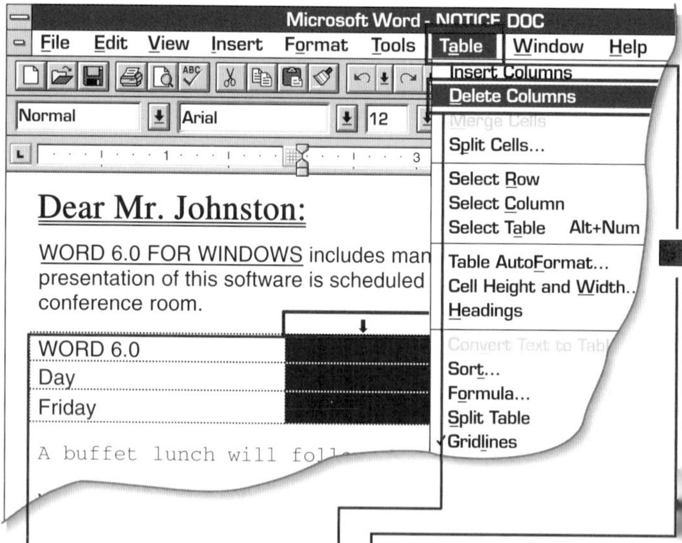

1 To select the column you want to delete, move the mouse I to the top edge of the column (I changes to ⬇) and then press the left button.

2 Move the mouse over **Table** and then press the left button.

3 Move the mouse over **Delete Columns** and then press the left button.

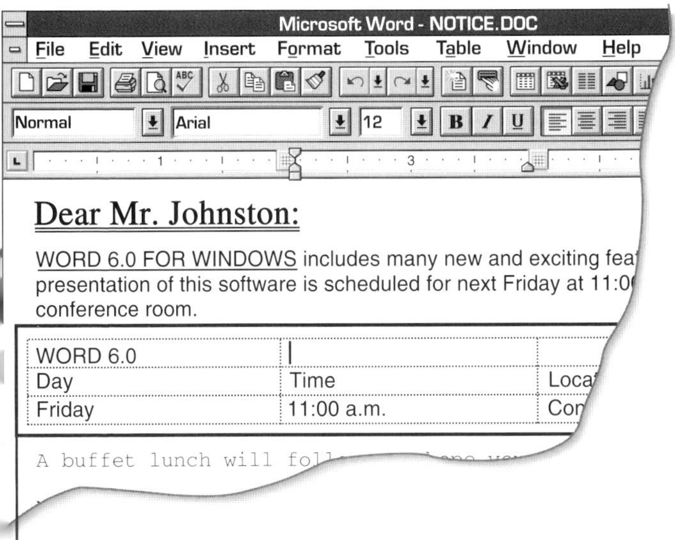
Microsoft Word - NOTICE.DOC
File Edit View Insert Format Tools Table Window Help
Normal
Arial
12
Dear Mr. Johnston:
WORD 6.0 FOR WINDOWS includes many new and exciting fea
presentation of this software is scheduled for next Friday at 11:0
conference room.
WORD 6.0
Day
Time
Loca
Friday
11:00 a.m.
Con
A buffet lunch will fol

The column disappears from your table.

CHANGE COLUMN WIDTH

You can adjust the columns in your table to make them wider or narrower.
Dear Mr. Johnston:
A buffet lunch will follow. We hope you

CHANGE COLUMN WIDTH

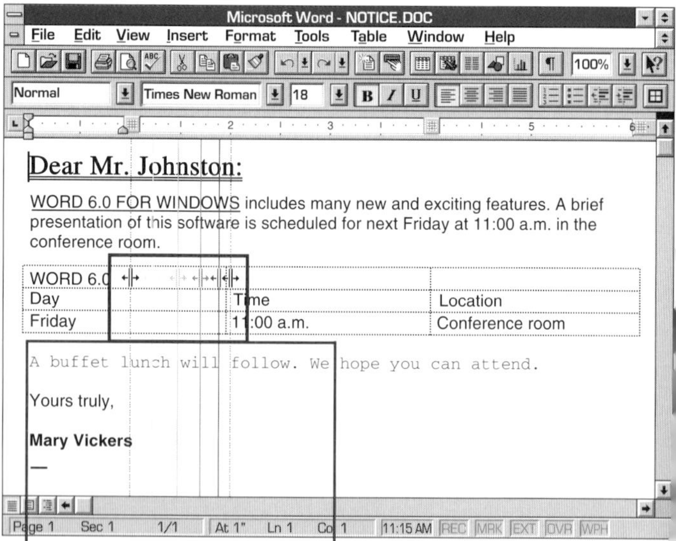

Microsoft Word - NOTICE.DOC
File Edit View Insert Format Tools Table Window Help
Normal
Times New Roman
18
100%
Dear Mr. Johnston:
WORD 6.0 FOR WINDOWS includes many new and exciting features. A brief presentation of this software is scheduled for next Friday at 11:00 a.m. in the conference room.
WORD 6.0
Day
Time
Location
Friday
11:00 a.m.
Conference room
A buffet lunch will follow. We hope you can attend.
Yours truly,
Mary Vickers
Page 1 Sec 1 1/1 At 1" Ln 1 Col 1 11:15 AM REC MRK EXT OVR WPH

1 Move the mouse I over the right edge of the column you want to change (I changes to ↔).

2 Press and hold down the left button as you drag the edge of the column to a new position.

◆ The dotted line indicates the new position.

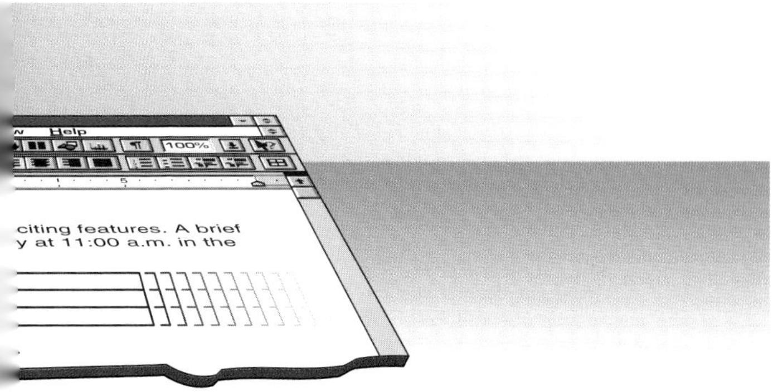

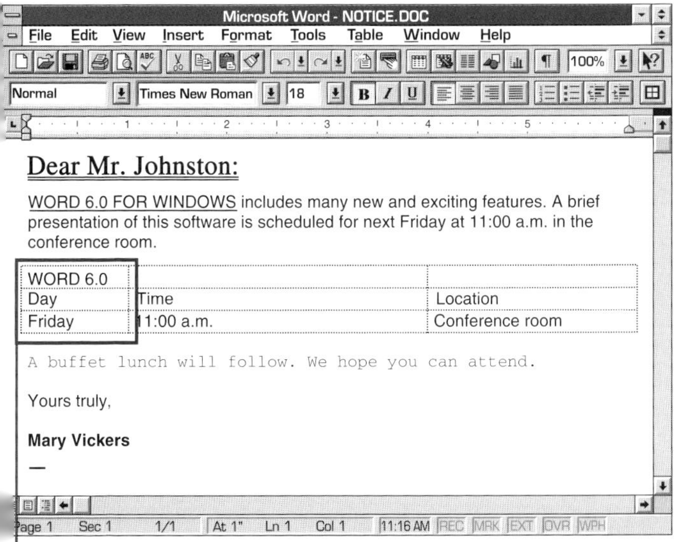

3 Release the button and the new column width appears.

Note: The width of the entire table remains the same.

CHANGE COLUMN WIDTH

You can have Word adjust a column width to fit the longest item in the column.

CHANGE COLUMN WIDTH AUTOMATICALLY

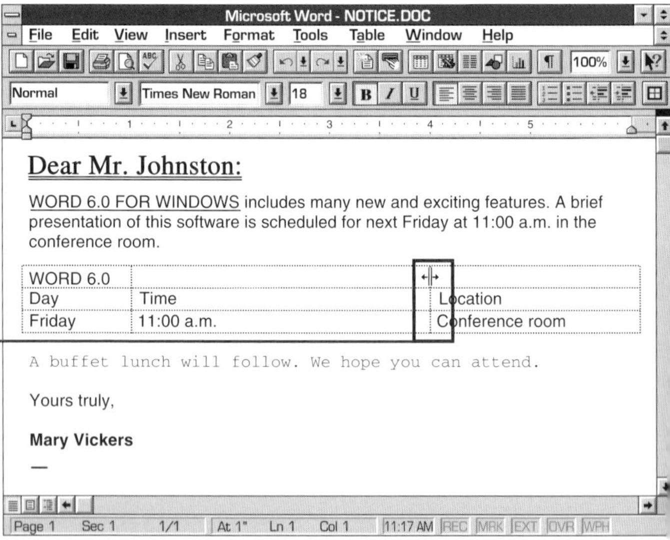

Microsoft Word - NOTICE.DOC
File Edit View Insert Format Tools Table Window Help
Normal
Times New Roman
18
100%
Dear Mr. Johnston:
WORD 6.0 FOR WINDOWS includes many new and exciting features. A brief presentation of this software is scheduled for next Friday at 11:00 a.m. in the conference room.
WORD 6.0
Day
Time
Location
Friday
11:00 a.m.
Conference room
A buffet lunch will follow. We hope you can attend.
Yours truly,
Mary Vickers
Page 1 Sec 1 1/1 At 1" Ln 1 Col 1 11:17 AM REC MRK EXT OVR WPH

1 Move the mouse I over the right edge of the column you want to change (I changes to ⟺).

2 Quickly press the left button twice.

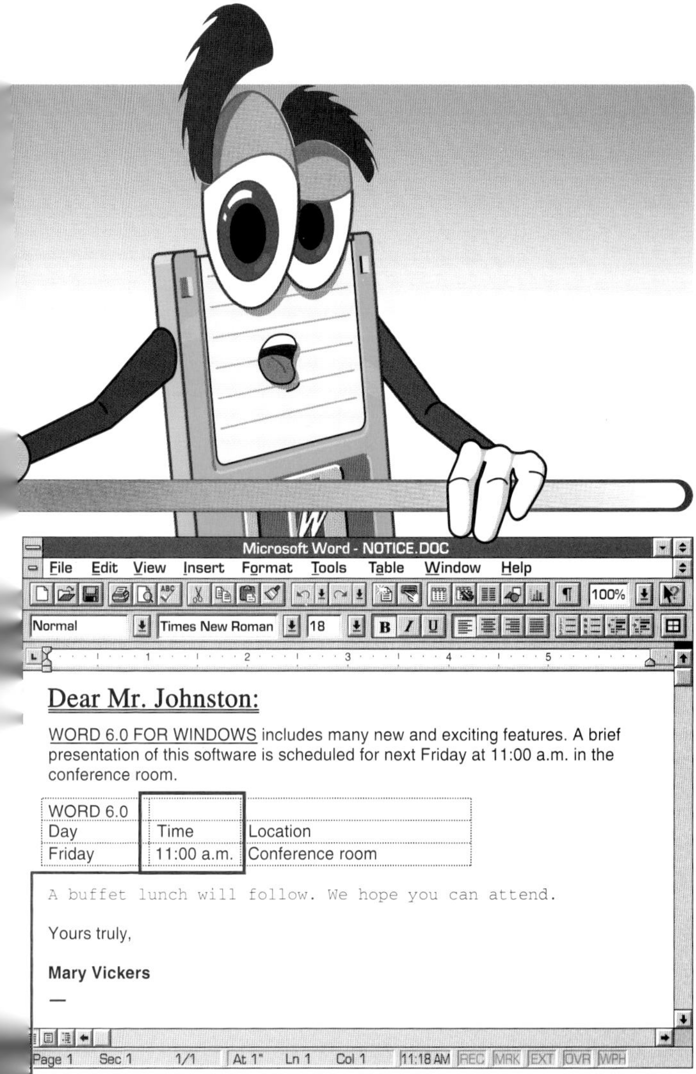
Microsoft Word - NOTICE.DOC
File Edit View Insert Format Tools Table Window Help
100%
Normal
Times New Roman
18
Dear Mr. Johnston:
WORD 6.0 FOR WINDOWS includes many new and exciting features. A brief presentation of this software is scheduled for next Friday at 11:00 a.m. in the conference room.
WORD 6.0
Day
Time
Location
Friday
11:00 a.m.
Conference room
A buffet lunch will follow. We hope you can attend.
Yours truly,
Mary Vickers
Page 1 Sec 1 1/1 At 1" Ln 1 Col 1 11:18 AM REC MRK EXT OVR WPH

The column width hanges to fit the longest em in the column.

Note: The width of the entire table changes.

FORMAT A TABLE

FORMAT A TABLE

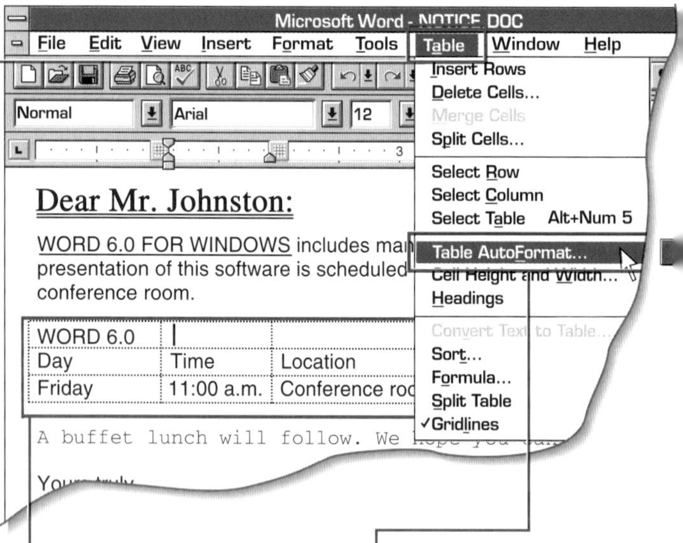

1 Position the insertion point anywhere in the table you want to format.

2 Move the mouse ⇖ over **Table** and then press the left button.

3 Move the mouse ⇖ over **Table AutoFormat** and then press the left button.

Word provides a selection of designs that you can choose from to format a table in your document.

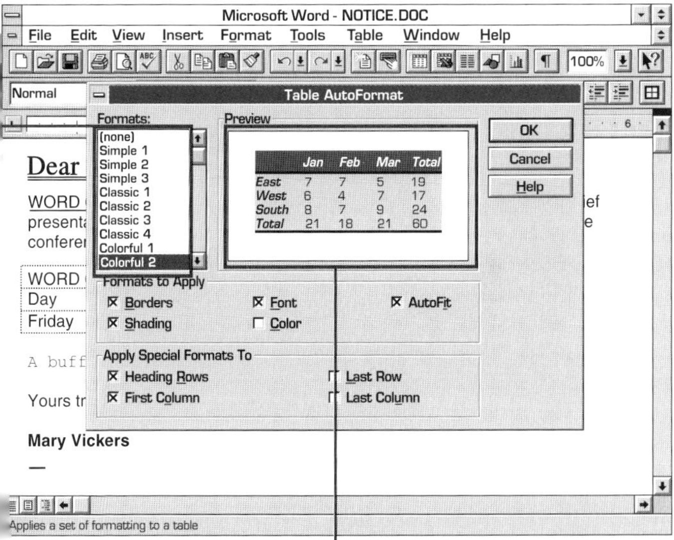

- The **Table AutoFormat** ialog box appears.
- The **Formats:** box isplays a list of the vailable table designs.

4 Press ↓ or ↑ on your keyboard until the **Preview** box displays the design you want to use (example: **Colorful 2**).

Note: To continue, refer to the next page.

FORMAT A TABLE

FORMAT A TABLE (Continued)

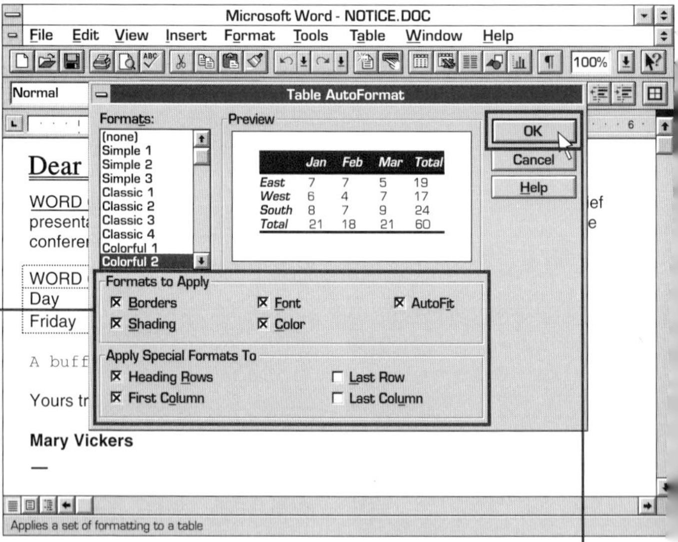

5 To apply or remove a format, move the mouse over an option (example: **Color**) and then press the left button.

Note: ☒ indicates an option is on.
☐ indicates an option is off.

6 When the **Preview** box displays the desired table appearance, move the mouse over **OK** and then press the left button.

The Table AutoFormat feature will enhance the appearance of your table.

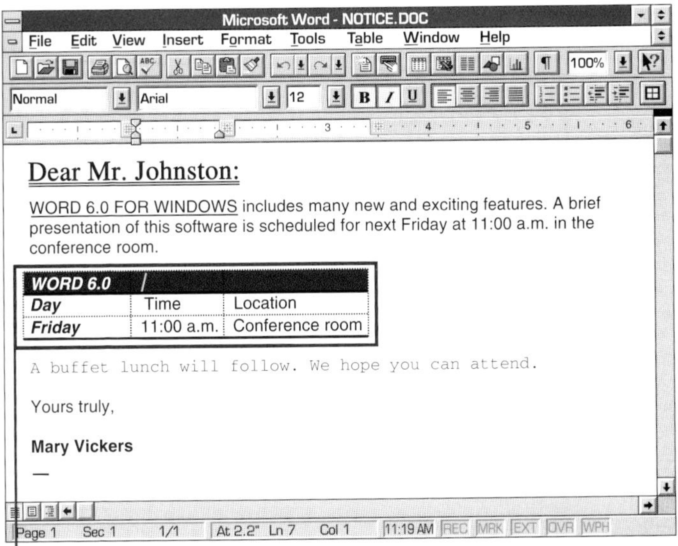
Microsoft Word - NOTICE.DOC
File Edit View Insert Format Tools Table Window Help
Normal
Arial
12
100%
Dear Mr. Johnston:
WORD 6.0 FOR WINDOWS includes many new and exciting features. A brief presentation of this software is scheduled for next Friday at 11:00 a.m. in the conference room.
WORD 6.0
Day Time Location
Friday 11:00 a.m. Conference room
A buffet lunch will follow. We hope you can attend.
Yours truly,
Mary Vickers
Page 1 Sec 1 1/1 At 2.2" Ln 7 Col 1 11:19 AM REC MRK EXT OVR WPH

◆ Word applies the formats you selected to the table.

REMOVE FORMATS

To remove the formats from the table, perform steps 1 to 3, select **(none)** in step 4 and then perform step 6.

MERGE CELLS

Tables

MERGE CELLS

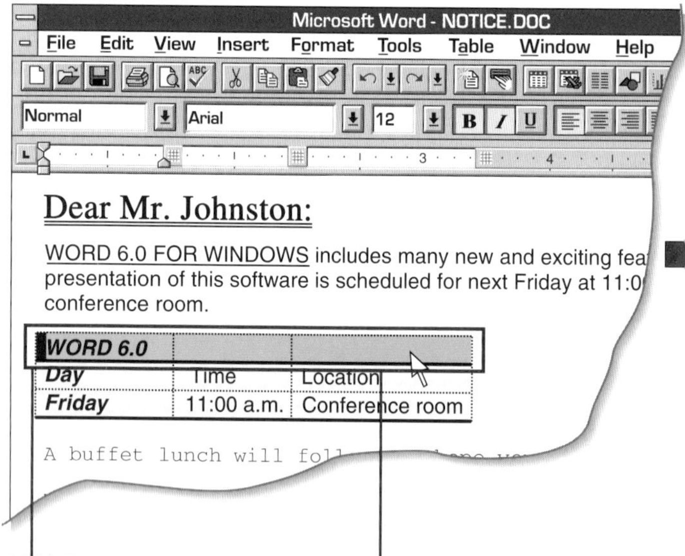
Microsoft Word - NOTICE.DOC
File Edit View Insert Format Tools Table Window Help
Normal
Arial
12
Dear Mr. Johnston:
WORD 6.0 FOR WINDOWS includes many new and exciting fea
presentation of this software is scheduled for next Friday at 11:0
conference room.
WORD 6.0
Day
Time
Location
Friday
11:00 a.m.
Conference room
A buffet lunch will fol

1 Move the mouse I over the first cell you want to join with other cells.

Note: You can only join cells in the same row. You cannot join cells in the same column.

2 Press and hold down the left button as you move the mouse I to highlight the cells you want to join. Then release the button.

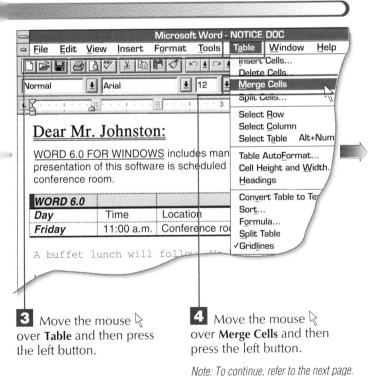

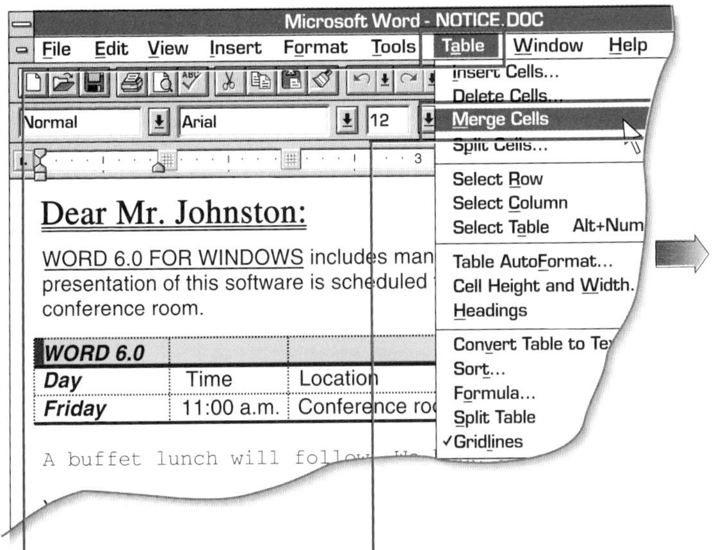

3 Move the mouse over **Table** and then press the left button.

4 Move the mouse over **Merge Cells** and then press the left button.

Note: To continue, refer to the next page.

Tables

MERGE CELLS (Continued)

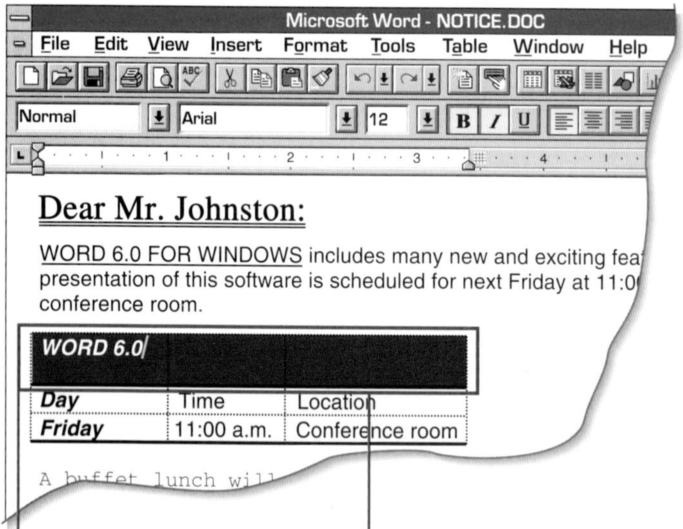
Microsoft Word - NOTICE.DOC
File Edit View Insert Format Tools Table Window Help
Normal
Arial
12
Dear Mr. Johnston:
WORD 6.0 FOR WINDOWS includes many new and exciting fea
presentation of this software is scheduled for next Friday at 11:0
conference room.
WORD 6.0
Day
Time
Location
Friday
11:00 a.m.
Conference room
A buffet lunch will

◆ The cells merge into one.

Note: To deselect the cell, move the mouse I outside the table and then press the left button.

◆ If a blank line appears in the row, you can remove the extra line. To do so, position the insertion point to the right of the text in the cell and then press **Delete**.

The Merge Cells feature is useful when you want to display a title at the top of your table.

SPLIT CELLS

You can split one cell into two or more cells.

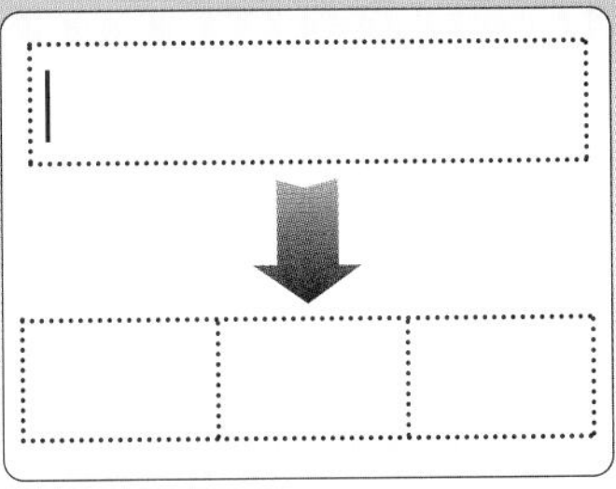

1 Position the insertion point in the cell you want to split.

2 Move the mouse over **Table** and then press the left button.

3 Move the mouse over **Split Cells** and then press the left button. The **Split Cells** dialog box appears.

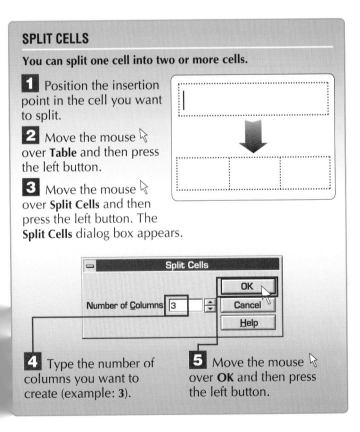

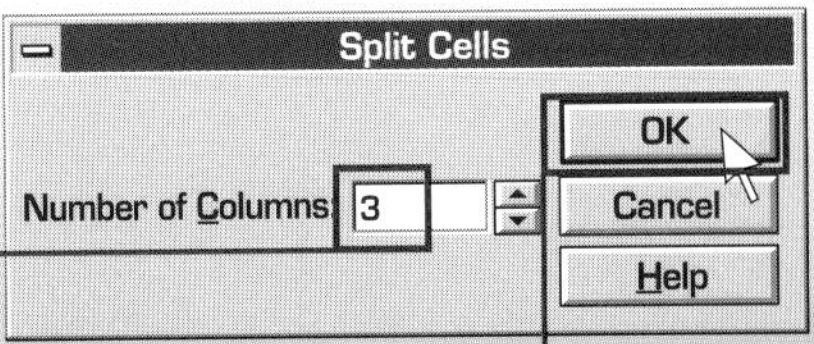

4 Type the number of columns you want to create (example: **3**).

5 Move the mouse over **OK** and then press the left button.

INDEX